TURN MY HEAD INTO SOUND

a history of

kevin shields

and my bloody

valentine

andrew perer

**TURN MY HEAD INTO SOUND
A HISTORY OF KEVIN SHIELDS
AND MY BLOODY VALENTINE
ANDREW PERER**

A Jawbone book
First edition 2025
Published in the UK and the USA by
Jawbone Press
7 Orlando Road
London SW4 0LE
England
www.jawbonepress.com
books@jawbonepress.com

ISBN 978-1-916829-14-5

Printed by Short Run Press, Exeter, Devon

2 3 4 5 29 28 27 26

table of contents

'From pure sensation to the intuition of beauty, from pleasure and pain to love and the mystical ecstasy and death—all the things that are fundamental, all the things that, to the human spirit, are most profoundly significant, can only be experienced, not expressed. The rest is always and everywhere silence.

After silence, that which comes nearest to expressing the inexpressible is music.'

ALDOUS HUXLEY, 'THE REST IS SILENCE,' 1931

'Turn my head into sound ... You will see, oh now, oh the way I do.'

'SOMETIMES,' WORDS AND MUSIC BY KEVIN SHIELDS, 1991

•

For my mother, father, and Neva G.

introduction

about bloody time

'As composer and bandleader of My Bloody Valentine, Shields has created expression which goes beyond language and tapped into the myths, symbols, and archetypes which Carl Jung saw as uniting humankind. Though Shields's music transcends language, he was kind enough to use language when he spoke with us.'

IAN SVENONIUS, *SOFT FOCUS*, 2007[1]

On June 16, 2008, Colin Newman, best known as the lead vocalist of the post-punk band Wire, took the stage at the Brewery in London to present *Mojo* magazine's 'Classic Album' award to *Loveless*, which duly joined the company of such trailblazing albums as Can's *Tago Mago*, Television's *Marquee Moon*, The Stone Roses' self-titled debut, and Bob Marley's *Exodus*. At one point in his presentation speech, Newman asserted, 'There was a period in the early 1990s when the band in question were really the cultural deciders. You either loved them or you hadn't heard of them.'[2]

After Newman's speech, MBV—Kevin Shields, Bilinda Butcher, Deb Googe, and Colm Ó Cíosóig—approached the podium to accept their award, looking casual but engaged: Shields in an unbuttoned dress shirt over a dark T-shirt with thin horizontal lines, Googe in a black short-sleeved T-shirt with white letters spelling out 'little black dress,' Butcher in a tomato-red dress and button-down black sweater, Ó Cíosóig in a brown patterned shirt and dark jeans.

Shields, much as when he performs, appeared cordial but self-conscious about being the center of attention. 'Thanks,' he said, before noting, 'it sounded kind of weird'—a critique of the audio of the footage that was part of the presentation.[3] Leave it to him to notice subpar audio quality at an awards ceremony.

During an on-camera interview after the ceremony, Butcher and Googe were asked whether *Loveless* was the record they were most proud of. 'Well, of the two,' Googe responded, without missing a beat, laughing and then wincing at the thought of the band's anemic output over the previous seventeen years, before deciding, 'It's fifty-fifty.' (A few moments later, Shields would joke, 'Half our albums are classics.') Googe then looked to Butcher for her take. 'Of the two albums,' she said, seeming a bit unsure, 'it's probably … well, I do like a lot of the songs from *Isn't Anything*.'

Googe and Butcher then answered some questions about whether they were ready to start playing live again, and about the upcoming Fuji Festival in Japan. Googe reflected on how it had been sixteen years since they last toured and talked about how much she had enjoyed getting to know Butcher again. Then they paused and gave each other a quick, heartfelt embrace.

The camera then moved to Shields, who at approximately six foot two had to lean over to speak into the microphone. When an interviewer asked him who in the audience he was most excited to see, he reeled off a litany of iconic figures—John Lydon, Nick Cave, Jimmy Page, Mark E. Smith, Terry Hall—who had firmly left a mark on popular music. The ceremony was confirmation that Shields had finally taken his proper place among them. He must have been grateful that there were no tiresome questions about *Loveless*'s troubled birth or any of the other spurious rumors that were often bandied about when people talked about the record. The album had finally transcended all that, and his name had the kind of currency that only a small minority of artists ever achieve.

As Shields spoke with reporters, he revealed that, like so many other people, he viewed music through the prism of The Beatles. As he saw it, with *Loveless*, MBV only got as far as their *Revolver* phase. 'We can't finish there completely,' he said. 'We've got to do at least two really good records, and then we can get old and die.'

•

In a 2018 interview with Fender.com, Kevin Shields was asked what he wanted people to take away from his music. Having read so much about him and his band over the past thirty-five years, I wasn't too surprised by his answer. 'Nothing, really,' he said. 'Just that it makes people feel more connected to everything than less connected and less isolated. That's what it's about.'[4]

While he wanted to be recognized as an original with something to say, he certainly didn't start MBV to get rich, meet women, or become a celebrity. Rather, sound is foundational to his way of being—it's the natural lens through which he views pretty much everything in the world—and his primary goal as an artist has been to give the gift of that sonic vision to other people so they can feel it too.

Ultimately, it's about the drive to connect. And connect he has. His work as a guitarist and producer—his forays into *all* of sound's transportive qualities, his blurring of the lines between music and noise, and his use of sound as a type of language—has created brand-new vocabularies for thinking and talking about what music is and what it can be.

Countless musicians and fans have discovered something in his music that has spoken deeply to them. The following comments from Italian avant-garde composer Caterina Barbieri are typical of the type of praise and devotion Shields has drawn from other musicians:

> It's amazing how music can introduce what feels like a new emotion. I felt like that the first time I heard My Bloody Valentine…I bought *Loveless* and it was such an enlightening experience. It was like some alien record. It has such a different perception of time and space. You can almost disappear into the sound. There's a feeling of self-surrender to the wall of noise. That feeling of immersion in music was a big influence on me.[5]

Barbieri's description of *Loveless* isn't what makes this passage stand out. Lots of people consider it to be one of the best records ever made. What's so striking is her sense of surprise at how Shields was able to show her—an accomplished musician—that it was still possible to experience music and reality in ways she had never imagined.

Barbieri isn't alone. For many other musicians, critics, and fans, Shields's studio recordings, live shows, remixes, and production work have brought forth a world of sound that had previously been sitting somewhere in our consciousness but had yet to be manifested into our overlapping aural reality.

It may seem puzzling that Kevin Shields isn't more well known than he is until you consider how much more fragmented the world has become over the last twenty years. A headline in the *Toronto Star* got it right at the time of the band's 2008 reunion tour, billing MBV as 'Legendary But Obscure.' Things have changed since then in meaningful ways. In 2023, the *Irish Independent* named *Loveless* the best Irish album of all time, after tallying the votes of more than one hundred musicians, producers, broadcasters, critics, publicists, and other industry insiders, beating out everything on offer from U2, Van Morrison, The Pogues, The Cranberries, Enya, and Sinead O'Connor (and outranking the second choice, *Achtung Baby*, by a significant margin.) And yet, while it would be easy to see almost any rock fan picking Bono, Shane MacGowan, or Dolores O'Riordan out of a lineup, they'd be hard pressed to recognize Shields in the same way.

Despite continual coverage by the *New York Times*, the *Guardian*, the BBC, NPR, and their counterparts across the Western world whenever anything worthwhile happens, there remains a strange disconnect between the magnitude and reach of Shields's innovations and contributions as a musician and the number of people who know about them. It's also led to a gap between the lore surrounding 'Kevin Shields' and who the man really is. The countless YouTube posts and other unsourced pieces online are often wrong and give little context. They miss so much about who Shields really is as a creative practitioner: his state of mind and thought processes as an artist; his sacrifice and unwillingness to compromise his music, often at great personal expense; and his genius as a songwriter, engineer, producer, remixer, and collaborator.

That's where this book comes in.

I was born in 1972, and I first heard MBV in 1988, when the *You Made Me Realise* EP came out. Sixteen is when music really starts to become imprinted on your brain—it's the time in life when people often find those bands and artists that will stick with them forever. Before I heard *You Made Me Realise*, I had been obsessed with The Smiths (Johnny Marr, in particular), Joy Division, and The Velvet Underground (especially *White Light/White Heat*). All these bands were foundational—it's almost impossible to think of the history of rock music without them—but they were all before my time. By contrast, *You Made Me Realise* seemed to signal the arrival of a band hitting their artistic stride at the *exact* moment when discovering new music was most important to me. And though I may not have been able to articulate it at the time, I heard something special in the way the title track brought together an American hardcore dynamic, a super-catchy melody, and an uncommon authenticity. I'd never heard anything quite like it before.

The same could be said of MBV's next EP, *Feed Me With Your Kiss*, which again deftly combined melody, noise, and genuine allure in ways that were also new to me. MBV offered something no other band could come close to. I've listened to lots of other iconic rock music, but the blend of melody, noise, and seduction on *You Made Me Realise* and *Feed Me With Your Kiss* felt alien. These were records that felt radically *new*, music that uniquely captured all the ways sexuality, youth, and freedom were changing at the time. And I haven't stopped thinking about Shields and MBV since. But as much as I have loved Shields's music, I also always knew he was a human being, and that it is wrong to confuse the work with the man. Shields may be a musical genius, but to paint him as a perfect human would be to get the story wrong. So, my goal here is to tell his entire story, once and for all.*

•

---

* The other three members of MBV are mentioned primarily in terms of the way their actions relate to Shields and MBV. I don't wish to minimize the roles of Colm Ó Cíosóig, Debbie Googe, and, perhaps most crucially, Bilinda Butcher. But without Shields, the MBV we know simply wouldn't exist.

If you know the story of how *Loveless* came to be, you know it's pretty amazing that the album exists at all. By the time Lennon and McCartney had recorded *Revolver* and *Sgt. Pepper*, The Beatles were extremely well-off financially and had an array of assistants at Abbey Road to help them. Brian Wilson was in a similar situation when he made *Pet Sounds*; he was able to spend months assembling 'Good Vibrations' at three of the premier studios in Los Angeles. When these artists were creating their masterpieces, they never had to deal with flawed recording desks or subpar instruments, nor did they have to worry about where their next meal was coming from. What's worse is that when Shields was making *Loveless*—and regularly arguing with engineers about proper recording techniques—the band members didn't even have a stable home to lay their heads. It's no wonder the album took two years to finish. But they prevailed, completing *Loveless* without compromising their vision.

Over the years, it's become clearer and clearer that the immense expectations set by *Loveless* have been both a curse and a blessing. Because the album looms so large in the rock pantheon, it has certainly taken the air out of the room at many points, leaving little time for critics and fans to talk about *Isn't Anything, m b v*, or the four revelatory EPs the band put out while they were signed to Creation. As such, though the talk and hype that surrounds *Loveless* is justified, a good number of MBV fans are missing out on so much more of their work. *Loveless* is really only about twenty percent of the whole MBV story.

Just as *Loveless* overshadows and obscures MBV's other releases, Shields's position in the band obscures some of his many other gifts. He's collaborated with Patti Smith, Brian Eno, and Sofia Coppola, and his remixes demonstrate he is one of the most innovative people to ever work at the intersections of rhythm and tonality. So if you're coming into this book knowing only his work with his MBV family, you'll find hours more of his music to explore.

By 2008, Shields finally seemed to have concluded the most difficult period of his life, and all the difficulties and misery had finally led to the type of recognition that few bands get to experience. Indicative of this newfound respect was an offer of $300,000 for the band to reunite and headline the Coachella Valley Music & Arts Festival a year earlier. The concert's organizers had since upped their offer to a cool million. For Shields and company, the hard-won recognition came as both a relief and an overdue reward. It was also a sign that their unwillingness to take any shortcuts had been the right move. It finally seemed that the world had caught up to his singular sonic vision.

Technology also played a key role in their renaissance. Although MBV were out of the limelight between 1993 and 2007, word about the band spread, and their fan base grew as technology continued to make the world smaller amid the explosive growth of the internet and online media. As one blogger put it, 'At this point, it seems a bit silly to call Kevin Shields underrated. Though MBV may have been an underground band at one point, the information age has lifted them out of obscurity and lauded them with an almost comical slew of superlatives.'[6] Without the benefit of the internet, The Velvet Underground had to wait twenty-three years after their breakup in 1970 for the world to catch up with them, resulting in a lucrative European reunion tour in 1993. MBV only had to wait until a decade after their dissolution to get the recognition they deserved.

The years following the band's appearance at the *Mojo* Music Awards were filled with shows that took MBV all over the world. Their reunion began with two warm-up concerts for an invited audience of approximately 350 friends and family members in London on June 13 and 14, 2008. During their first rehearsal, it took the band four hours to get through twelve songs. Though they had played them all live back in 1992, they now had to deal with a vast array of new equipment, and while Shields finally had a PA system to match his ambitions for the live shows he'd envisioned earlier in their career, it took some time to integrate everything. By June 14, they were able to get through their fourteen-song set in an hour and a half. The two private warm-up shows were followed by five sold-out shows at the Roundhouse, also in London. And although a couple of songs fell apart at various points, there were no requests for refunds.

Over the next few years, MBV earned hundreds of thousands of dollars playing festivals and touring America, Europe, and Asia. *Billboard* magazine, the bible of the music business, reported that they had been assured six-figure fees per show, in addition to merchandise sales. Seven shows in America brought in well over a million dollars. Who would have thought they would get to this position when Shields and Ó Cíosóig were teenagers who didn't know how to tune a guitar or keep a basic rhythm? And who could have predicted this kind of cachet and financial security after the band had gone through such a rough patch between 1997 and 2007?

In interviews, Shields has always emphasized how things have a way of looking after themselves, no matter the missed deadlines or seemingly interminable detours. 'Everything works out in the end,' he confidently pronounced in 2008—just as everything was falling into place, and all the peril was being left behind.[7] But what was he thinking at his lowest point, a decade earlier, when the other three members had left the band and Island had cut off his money supply? Was he just as assured about his ultimate success when he was still under contract to Island Records? He owed the label over a million dollars (adjusted for inflation), and he wasn't in any condition to make new music. We know the answers now, of course, but at the time, it certainly didn't look like overcoming these obstacles would be easy.

It took twenty-one years for My Bloody Valentine to release *m b v*, which followed *Loveless* but was not the proper follow-up to *Loveless*. Since then, it's been twelve years without new music. New songs have shown up in their live sets since 2018, which typically serves as an indication that a song has been recorded and should give fans some comfort and reasons to be optimistic. The interest is there, and it only continues to grow, as proven by the hysteria surrounding the recently announced shows that will begin in November of 2025 (and which quickly sold out). But the obvious question remains: when will Shields and his bandmates release the various follow-up albums and EPs he's promised? And, if they do arrive, will they, like so many other reunion projects, be a pale imitation of the band's former heights? Or will we get MBV's *White Album* and *Abbey*

Road—masterpieces that more than make up for the band's many years without releasing anything new, making good on Shields's prediction that 'the last bit is the best bit'?[8]

•

When I started this book, I thought I had the basic arc of Shields's life figured out.* Looking back now, six years later, I can see how wrong I was. Many details clashed in ways I'd never noticed before. Only by writing it all out was I forced to figure out where the contradictions and gaps were, where more research was needed, and what I needed to ask other people about. It now seems obvious to me why Shields balks at some of the more exotic descriptions of his music. He always preferred to think about his work in much simpler terms. As he explained in one interview, 'More than erotic or psychedelic, I think our music is kinda human, y'know?'[9] I couldn't agree more.

---

* If at any point you need a better sense of the major events in that arc, there is a timeline at the end of this book.

chapter one

Kevin Patrick Shields was born on May 21, 1963, at Jamaica Hospital in Queens, New York. His parents, Tom and Mary Dolores Shields, had emigrated to the United States as teenagers in the 1950s, as part of a wave of five hundred thousand Irish immigrants—many of whom ended up in America—who were looking to escape an irreversible decline in rural farming that had devastated the Irish economy. His father eventually worked in a managerial capacity for the A&P grocery chain, while Mary worked as a nurse before becoming a full-time homemaker.

After Kevin was born, Tom and Mary had four more children, the last of whom, Eileen, was born in 1970. Although the family resided in Flushing, Shields's main memories of the New York of his childhood are of Brooklyn, where he often visited relatives. In 1967, the family moved to Long Island, where they stayed until 1973, at which point they left their Irish American enclave in New York for good and returned to Ireland to be closer to family. According to Shields, they had very little money and lived in a rented row house next to other A&P employees.

Shields's parents encouraged their children's pursuits in the arts and education, and all five would end up involved in those fields in some way.* At a young age, Kevin was interested in The Beatles, The Monkees, The Partridge Family, and other pop groups that he came across on their own branded television shows. The first album he recollects owning was a cassette of The Beatles' *1967–1970* compilation. By the age of ten, he knew he wanted to make music his life's pursuit. He even daydreamed about starting a Partridge Family–type band with his four siblings, miming along to songs while using pillows and other household props as instruments. In hundreds of interviews over the years, Shields never once mentioned his parents pressuring him to abandon music to take up a trade. But he did note their relief that he shared an interest in music with other boys his age.

One of Shields's earliest memories of creating music was when, at eleven years old, he recorded a vacuum cleaner with a Dictaphone, then rerecorded the replayed sound with a portable cassette player. He went back and forth between the two devices, engaging in a kind of tape-on-tape experiment, listening to how the sound changed and warped as it got further from its original source. It was one of the first times he grew totally obsessed with something having to do with sound.

When his family moved from New York to the Dublin suburb of Cabinteely in 1973, Shields experienced a kind of culture shock, later remarking that it felt like stepping twenty years into the past. Dublin, he noted, was just catching up with the 'junk culture and selling garbage to people' he had witnessed in America.[1] Unlike the USA, where capitalism had been given the opportunity to run amok and where there was no common culture to slow the race to the bottom, Ireland was an actual nation state with traditions and societal norms that kept capitalism in check.

---

* At the time of writing, Ann-Marie is head of careers, industry, and events at the British & Irish Modern Music (BIMM) Institute in Dublin, where she oversees graduate programs and live festivals based on her years involved in all elements of the music business. Kevin's younger brother, Jimi, has also done noteworthy work as a musician, but he has truly distinguished himself in the field of landscape architecture; his company, Thirty-Three Trees (TTT), which he co-founded in 2004 with his wife, Maria Vlahos, joins horticulture and architecture to create unique urban spaces. Eileen first rose to prominence by establishing Donna Karan's shoe lines before launching her own successful high-end shoe brand in 2004. And Siobhan is a Montessori teacher and lecturer at the Aughrim Montessori School in Ireland, which she founded.

Despite the accepted precept that unbridled capitalism was supposed to offer wider choices wherever it reared its head, Ireland and the UK had a great deal more to offer young people when punk was being born. While Dublin is in the Republic Of Ireland and therefore not part of the UK, its inhabitants received many of the same radio and TV networks—including the BBC and ITV—and with them music programs like *Revolver*, *The Old Grey Whistle Test*, *Top Of The Pops*, and *Something Else*. These shows exposed young people in Ireland to American and British punk and post-punk acts years before teens in the USA got to see these bands in the national media.

Shields remembered being inspired by glam rock, which never really took hold in the United States. But his most affecting musical memory was seeing the Ramones play 'Swallow My Pride' on television as a teenager in Dublin. 'The Ramones for me were THE revelation,' he recalled. 'Suddenly I realized he [Johnny Ramone] wasn't playing guitar—he was generating the sound. He was doing what he had to do to make that, but there was no "playing guitar" involved.'[2] In an interview outtake for Pitchfork, he added, 'And there was no lead guitar; I'd heard punk rock up to that point, but there was too much lead guitar. I went through a huge hatred of wanky guitar solo horribleness when I was around thirteen, just this image of the guy with the Les Paul whittling away, Jimmy Page style.'[3]

Watching Johnny Ramone, Shields saw a way he could play guitar without having to be a cheesy guitar hero—all of a sudden, the instrument didn't look so intimidating. In 1979, when he was sixteen, he would get his first guitar, a Hondo SG, for Christmas. He would learn to play it along to the Ramones' 1977 live album *It's Alive*.*

---

* The following names have consistently come up when Shields talks about the guitar players who were particularly influential during his formative years: Johnny Ramone, Rowland S Howard (The Birthday Party), Steve Diggle and Pete Shelly (Buzzcocks), Kid Congo Powers (Gun Club/The Cramps), Poison Ivy (The Cramps), John Lennon, Thurston Moore and Lee Ranaldo (Sonic Youth), William Reed (Jesus & Mary Chain), Jimi Hendrix, Fred 'Sonic' Smith (MC5), Ron Asheton (Stooges), Geordie Walker (Killing Joke), Robert Smith (The Cure), and John McGeoch (Siouxsie & The Banshees/Magazine).

After Johnny Ramone, the next person to shape Shields's musical odyssey was Colm Ó Cíosóig, born on October 31, 1964. They first met in the summer of 1978 when they both answered an ad looking for people to join a band. Unlike Shields, Ó Cíosóig (pronounced *KEY-Soy-Ig*) grew up in Ireland, having been born in the Glenageary neighborhood of Dublin. The two young men met right around the time that they each got their first instruments, and they soon forged a very close personal and musical partnership. For the next twenty years, almost every single musical project Shields was involved in would involve Ó Cíosóig as well. They started very much from square one. For months, during their first 'rehearsals,' Shields would tune the top two strings of his guitar incorrectly (in line with the other four strings) and Ó Cíosóig, who started on bass before switching to drums, bashed out a series of primitive, erratic patterns.

Shields and Ó Cíosóig played their first gigs together in a short-lived venture called The Complex, their sets featuring covers of Ramones and Sex Pistols songs. Then, as A Day In The Life, and with a rotation of other band members, they performed material that leaned in a gothic, post-punk direction. Other short-lived groups would form and dissolve. One anecdote from these days stands out as a harbinger of Shields's genuine obsession with sound. Playing with another random group, he came into contact with a phaser pedal for the first time. It fascinated him, and he didn't want to stop playing around with it. He recalled. 'I enjoyed moving past the point of reason.'[4] He was so distracted and obsessed with the pedal's sound that he was not invited back.

Like many other aspiring musicians of the time, Shields got a TASCAM Portastudio—a truly revolutionary device on its release in 1979 for the way it opened up the potential of home recording. He and Ó Cíosóig would use it in a variety of ways, including early experiments with pitch bending that started as far back as 1981. Shields also used it to record vocals and guitars for other bands at his home—his first forays into the world of recording, mixing, and equalizing.

Dave Conway, born September 23, 1963, became the next piece of the puzzle when he joined Shields and Ó Cíosóig's loose collective of musicians after answering an ad placed by bass player Mark Ross in July 1983. Forty years on, he vividly remembered his first meeting with Kevin and Colm at Shields's home: some amps and a drum kit had been set up while the adults were away on holiday. Upon hearing them play, he realized they shared his feelings of being an outsider in their hometown, and he was immediately drawn to them, recalling, 'At this point, Kevin's guitar style was mostly dominated by heavy chords and riffing filtered through layers of distortion, chorus, and analog delay effects—a big, scary wall-of-sound, I think you could say. Colm's drumming style was already in evidence: a really driving, atavistic attack.'[5]

As far as the Dublin scene was concerned, they were outsiders, like him, and he sensed their real commitment to going against the grain. The new group's first gig took place on August 18, 1983. They had yet to settle on a name, so Conway suggested My Bloody Valentine. The rest of the band members found it funny, though they also had to admit it was a good fit with their gothic leanings. At the time, Shields had no idea about the slasher horror movie of the same name, and it's safe to say that at this point, no one was thinking all that much about how the name might play out over the long term.

The band continued to experiment, playing live and recording songs on the Portastudio. They were young, restless, and looking to make progress. And they knew that wasn't going to happen in Dublin.

•

For a short time in the mid-70s, Bono and The Edge of U2 and Gavin Friday of The Virgin Prunes were part of an arts collective in Dublin known as Lypton Village. The group included artists who were interested in music and theatre, united in their apathy for the 'banal cultural wasteland' they felt Dublin had become.[6] Ó Cíosóig later recalled seeing U2 perform a Ramones song very early in their career.

U2 and the Prunes (whose members included Dik Evans, brother of David Howell Evans, aka The Edge) would eventually go in radically different directions, U2 selling millions of records across the next four decades while the Prunes stayed together for less than a decade. But the latter group followed a far more experimental path, which spoke to Conway, Ó Cíosóig, and Shields.[*]

Much like when Nirvana broke out in Seattle in the 1990s, U2's relatively rapid ascent led to many young Dublin bands being signed to major labels with unrealistic expectations. For every success story, there were a hundred failures who were never heard from again, and they usually ended up in debt to large record companies. Shields called the fallout from U2 a 'sad situation'; for artists with a long-term, outside-the-box perspective, Dublin seemed to offer little opportunity.[7]

Looking back on this period in a 1989 interview with the Dublin-based *Hot Press*, Ó Cíosóig and Shields didn't hesitate to call Dublin a 'shithole' due to its stifling atmosphere when they were growing up. 'That's why we left,' Shields explained. 'There was no room for us.'[8] In 1991, Ó Cíosóig confirmed that impression, describing the city's provincialism as a barrier to creativity: everyone gets along just fine when you're on the same page, but once you do something just a bit different, it's as if no one knows you. 'The Virgin Prunes made some headway for a while ... but apart from them, there's been no one,' he recalled.[9]

Both Shields and Ó Cíosóig have been clear in their admiration for the Prunes, who were the only band challenging what had gone before and demonstrated a sense of adventure. 'For about two years in the early 80s, they were the most amazing thing anywhere,' Shields has said. 'They were the prototype of what My Bloody Valentine are about.'[10] In a later interview, Ó Cíosóig noted, 'Gigs you can remember can become some of the most important things in your life.' Shields added, 'If there was ever an Irish Sex Pistols, the Prunes are definitely it.'[11] So, when MBV was first seeking advice about how they should proceed, Friday was the obvious person to turn to.

Friday had recently been interviewed for a fanzine put out by Jon

---

[*] U2 also spoke to them in that they represented conventions—in particular, Bono's exasperated passion—that MBV wanted to avoid. Shields was a much bigger fan of the more subdued vocal stylings of Ray Davies and Syd Barrett.

O'Brien, an acquaintance of Conway's. After the interview, Friday mentioned to O'Brien that any Irish band looking to do anything outside the mainstream (which at the time included acts like U2 and The Police) should consider going abroad. He also hinted that he'd pass on whatever resources he had and what he'd learned from touring.

Conway had grown up very close to Friday's childhood home, where the singer still lived, and knew him by sight. With O'Brien's encouragement, he called up the Prunes frontman, who invited him over. Friday was 'complimentary and quite enthusiastic' about the recordings Conway, Ó Cíosóig, and Shields had made on their Portastudio, which exhibited the influence of The Cramps, the Stooges, and The Birthday Party (all of whom were then in the process of becoming influential cult acts).[12] He recommended that MBV first try their luck in the Netherlands. There were a large number of small and midsized clubs there, and because they received government subsidies, most of the young bands who played throughout the country would receive some sort of remuneration for their work. In Dublin, bands who were just starting out would typically *lose* money playing live to small audiences once the rented PA was accounted for.

When Shields and his bandmates found out they might actually get paid for playing in the Netherlands, it sounded promising. Friday put them in touch with another acquaintance, who gave them a list of forty venues in the Netherlands that might be open to booking them. When a club in Tilburg offered them a gig, that was all it took for them to leave Dublin.* Thus begins the proper story of My Bloody Valentine 1.0.

•

Of the informal collective of musicians that were playing intermittently with MBV at the time, only four were willing to make the trip to the Continent in the late summer of 1984: Shields, Ó Cíosóig, Conway, and Conway's girlfriend Tina Durkin, who played keyboards. After playing that one gig and squatting in Amsterdam for a month, they were broke,

---

* He also warned them against signing any kind of significant record deal in the speculative rush that took place after U2's success.

and things did not look promising. Shields even found a laborious job, probably his first and last, cleaning out cowsheds. They got lucky when they made the acquaintance of a Dutch club owner who felt very paternalistic toward them due to their dire straits and offered them his cottage in South Holland for three months, complete with an expansive record collection, while he was away. A few more gigs followed, but with the band unwilling to impose on him or anyone else further, after a few more gigs, they hit a dead end—in particular, residency requirements and documentation—that made it clear that staying in the Netherlands wasn't going to work in the long term.

Fearing they would remain completely under the radar if they went to London at this point, and inspired by The Birthday Party's escapades in Europe, the quartet next moved to Berlin in the winter of 1984. By this time, The Birthday Party had split—Nick Cave had begun his new band, The Bad Seeds, while Rowland S Howard formed Crime & The City Solution. But these Australians were still shaking up Berlin.[*]

Shields would also mention the importance of attending shows at the first iteration of the Berlin Atonal Festival in late 1984. by which time they knew people involved with or playing at the festival. In early 1985, they saw Einstürzende Neubauten and other radical acts who profoundly affected their outlook. Neubauten's cover of the Lee Hazelwood / Nancy Sinatra duet 'Sand' made a particularly large impression. 'That, for me, was a huge click moment,' he later recalled, 'because they were literally having Molotov Cocktails onstage, and it was just the sound of…war and chaos, but with this amazing song. Experiencing that, you know, the hugeness of it. It was so non-traditional. And yet with a really great traditional kind of song.'[13]

Dimitri Hegemann, the organizer of the Berlin Atonal Festival, asked for and got a tape of MBV's homemade demos. At the time, he was working with a label called Dossier, which had sporadic success with the American sci-fi proto-industrial band Chrome. He was sufficiently impressed by

---

* The filmmaker Wim Wenders was, in part, inspired to make *Wings Of Desire* after moving back to Germany in 1984 and witnessing its lively music scene. Both offshoots of The Birthday Party perform in the movie.

their tape that he offered them the chance to record an LP for his offshoot label, Tycoon. Short of songs, they recorded a mini-album instead, *This Is Your Bloody Valentine*.

Recorded in December of 1984 and released the following January, the LP documents a very young but competent and melodious band. As it was with all of their recordings from this time, Shields wrote all of the music and titles, and Conway wrote the lyrics. Although Shields has tried to warn fans away from listening to anything he made before 1987, *This Is Your Bloody Valentine* is actually the most realized of the group's releases from the period when Conway was their vocalist. Nothing would match it until 'Strawberry Wine' came out in 1987.

The band had been given access to a proper studio—paid for by the label—for five days, though the songs were all mixed in an afternoon (one of them reportedly in ten minutes) without their input. They were left in the dark for much of the recording process, and they only heard the completed recordings when they received payment in the form of four copies of the album. Nonetheless, it was recorded relatively well—especially when judged against their next four studio EPs—and compares favorably with albums by other bands of the time who were also trying to play a particular brand of gothic rockabilly. Reviewing the mini-album for *Sounds* magazine, Roger Holland noted 'enough deft touches to promise a healthy future' and gave it four and a half stars. But he also homed in on the band's influences, which were readily apparent:

On 'Don't Cramp My Style,' My Bloody Valentine preempt a lot of the criticism they are likely to attract. It's a ridiculously c[r]amped-up swamp-stained rant which will presume admits the influence while sending up anyone who thinks it overly important. . . . They are not exclusively Cramps-orientated, of course. 'The Last Supper' for instance derives quite blatantly from The Doors. But My Bloody Valentine are equally obviously steeped in the traditions of mentally disturbed Americans, which only goes to make *This Is Your Bloody Valentine* a merrily dark and powerful record.[14]

MBV's next official recording, *The Man You Love To Hate*, captures their performance at the Die Kwahl festival on March 9, 1985. It went on sale later that month, released by the tiny cassette-only label Schuldige Scheitel Tapes, featuring four songs from the mini-album and four songs from their live set that they would never formally record in a studio. At most, a few hundred copies were dubbed and prepared for release. (Another nine live tracks from the same show, including an early version of 'Sunny Sundae Smile,' would later find their way onto bootlegs and illegal peer-to-peer networks.)

Comparing these first two releases, it's not immediately apparent how much more exciting the band could be as a live act or in rough demos compared to the more staid, professional songs done in the mid-level studio for *This Is Your Bloody Valentine*. But when the band began using inexpensive studios with less guidance after moving to the UK—leading to dull, stilted results—it became painfully obvious just how much they still had to learn.

MBV ended up staying in Germany until funds ran low and the band members realized they were not eligible for public assistance. After some more gigs in the Netherlands, they had all ended up in London by the middle of 1985. Shields then took a short break in Dublin; despondency had set in, and he and the other band members were unsure if they would continue. When he eventually returned to London, he and Ó Cíosóig got a place together. Through chance or kismet, they ended up living within just a few minutes of Conway and Durkin, which made their future endeavors that much simpler once they decided to carry on together.

London's squatting scene and the UK's public assistance programs of the time meant that housing and money were readily available—an ideal situation for young bands who were just starting out with lots of time and ambition. Tim Gane, the co-founder of Stereolab and a contemporary of Shields's, was another musician who came to London for the 'free' housing and public assistance, which enabled him to pursue music full-time. He later speculated that the dole supported ninety percent of the bands in London, including The Jesus & Mary Chain, Pulp, and Primal Scream. 'I've never done a job interview in my life,' he said.[15]

Ó Cíosóig and Shields have both subsequently mentioned how, without the squatting scene, MBV would have been forced to take menial jobs and would not have had the time to hone their craft. To this day, they look back on the community and their earliest gigs (at squats) affectionately. Ultimately, it enabled them to make a considerable amount of progress in a short amount of time.[*]

•

Around this time, Tina Durkin stopped playing in the band, having only ever done so as a favor to her boyfriend and the others, and for the adventure of it all. In need of a proper bass player, the remaining members were given the name of Deborah Ann Googe, born October 24, 1962, who had just moved to London from Somerset.

Googe (pronounced 'Goodge') was born in Bristol, the youngest of six. Like MBV's other members, she had had no formal musical training—an asset when punk burst onto the scene. Comparing her first attempt at playing in a band to that of The Shaggs, she has said that she initially felt hemmed in by knowing only three chords, but then everything changed. 'Fortunately for me, punk happened, and that just totally shifted the goalposts,' she recalled. 'Suddenly it wasn't about musicianship so much as attitude, and as a fifteen-year-old musical illiterate, you can imagine that was very appealing. So I adopted anarchy, concentrated on one string instead of pretending to play four and that was it, really.'[16]

Googe was taken with punk in Somerset in much the same way Shields and Ó Cíosóig were in Dublin. She gigged around and participated in a fanzine and record label, her most recent endeavor being an all-girl venture called Bikini Atoll. Shields, Ó Cíosóig, and Conway had gotten her name

---

[*] Squatting has a long history in the UK, and in London in particular. In *The Autonomous City: A History Of Urban Squatting*, Alexander Vasudevan explains its initial sociological role and how the practice changed over time: 'The "movement" of the 1970s was a mass housing movement. The various identities it produced and the radical social relations it prefigured were forged within a wide-ranging landscape of protest and resistance. Squatting in the 1980s and 1990s was, in contrast, characterized by the formation of dynamic albeit highly localized micro-communities and subcultures.'

from Anne Lloyd, an ex-girlfriend of Googe's who lived in Berlin. Ó Cíosóig left several phone messages for her in his thick Irish brogue, and Googe eventually deciphered enough of his words to meet up with the group. For the next six months, she regularly attended practice sessions at Salem Studios in Euston, a rehearsal room run by members of the band Kill Ugly Pop, who put out a dozen records on their Fever label. Band members Paul and Jools were sufficiently impressed to offer them the chance to make a record, so long as the band financed it themselves. Even at this late date, Googe was never really told if she was in the band; the three others would simply tell her the day and time of their next practice and welcome her to come along if she wanted. It was only after the December 1985 release of the *Geek!* EP, which credits her on bass and features her picture on the sleeve with the other members, that she safely assumed she was officially part of the group.

Although the band received another write-up in *Sounds* after *Geek!*'s release, Shields was largely disappointed by the endeavor. In particular, the band had encountered problems when it came to cutting the recordings to vinyl, having been told that many of the guitar frequencies they used were impossible to press and had to be discarded. This is one reason why *Geek!* is the weakest studio recording by any iteration of the band. It is the sound of a band in transition, though at the time it wasn't clear where they were going or whether they would even stay together. Shields even considered moving back to the USA to live with some relatives there, but he soldiered on, despite his disappointment about the band's lack of progress.

•

As with so many of their contemporaries, MBV were deeply affected by the release of the first few singles and debut album, *Psychocandy*, by The Jesus & Mary Chain. The band's rise in 1984–85 coincided with MBV's move to London, and Shields has made clear that their early records were a seminal influence:

> MBV used to be more garage-y, like The Birthday Party and Cramps, but 'Never Understand' took us in another far more

modern and radical direction. . . . I used to play *Psychocandy* to people to see their reaction, even my parents, because to me they were so revolutionary—did people realise what was happening here? People used to go on about the Velvets, but they didn't come close to what the Mary Chain did with noise and feedback. *Psychocandy* took the idea of noise and put it into a pop area, where it hadn't been before.[17]

Jim and William Reid of The Jesus & Mary Chain lived near to where Shields and Ó Cíosóig were staying, though they largely ignored them. They made it clear they were not impressed by MBV back then, likening them to 'Freddie & The Dreamers with noise' in a fanzine interview.[18] (This would all change with the release of *You Made Me Realise* in 1988, while in 1992, the Mary Chain would invite MBV onto their Rollercoaster tour.)

In September 1986, MBV released another four-song, twelve-inch EP, *The New Record By My Bloody Valentine*, on another label, Kaleidoscope Sound. Label owner Joe Foster later explained that he'd signed the group to help them make a record that was more in line with how they sounded onstage—a sound he found astounding. Foster tried to influence the EP's sound in an effort to better capture the group's dynamic live performances, eventually giving himself a production credit, but the overall feel of the record was ultimately determined by the band and engineer Steve Nunn. The results, like MBV's other early studio efforts, don't quite capture the energy that was a signature part of their live shows (as can be heard on various bootlegs), but it was certainly an improvement on *Geek!*

Foster lost money on the EP and was unwilling to invest in another recording, so MBV next signed a contract with Lazy Records for two EPs and a mini-LP. The first of these was *Sunny Sundae Smile*, recorded in late 1986 and released the following February. Conway was more satisfied with the EP than he had been with their previous efforts, but he had begun to realize that he wasn't interested in where the band's sound was headed. In retrospect, this last release by the first incarnation of the band sounds like the end of the band's beginning. And, like their previous records, it failed to make a significant positive impression on the public or the press.

From 1985 to 1987, the notoriously fickle English press would cover MBV regularly but rarely had anything positive to say. Wax O'Scratch called them the 'Funny Valentines' in his review of *Geek!* for *Sounds*, while the same magazine reviewed a 1987 live show under the headline 'Not Bloody But Bland.' Similarly, a review of *Sunny Sundae Smile* in the short-lived *Underground* magazine called it 'another piece of twangy fuzzed-out pop from the would-be Monkees of the 90s.'[19]

MBV weren't helped by the fact that many journalists had difficulties categorizing either their music or their look. During Conway's tenure as lead vocalist, they took a more 'conceptual' approach, with matching haircuts and sparkling tops, and lyrics about death, necrophilia, and incest sung loudly over bright melodies and harsh guitar frequencies. It felt subversive to them at the time, but it went over everyone else's head, leaving audiences unsure whether MBV were trying to be goth or punk or… what, exactly? It's not even clear whether Shields liked it; retrospectively, he has called this period the band's 'shit/anorak indie phase.'[20] Only after Conway bowed out did they drop the concepts and relax.

Shields later came to regard the band's early work as little more than juvenilia, especially in light of the direction they would eventually pursue. His main concern when discussing the music MBV made before Bilinda Butcher joined the band is to warn fans away so that they avoid paying a premium for it. In his mind, the early EPs represent the work of an entirely different band, barely related to the one the world would come to celebrate after *Isn't Anything* and *Loveless*.

Conway left the band in March 1987, after a tour in support of The Soup Dragons. He was dealing with gastric ailments and wanted to devote his time to writing fiction. Perhaps more importantly, he felt that his work with MBV had run its course and he really didn't have anything more to contribute.

Conway wasn't alone in his frustration about where the band were headed. According to Shields, they all felt discouraged. 'None of us really like the records, Dave especially. A few things came out okay, but in general, in our minds, it was crap. They would always seem to come out clinical and dull. None of these earlier records worked at all really, they were okay, but live, it was always so much better.'[21]

Conway left on good terms with the other members, and Ó Cíosóig and Shields certainly thought of his departure as a loss. 'Visually and live, [Conway] was a lot,' Ó Cíosóig has since pointed out, 'because he had a great voice and wrote good songs.'[22]

Conway's departure brought with it a number of other changes. The band no longer wore coordinating outfits or hairstyles; the more contrived 'pop' concepts fell away, and with them went the elements that they later believed were holding them back. The remaining members placed an advertisement looking for a new lead singer. Shields made the mistake of mentioning The Smiths in the ad, which meant the resulting auditions turned into a procession of 'fruitballs' doing poor imitations of Morrissey.[23] Ultimately, MBV found two new members through old-fashioned word of mouth. One would be gone from the band in the blink of an eye; the other would completely change the trajectory of MBV and indie-rock history.

chapter two

'Wayne used to tell me all the things we should do to be more professional. He said we had to make a commitment to him if we wanted to get on, and off the dole. We just couldn't agree with what he said though. We didn't want to end up as a second-rate Primitives. That was the last thing on our minds.'

KEVIN SHIELDS ON WAYNE MORRIS, 1988[1]

Bilinda Jayne Butcher, born September 16, 1961, was raised in London before moving to Golden Valley, a hamlet in Derbyshire. Unlike the other members of MBV, her introduction to music came via northern soul rather than punk. As a teen, she attended 'all-dayers' in the morning, being too young to stay up all night on amphetamines. In talking about her adolescence, her frame of reference was often the 20s and 30s, never bothering with current events. Her mother perceived her as living in another era, her head high up in the clouds.

At sixteen, Butcher moved to London to study dance and also started going to goth gigs by bands like Bauhaus and Sisters Of Mercy. For one of her auditions, she danced to the accompaniment of a song by Black Flag. She was not invited to attend. She eventually enrolled at the Laban Dance Centre, but she had difficulties completing her classes due to what turned out to be chronic bouts of cystitis.* It's clear from later interviews that the disappointment at not being able to complete her studies is something that stayed with her.

After leaving dance school, Butcher worked as a nanny for a French couple, but this endeavor too was cut short when her only surviving parent, her mother, passed away, requiring her to return to Derbyshire to put things in order. She returned to London in 1979, in time to see Joy Division, The Birthday Party, and Talking Heads. It was at this time that she began to date a Frenchman whom she has refrained from naming in interviews. The two of them moved to Paris for six months, living off her inheritance, before returning to London, specifically to a squat in Brixton.

According to Butcher, her French boyfriend first met Ó Cíosóig on a ferry from the Netherlands, most likely in early 1985. A couple of years later, in the spring of 1987, that same boyfriend, with whom she'd now had a son, Toby, let her know that MBV were holding auditions. It came down to a choice between her and a girl named Julie, the girlfriend of Douglas Hart, who played bass in The Jesus & Mary Chain. Butcher sang Dolly Parton's 'Bargain Store,' which quickly won over Googe. *'My life is likened to a bargain store / And I may have just what you're looking for'* was a prophetic line indeed for the person who would soon transform the band.

Unlike MBV's other members, Butcher had some formal training in the arts. Besides dance, she had also studied the guitar as a child, though she had long forgotten her lessons by the time she auditioned. It was her natural feel for rhythm and melody that Shields picked up on right away. His belief that innate ability could trump anything one might learn through rote practice is one of his core artistic values. 'The reason we got Bilinda in was that she understood the rhythmic side to playing in a band,' he later explained. 'You'd play something and she'd play in time and with a sense of how it should all fit together. That's rare. We may not have been

---

* Butcher's story will be familiar to any woman who has ever been dismissed or treated badly by a male physician who didn't take her seriously. She felt as though she was being written off as a promiscuous girl with recurring sexually transmitted diseases. By the time she received a proper diagnosis, she'd dropped out of the dance program.

technically very good, but I knew we had the right feel.'[2] He was also particularly impressed that she could sing in tune with little to no effort.

Around the time Butcher joined MBV, Joe Byfield, who would later form the band Gallon Drunk, briefly came in as the band's lead singer, but he was let go due to a lack of commitment after one show as a five-piece in Camden in April 1987. With Byfield gone before their next show in May, Shields was forced to take on lead vocal duties himself.

•

In the long tradition of outsider entrepreneurs, Wayne Morris, the founder of Lazy Records, was practical when it came to raising funds to launch his label. He was also more than willing to push boundaries and take risks; among other things, he sold T-shirts featuring the slogan 'Hitler's World Tour 1939–1945.' The money he made at his shop was put to good use, though, as he successfully managed and promoted The Primitives, which resulted in some hit singles and significant LP sales. He chalked up the band's success to his own business acumen, although it's impossible to know exactly what role his guidance played in putting them on the map. Nevertheless, he came to believe in his own infallible judgment, concluding that all any group needed was to be 'as cute and attractively packaged as a Milky bar.'[3]

These kinds of nakedly commercial ambitions never sat well with MBV, but despite this clash in worldviews, MBV still owed Lazy two more records. In July 1987, five months after Butcher joined the group, they recorded a single, 'Strawberry Wine.' It was originally planned as a five-song EP but ended up as a three-track single after the two other songs the band attempted failed to come together. It seems probable that had they just repeated what they had done in the past, all five songs would have been completed easily. The fact that they didn't, however, offers us a clear indication that Shields was becoming more ambitious and more willing to rethink things from the ground up.

In the band's previous iteration, Shields had ceded lyrics and vocals to Conway. Conway wanted to sing lead, and Shields wasn't particularly keen on being the center of attention. With Conway's and then Byfield's departures, he was forced to take on the role as lead vocalist; even as he still took input from other members, he also felt compelled to take the lead role in fundamentally shaping the songs to a much greater degree than ever before.

The band's first release with Butcher, 'Strawberry Wine' is a major demarcation point and the first fully realized song from any iteration of MBV. It is also the first for which the band began drawing material from their own lives. The song grew out of Shields's daydreams about a beautiful girl as he paced up and down the grimy street she lived on. He recalled that, like the real whisky cocktail of the title, 'It's about something that's sweet but heavy. Intoxicating. Which means, literally, poisonous.'[4] While the song lacks the dissonant timbres MBV would artfully add to the mix on the *You Made Me Realise* EP, it nevertheless transports you into a different realm, creating something that is greater than the sum of its parts.

Just a few weeks after finishing the single, MBV began work on a mini-album, *Ecstasy*. Recorded over two weeks during which the band slept for only a couple of hours a night, it would be the first album they recorded using sleep-deprivation techniques (and likely marijuana) as part of their creative process. Although they were happy with what they recorded, they were frustrated with Lazy, claiming that the pressing of *Ecstasy* neutered the sound because the tapes weren't cut to the master disc properly. Shields brought in his own engineer in an attempt to solve these issues, but Morris refused to invest any more money in the record.

'We did some really extreme things with the guitar—if you listen to *Ecstasy* really carefully, you can just about hear them,' Shields would later complain. 'It was the first time we'd actually played around properly in the studio, and we came out with some quite nasty guitar ideas. Very extreme.'[5] After the unsatisfactory pressing was finally released, the mini album seemed to disappear from stores after only two weeks. The 'Strawberry Wine' single, by contrast, remained available for a year.

Butcher's talent and originality led to her role in the band expanding with each release. She sang enchanting backup vocals, starting with 'Strawberry Wine,' and took over lead vocals for the first time on 'She

Loves You No Less,' *Ecstasy*'s opening track, where her sinuous voice plays off Shields's chiming guitar to great effect. Though the band may not consider it a fully realized effort in retrospect, it's indicative of what they were now aiming to create, and Butcher's vocals leave an indelible impression that is still a signature element of MBV's sound to this day.

Because the single and mini-album were recorded and released so close to one another, many outlets reviewed them together. Bob Stanley, who would later co-found the band Saint Etienne, was a young journalist at the *NME* when he gave 'Strawberry Wine' and *Ecstasy* a combined score of nine out of ten:

> Given one listen you might dismiss My Bloody Valentine as mere noisy upstarts, but bite through that crunchy exterior and you will find the sweetest honey at the core…
>
> Take 'Strawberry Wine,' the new single. It floats on a sea of sighed backing vocals, a lilac-covered love song, the sensuality implicit. You will hear few better singles this year. *Ecstasy* covers similar ground, entering a perfumed garden of pop where emotions are affected as if you were thumbing through a pile of fading snapshots.[6]

Blur guitarist Graham Coxon was also a fan, selecting it as a 'lost classic' in a 2012 feature for the same publication. 'I know Kevin Shields might hate me for picking this,' he noted, 'but it's the sort of music that I'm a big fan of: beautiful little pop music but it's very barbed, with a layer of white noise and big tambourines.'[7]

At first glance, the songs the band were writing around this time shared a number of attributes with the C86 music scene of the mid-80s, but there's something more sophisticated, lascivious, and arch running through the best songs on these last two Lazy releases.[*] They hint at what was to come.

---

[*] C86 was initially the title of a twenty-two-song cassette compiled by the *NME* featuring songs by bands like The Wedding Present, Primal Scream, McCarthy, The Pastels, and The Shop Assistants, among others. The name quickly became shorthand for the young, jangly independent UK guitar bands of the era.

It's important to appreciate how two things that happened around the same time—Butcher joining and Shields taking over most aspects of each song—radically changed the band's sound. With Conway gone, Shields found himself more responsible for the songs than ever before. 'When I started to sing,' he later noted, 'it gave me the freedom to do anything I wanted with the guitar because I didn't have to worry about a singer trying to sing along.'[8] These possibilities were further enhanced by having Butcher available to sing as well, either solo or in tandem with him.

'Strawberry Wine,' 'She Loves You No Less,' and '(You're) Safe In Your Sleep (From This Girl)' are sweeter-than-sweet confections that serve as captivating previews of the intense, melodic sound the group were now capable of creating. 'Claire,' which includes some fuzzy guitar tones and a dissonant loop made out of crowd noise from a recording of The Beatles at the Hollywood Bowl, is noteworthy as an important link to the band's key philosophy from 1987 onward, to be better realized upon signing to Creation Records: to combine 'pure noise and pure melody.'[9] It also served as a vehicle for experimenting with melody and noise each time they played it live. They would regularly end their sets by extending it from anywhere from five to sixteen minutes, creating a precursor to the extended 'holocaust' noise section that would mark their live performances of 'You Made Me Realise' from 1991 onward.

Upon the initial release of the single and mini-album, Shields began giving more thoughtful, detailed interviews. Clearly, something was afoot. Of *Ecstasy*, he told *Record Mirror*, 'It's a Hüsker Dü type of style we have. Very heavy but fragile melodies. The guitar is indistinct, there isn't much sense of playing guitar at all in fact.'[10] If one didn't know better, you'd think he was trying to describe the sound of *Isn't Anything*. Even if he couldn't yet fully realize his ideas and get them down on tape, it's clear he had inklings of where he wanted to be.

Another article in the *NME*, titled 'The Excellence Of Ecstasy,' showed that the band felt they'd captured something special with the mini-album, demonstrating Shields's newfound confidence in the band's songwriting. Asked if the album was an attempt at 'classic pop,' he replied, 'Most indie bands are tune-based, guitar hooks, but we try and base ourselves on noise.' Asked to explain the band's recent evolution, he responded, 'We grew up.'[11]

•

In later years, and as soon as MBV got their bearings with Creation in 1988, Shields would reframe these two Lazy releases in a much more dismissive, negative light. In 1991, for example, he portrayed them as hastily done demos that were further hampered by his inexperience at singing lead. Plus, he said, he had just recently been introduced to The Byrds, leading him to be a bit too enchanted with his twelve-string guitar and to writing songs that were 'too jingly-jangly.'[12]

A bootleg video from September 1987, shot at the University Of London Union, provides some insight into what the band sounded like live at the time. It was filmed about six months after Butcher joined and about a month after their final two recordings for Lazy were in the can but before they were released. The set list consists of 'Sylvie's Head,' 'Kiss The Eclipse,' 'By The Danger In Your Eyes,' 'Paint A Rainbow,' 'Strawberry Wine,' 'Thorn,' 'We're So Beautiful,' 'Never Say Goodbye,' 'Lovelee Sweet Darlene,' 'Sundae Sunny Smile,' 'No Place To Go,' and 'Mary Mary' (a Monkees cover). The band were still integrating Butcher into the lineup, and Shields was still learning to play and sing at the same time. But the performance is of particular interest when we compare it to footage of the band just twelve months later, after their sound had undergone a massive transformation.

Shields has since stated that the band were so unhappy with their final releases on Lazy that they considered breaking up altogether. It turns out that he was using the term 'breaking up' rather loosely, however; they never planned on quitting but instead considered taking a break and then returning under a new name and starting up again with a new roster of material. With the exception of a few worthy songs on the *Sunny Sundae Smile* EP, they didn't want their older recordings following them around. But their desire to keep playing live, paired with an inconsequential following, led them to soldier on under their original moniker, giving little thought to how their fortunes might change (and how quickly) or how their name might be perceived and exploited.

The name aside, however, this was a different band in every regard, and as 1987 ended, it was clear they were beginning to find their feet. Their new image—shown in the photos for *NME*'s 'Excellence Of Ecstasy' feature, without the coordinated outfits and bowl haircuts—was a welcome change. With Butcher's beautiful pre-Raphaelite looks, Shields's shaggy head of hair, and another handsome (platonic) couple with short hair bringing a kind of symmetry to their image, they were now an inviting-looking young band. And, regardless of how Shields later framed the songs of the period, they were making recordings that finally hinted at what MBV might be capable of.

When they undertook their first recordings with Butcher, the four members of MBV had only been playing together for three or four months. They had no firm vision of where they wanted to go next. Despite this, these sessions were a necessary exercise (or perhaps exorcism) that they had to endure. This was the step that allowed them to hit the ground running when 1988 rolled around and a new label entered the picture.

chapter three

'Up to that point, I had always believed they were a really wimpy anorak band … *not for us*. But I saw that show, and it knocked me out.'

ALAN MCGEE, 1991[1]

'It changed everything for us as a band. It was the point where My Bloody Valentine became My Bloody Valentine, so it's always going to be very dear to my heart. There's something about that time and the making of that record where we suddenly evolved from being one thing into another.'

DEB GOOGE ON *YOU MADE ME REALISE*, 2012[2]

'It was the first time I ever really had control. So the combination of that freedom . . . and Bilinda's personality and the way she sang influencing what I wanted to write … turned into the *Realise* EP.'

KEVIN SHIELDS, 1992[3]

Among the many histories of British independent record labels, Creation Records is one of the most genuinely rock'n'roll stories of them all. The label played a critical role in the careers of a diverse array of beloved and influential acts, including The Jesus & Mary Chain, Primal Scream, Felt, Teenage Fanclub, Super Furry Animals, and Oasis. It was also, of course, home to MBV's work in the late 80s and early 90s, and the role the label played in the making of *Loveless* shouldn't be underestimated. But one thing separates MBV from these other acts. MBV may have been the only ones that did as much for the label as the label did for them.

Creation came into being in 1983, through a £1,000 loan, with Alan McGee leading the way, Dick Green as second in command and an invaluable stabilizing force, and Joe Foster helping out here and there. Although McGee was originally from Glasgow, he often joked that he started Creation in London in part because it was where the best drugs were—a fact that would have both benefits and drawbacks as the label grew in stature. (In actuality, he initially moved to the city because he was in a band, The Laughing Apple, with Green and Andrew Innes, later of Primal Scream. They told him they were leaving for London, and, not wanting to be left behind, he picked up stakes and joined them.)

McGee and Green had achieved two notable financial successes before signing MBV, with the former's first noteworthy discovery being The Jesus & Mary Chain. Bobby Gillespie, a longtime friend of his from Glasgow, had heard the band's demo tape and called their front men, the Reid brothers, to say that his friend ran a label and wanted them to come and play a show at the Roebuck Pub in London. McGee heard something in that first performance that drove him wild, and he offered to record The Jesus & Mary Chain that night. After some initial struggles in the studio, Creation released the band's first single, 'Upside Down,' in November 1984. It quickly sold twenty thousand copies.

McGee hoped to turn The Jesus & Mary Chain into a fully fledged phenomenon by creating and courting controversy whenever possible. He succeeded in getting them a great deal of hype through word of mouth and by securing coverage in the music weeklies. The band wanted to be on a major label—they didn't see a future with Creation—but they wisely asked McGee to manage them. He got the attention of the majors, and he eventually helped them secure a deal with Blanco Y Negro, a label set up by Geoff Travis of Rough Trade fame but wholly owned and backed by the deep pockets at Warner-Elektra-Atlantic (WEA); this earned McGee a twenty percent management fee and helped put Creation on the map. And, crucially, the Mary Chain connection would play a vital role in MBV's desire to sign with the label.

McGee's other early moneymaker was The House Of Love, who sold a significant number of records for Creation before he got them a lucrative contract with a major as well. Playing multiple labels off one another, he eventually negotiated a contract with Fontana (a subsidiary of Phonogram) in 1987, securing an £80,000 management fee for himself. Soon after that, the band began to fall apart, but it was clear that McGee understood the game. In particular, he knew when to yield to the majors, with their deeper pockets and greater experience in distribution and marketing.

These two profitable deals allowed Creation to continue signing other bands and producing records. Most of the acts the label signed would break even, and any sales revenues were put back into the pot to fund future releases. But as the label looked to sign more ambitious bands, it was clear that capital was always going to be an issue.

In 1987, Creation's roster included TV Personalities, Felt, The Weather Prophets, The Loft, Heidi Berry, Nikki Sudden, The Jazz Butcher, and Primal Scream (still several years away from *Screamadelica*). They had more than a few quality singles, EPs, and LPs among them, but other than 'Upside Down,' Creation hadn't put out anything that really excited the music press or the public. That would soon change.

There's no real mystery about why Creation succeeded in the way it did. The label's success stemmed from McGee's knack for discovering great unknown bands in combination with his business smarts. *Upside Down* was only the eleventh release by Creation, but his ear for talent, promotion, and his general business acumen were all on display already. A fixture on the London music scene, he decided who to sign based on his own intuitive connection to their music. And, because he wasn't part of some larger corporate structure, he could move quickly.

Before McGee's own band, Biff Bang Pow, were invited by Shields to open for MBV, McGee had only seen them when they were fronted by Dave Conway. He first balked at the offer, labeling them as 'twee'—a joke band—despite their efforts to stand out. 'Not for us' was his unequivocal verdict when thinking about Creation Records and My Bloody Valentine.[4] Reminiscing later about being invited to play on the same bill, he quipped, 'I thought, Supporting *them*? They're fucking anoraks. They're like a bad Pastels. A bad Pastels; can you *be* a bad Pastels? Anyway, fine, I said, but we're headlining.'[5]

When MBV agreed that he could headline, McGee relented, and the show was set for Chatham Town Hall in Kent, fifty miles or so from London, in January 1988. What McGee didn't understand back then was that due to MBV's relatively recent lineup change, he was, in effect, playing with a completely different band from the one he was familiar with. In his autobiography, he recounts how his insistence on headlining was a mistake; Shields's deference didn't seem so magnanimous on reflection. MBV proceeded to destroy the place. 'The power was so amazing,' he recalls. 'It was so raw. The feedback hadn't emerged yet, and they sounded like a psychedelic Motörhead.'[6] Astounded, McGee leaned over to Dick Green after two songs and said, 'For fuck's sake, this is like the English Hüsker Dü.'[7] As soon as MBV stepped offstage, McGee offered them a one-off record deal.

At this point, Creation had no written contracts and no proper accounting system. Everything was done on a handshake. Profits were split fifty/fifty, which was generous and atypical (and would ultimately prove unsustainable). The accounting aspect wouldn't become much of an issue until two years later, when Creation switched distributors, disrupting the label's cash flow just as MBV began work on *Loveless*.

To get an idea of what MBV sounded like around this time, your best option is probably a bootleg recorded on March 12, 1988, in Hanau, Germany, at the Kultur-Basar Club, six weeks or so after the group opened for Biff Bang Pow. One can hear how songs like 'Sylvie's Head,' '(Please) Lose Yourself (In Me),' and 'I Don't Need You' have been transformed from the original recordings by both the group's aggressive performance and the live mix in the room.

Signing a deal with Creation was the type of change the band was looking for. 'We were together about six months when we started hating what we were doing,' Shields recalled. 'We felt like we may as well break up, because we never felt like, *This is it.*'[8] But the first Creation EP would finally provide a truly definitive 'this is it' moment—the instant when the band transformed from a caterpillar into a butterfly.

As before, Shields was probably using the term 'break up' lightly, as a way to signal that the band were thinking about taking a hiatus and regrouping. More than anything, his comments speak to the desperate straits they were in when they got McGee's offer. Being given the chance to put out a record on a label with Creation's reputation really did represent a concrete sign that things might be changing for the better.

Upon agreeing to do the one-off EP, Shields made it clear to McGee that whatever they did now would not sound like the band's previous studio recordings. McGee told them to do whatever they wanted.

•

With Creation footing the bill, MBV recorded the *You Made Me Realise* EP at Bark Studio in Walthamstow, East London. It saved the label money due to Bark's early adoption of Sony DAT technology in place of high-maintenance quarter-inch tape. In a 2013 interview, McGee said that the five songs cost a paltry £1,000 to record (the equivalent of around £3,500 today). The session lasted five days, with the band using borrowed equipment, most notably a Fender Jazzmaster that was in good working order.

While Shields has often remarked that the band would go into the studio with 'nothing' prepared, this isn't quite accurate. Butcher and Ó Cíosóig have both mentioned in passing that some of the songs from *You Made Me Realise* were written in their squat. In the majority of cases, Shields would have the chord changes and melodies sketched out on acoustic guitar, though it makes sense that he could only begin to truly define each track and color in its nuances once he was in the studio and had a sense of the guitars, amps, and other equipment that were available. Even so, while the band may have had only the roughest outline of what a song would look like, they didn't go in completely unprepared.

Creation's support made a huge difference to how the band approached this new session. Shields recalled, 'This was the first time we'd never had to worry about recording costs and budgets. We could spend all our energy on the making of the record. We could do anything, use anything, so we did. Incorporating samples using equipment with which we'd never had access to, backwards guitar sounds, and different effects on the vocals.' It was also the time he'd used Fender transistor amps—a direct result of wanting to get the midrange hardness he heard on the first two Public Enemy albums. 'We mostly concentrated on the song "Slow" for that EP, even though Debbie thought it sounded like Jefferson Starship,' Shields continued, 'but when it came out, no one took much notice of it. They all went for "You Made Me Realise."'[9]

Based on other comments Shields made at the time, 'Slow' was a crucial song in the MBV catalog because it was his first deliberate foray into what he would soon call 'glide guitar.' (Subsequent comments would tell a much different story, suggesting Shields did not yet fully understand what he had on his hands.) He had already experimented with 'reverse reverb' on 'Strawberry Wine' and *Ecstasy*, his curiosity piqued by an interview by Hüsker Dü frontman Bob Mould. It's noteworthy, though, that there was no tremolo arm involved. But through a series of random events over the next year, the band were about to take the next key step in finding their sound.

The first change of note was the insistence of Shields's friend Bill Carey (from the Creation band Something Pretty Beautiful) that he try using some decent equipment. In particular, Carey urged Shields to borrow his overhauled Jazzmaster, complete with tremolo arm. In any other situation, this wouldn't have been of any great consequence, but because Carey had just had his guitar refurbished, the tremolo bar was unusually high. 'It had a re-made tremolo that was really big,' Shields recalled. 'So I put tape on it to keep it from going all the way into the socket.'[10]

Although the results of his experiments with reverse reverb on the Lazy recordings had proven unexceptional, Shields's curiosity grew after he noticed the way Thurston Moore and J Mascis used their tremolo arms, typically in conjunction with various pedals and other processors. Rowland S Howard had made an impression as early as 1983 with his distinct use of a Fender Jaguar, and Shields wanted to push his own experimentation further, now that his guitar had been upgraded.

Normally, with a tremolo arm in its stock position, you can't strum quickly. The range of motion is also limited by the fact that the arm is designed to remain parallel to the guitar body. But by using gaffer tape to loosen the arm's connection, you can strum quickly and across more planes, allowing for a much wider range of sounds. This was a key innovation and the first step toward something wholly new.*

Shields would later recall that while recording 'Thorn,' the tremolo arm made the strings 'shiver.'[11] In that moment, something jumped inside him as he realized how profoundly sensitive the setup was. After an hour or two of messing around with reverse reverb on 'Thorn,' he moved on to 'Slow,' where more elements came together. He turned the tone knob on the guitar all the way down to get what he would describe as a 'liquid' or 'melted' sound that altered both the pitch and the tone as he held the tremolo arm in his hand while strumming, locking the arm in the down-only position. In the song's first few seconds, you hear nothing but the blurry, wavy, tone-bending sounds Shields gets by manipulating the tremolo arm. The guitar caresses your ears for a few bars before the bass and drums drop in and get things going.

At the time, Shields didn't really comprehend the full potential of what he was doing, seeing it instead as a one-off setup for one specific song. As he put it thirty years later, during an extensive interview with Fender online, 'It was just some new thing, y'know, whatever.'[12] It was not until the band's next recording session, in Wales, that he began to really understand its potential.

'Slow' contains other innovations that at that moment were of more interest to Shields at the time, and they really grab the listener's attention. In particular, he was excited by the chance to bring a genuine hip-hop

---

* Other guitar players had put tape on their guitars before, but Shields was going to use this hack in a different way—one that would soon lead to an infinite number of new sounds.

feel to a rock song. He wasn't trying to rap, per se, so much as to sing in a percussive way—his take on what he described as 'early, very stark hip-hop, like LL Cool J—really raw and unpretentious.'[13] He then paired this with a low-down, grinding bass line and an underlying beat, with an early iteration of the pitch-bending reverb running through the song.

Shields would later claim that no one took much notice of the track, insisting that they were drawn instead to 'You Made Me Realise,' but that's not entirely true. After the band performed 'Slow' at Creation's 'Doing It For the Kids' festival in August of 1988, *Melody Maker*'s Simon Reynolds named it the 'sex song' of the year. 'With its colossal "Sidewalking" bass, disorientating drones, and languorous, enervated vocals,' he wrote, referencing a recent single by The Jesus & Mary Chain, 'it conjures up a honeyed, horny lassitude of desire to rival AR Kane.'[14]

A month later, Paul Oldfield, also of *Melody Maker*, singled out 'Slow' again:

When they play 'Slow' . . . it's also an almost unbearable release. It's a slow pestle and mortar action; a great abrasion that leaves nothing behind and keeps lapsing in utter solarised noise. If it's the sexiest song ever written, that's because it's both a grind—puts up resistance—and a slippage. It's as viscous as a body amidst its own secretions, or as mucous as the inside of the body. 'Slow' *is* a sex act you lose yourself in.[15]

Nonetheless, Shields is right that it was the EP's lead-off track that generated the most attention from record buyers. Surprisingly, however, had it been left up to the band, 'You Made Me Realise' would not have been the single. As McGee later recollected, 'I think they wanted "Cigarette In Your Bed" as the A-side, and I was like, No, you don't understand, we're going with "You Made Me Realise" . . . I remember picking up the phone to Kevin, and it was just so obvious that was the single. Luckily, at that point I had enough sway over them that I could actually get my own way so that it was the single.'[16]

According to McGee, while many bands came to him in need of a great deal of guidance, MBV were self-assured from day one. Making 'You Made Me Realise' the lead track on the EP was the only piece of guidance they took from him. Ultimately, Shields felt it was the right decision. 'The title song had a very immediate impact on people because it was very instinctive on our part,' he noted in 1991.[17]

You Made Me Realise represents a clean break from the band's past and signals the emergence of a group unencumbered by any of their previous misguided concepts and free of any of the trends that were evident in the music of their peers. The lyrics and music mirror their real lives and their real feelings. And the opening track was the perfect way to announce the band's new beginning, even if they didn't consciously know it.

Shields has always been loath to talk about what his lyrics mean, usually just offering general descriptions of overall themes. However, it is apparent that by this point in early 1988, Butcher and Shields had become a couple. Was it her, in her role as collaborator and muse, who made him realize what the band were now capable of? Perhaps the lyrics are about the band's shock at finding their new voice. In that sense, it is nothing less than a declaration of their arrival—the 'this is it' moment that Shields had long desired.

It's also a declaration of independence—a transition to a mindset whereby the only thing that matters to the band is pleasing themselves. The song paints a picture of a narrator turning to his lover and asking for some sort of fidelity, while also harboring feelings of confusion, desperation, fear, and ultimately, recognition. Everything in it—the melody, the rhythm, the lyrics, the structure—seems to be trying to convey the drama that this is a now-or-never, make-or-break moment.

The lyrics stutter along, questioning or contradicting the previous lines, the protagonist unsure which way is up. But despite his disorientation, he seems to be asking his lover, *Are you in?*

This is all set to one of Shields's signature earworm melodies, which rises and falls each time as the song gets to the razor's edge of the verses. Finally, with the song on the verge of its wordless climax, we arrive at the coup de grâce, where the music stops and only the vocals remain to attest to the narrator's clear-eyed understanding. Each syllable is dragged out as he reveals, '*In-sane eyesssss / You made me re-a-lise.*' The percussive chorus then hits three times in succession before the song dives back into the maelstrom and confusion of the verse.

With this EP and the other records that would follow later in the year, MBV brought something vital that was missing from British guitar rock at the time: a sense that intense melodies could deeply move you if they were tied to noise and rhythm. In Shields's estimation, many rock bands, particularly in the UK, weren't concerned with the whole track but were focused solely on the guitar and vocal parts. But he was keenly aware that it was just as important to consider how the sound makes your body feel (as you would with rap or dance music) alongside what you experience through your ears.

Martin Carr of The Boo Radleys has talked about how *You Made Me Realise* took him by surprise, particularly in light of the somewhat more conventional release, *Ecstasy*, that preceded it. He has also made some convincing arguments about the rhythmic deficiencies of other bands of the time, noting in 2014:

> I don't think any of us expected *You Made Me Realise*. I got it home and I played it, and I had to play it again, check the speed. .... I didn't really know what I was hearing. I'd heard [Sonic Youth's] *Daydream Nation* and loved it, and you could see they were going for kind of like, 'Silver Rocket,' where there's that big noise bit in the middle. But the melody sounded like The Byrds, and it was just so HEAVY. The bass was so HEAVY. That's what the Mary Chain were missing, any kind of bass presence.[18]

Carr is correct in viewing MBV as one of the first guitar bands to graft melody and noise onto a compelling rhythm, creating songs that cover all the different elements both your mind and body want.

Shields has always appreciated how to employ some of the harshest, most dissonant guitar tones without putting off the listener, if those tones are paired with the right rhythm and a sweet, catchy melody. A few years later, he explained why the band's music from 1988 was so different from everything that had come before. Previously, they had been afraid of doing anything too extreme or too closely reflecting their influences. But now, perpetually on the verge of splitting up, there was nothing to stop them from trying whatever they wanted. As a result, they ended up with something much more original and much more fun.[19]

Ironically, it was Shields's obsession with originality that had previously held him back. At one point, he was so discouraged by his progress on the guitar that he switched to keyboards. It was only after he decided that he had nothing to lose that he felt comfortable putting *all* his various influences into the mix, and only then did he surprise himself with the unique voice that emerged as a result. The band became looser, freer, and more themselves—and the music was better for it. Their next task would be to prove that the *You Made Me Realise* EP was no fluke. They would make that case with another EP and their first long-playing album.

interlude one

Long before MBV made *Isn't Anything* and *Loveless*, Kevin Shields's natural curiosity about sound led to him incorporating and experimenting with a wide range of musical influences. Ultimately, the group's sound is *sui generis*, but it wasn't always like that, and Shields didn't invent it out of thin air.

Some of those influences date back to the earliest days of his life. He has mentioned, for example, how the degraded, wobbly television footage of Jimi Hendrix lighting his guitar on fire at the Monterey Pop Festival had long stuck in his mind, or how hearing the DAF song 'Der Mussolini' in 1981 showed him an early example of pitch bending. While the emergence of The Jesus & Mary Chain in the mid-80s profoundly changed his ideas of what music could be, his next major sources of inspiration came from America, particularly the bands who were gaining a following in the UK due to the zealous advocacy of Englishman Paul Smith.

Smith, who eventually went on to help manage Sonic Youth, set up Blast First as a sublabel of Mute Records in 1985, distributing releases by American underground and indie labels like SST, Touch & Go, and Homestead, by bands like Dinosaur Jr., Big Black, and the Butthole Surfers. His tireless promotion eventually turned Blast First into a label that punched way above its weight. According to music historian Richard King, it 'singlehandedly brought the cream of a generation of American bands into the UK and Europe ... reconfiguring the British guitar underground in a manner that sent shockwaves through their C86 contemporaries and inspired a new generation of British bands to explore noise, aggression and distortion.'[1]

MBV certainly benefited from this transatlantic exchange, and when asked about bands they felt a connection with, they would regularly mention the bands Smith had championed. In a 1987 fanzine interview, Ó Cíosóig cited MBV's affinity with 'some American bands: Dinosaur, Sonic Youth, Hüsker Dü.'[2] To that list, Shields added Suzanne Vega, Pussy Galore, and the short-lived British band World Domination Enterprises.

During the period when MBV were recording for Lazy and then making the transition to Creation, they were just finding their feet, and they had to consciously push back against claims that they were merely ripping off other bands on the US and UK indie scenes. 'People think we're crap,' Shields told *The Catalogue* in early 1989, 'that we're trying to sound like the current American bands, like Sonic Youth, or something like the Mary Chain. That we're a second-rate Dinosaur Jr.'[3] Criticism came from other quarters as well, even after the band had shown they were up to something unique on *Isn't Anything* and *Glider*. While promoting *Daydream Nation* in *Sounds* in 1990, Thurston Moore, discussing the current crop of bands being celebrated in the music weeklies, quickly dismissed the Manchester 'Baggy' scene, including Happy Mondays and The Stone Roses, but also took the time to single out MBV. 'Take a band like My Bloody Valentine, who would totally change their musical style from one day to the next,' he said. 'To us, that's like, forget it, just cross it out. That's why we're so cynical about bands who jump sound bandwagons.'[4] Coming some six months after the release of MBV's *Glider* EP, however, these sentiments seem like sour grapes.

Fortunately, for every detractor, MBV had a greater number of fans who understood in one way or another that they were following their own unique vision. Kurt Heasley, the main man behind the band Lilys, heard something profound happening with the band's early Creation releases. He understood how MBV's new music was related to the American bands he followed but also how it showed the group forging their own path. 'They took what I loved about Dinosaur Jr. and Sonic Youth and put it into this level of melody, suspended dissonance, and tonal resolution that had no comparison,' he said. 'They were the blue angels of noise, and you could feel it in the marrow of your bones.'[5]

Shields has said that the comparisons people have drawn between MBV and some American bands aren't so strange considering he spent his early years in the USA and shared many of the same influences as his peers from across the Atlantic. Like J Mascis and Thurston Moore, he had heard the Ramones and Hüsker Dü during his formative years and felt a kinship with the post-punk sound that developed there. 'I feel Irish,' he explained, 'although I only lived there for ten years. I spent the first ten years in America, and a lot of things come out in our music that people think we're just copying from various American bands. It irritates me occasionally because, whatever they've got, I've got just as much of.'[6]

Both Shields and Ó Cíosóig have made no bones about being fans of the US post-punk scene. Shields particularly loved Dinosaur Jr.'s *You're Living All Over Me*, while Sonic Youth's *EVOL* and *Sister* were in regular rotation at the squat he shared with Ó Cíosóig. Unlike the latter group, however, he made clear that he wasn't interested in doing anything self-consciously avant-garde for its own sake. 'That's one of the great misconceptions about [MBV],' he later noted, 'that everything is intellectual and there's an awful lot of time spent perfecting things.'[7]

Even if Shields never saw a strong overlap in terms of the songs they were creating, American bands altered his creative approach to music, giving him more confidence to indulge his truest vision and pursue the particular sound he was after. 'If there is a similarity, it would be one of attitude,' Shields put it. 'The people involved don't have any respect for the *correct* way of playing the guitar but are more interested in getting new sounds out whichever way they can.'[8]

•

Shields's other big contemporary inspiration was the emerging world of hip-hop and house music. As far as guitar acts go, The Stone Roses and Happy Mondays were the most prominent UK indie pop music acts to manifest the influence of American dance and hip-hop early on. But MBV were one of the first guitar-heavy bands to really understand the innovations that were happening at the time in rap, house, and techno and integrate them into their own sound.

On the free seven-inch that was included with early copies of *Isn't Anything*, 'Instrumental No. 2' is built around a sample of Public Enemy's 'Security Of The First World,' though it is utterly transformed by the guitar Shields laid over it. It is one of the most direct signs of the importance the group played in Shields's development as a musician and producer. Rappers Chuck D and Flavor Flav, the most recognizable faces of the group, have often taken center stage in the public's mind, but the revolutionary backing tracks and sampling techniques created by Hank Shocklee, his brother Keith Shocklee, and the rest of the Bomb Squad were equally important, both to the hip-hop records and dance music in the USA and the UK and to the direction MBV was headed in when they made the jump to Creation.

As Jeanette Leech explains in her excellent book *Fearless: The Making Of Post-Rock*, 'Before long, sampling would flex its muscles in rock music, and it was Hank Shocklee's work on *Yo! Bum Rush The Show*, *It Takes A Nation Of Millions To Hold Us Back*, and *Fear Of A Black Planet* that opened it up radically in this direction. He put sounds to new uses, strained the limits of technology, but kept the feel of a careful construct: a black sculpture in the hour of chaos.'[9] Around the time MBV first employed samplers in their recordings for Creation, they were being used in vibrant ways by Prince Paul on De La Soul's first album, *3 Feet High and Rising* (March 1989), and by the Dust Brothers on the Beastie Boys' *Paul's Boutique* (July 1989). 'It was the weird sampling in hip-hop records that inspired us to create eerie guitar effects in the first place,' Shields explained. Songs like 'Slow' and 'Soft As Snow (But Warm Inside)' offer twisted new takes on the guitar with vocals refashioned by Shields's own unique aesthetic, adapting the charisma of rap's punctuated delivery. Taken together with more amorphous songs like 'Instrumental No. 2' and 'Soon,' he was demonstrating the most creative yet subtle take on rap and house by any white rock band.

Shields was particularly inspired by Shocklee's subtler and more esoteric sampling strategies. The Bomb Squad often combined samples that might be a micro-tone or two off, or that might not quite line up with other samples but created a dissonance that somehow worked. Shields's guitar playing was similar; he would let notes go in and out of tune and focus with each strum whenever the whammy bar was in his hand (which it almost always was). He was attracted to layered samples 'that were half-buried or muted, a real sense of sounds being semi-decayed, or destroyed, but then re-used.'[10]

But it was also the overall *sound* of hip-hop—and, in particular, Shocklee's exploitation of midrange frequencies—that had the most profound impact on Shields. In a 2018 interview, Shocklee reflected on the origin of his attraction to midrange sound, noting that it's not as ear-fatiguing as digital while also emphasizing the way it can better leave an impression on the whole body. 'The reason why we love those records was that midrange that was there … we didn't have a lot of extra bottom end on the low, and we didn't have that crunchiness on the top—but the midrange was unbelievable. … The sources are more aligned with the human ear and the human soul because you don't just hear with your ears, you also hear with your body.'[11]

Through the early 90s, Shields's preferred way to listen to music was on cassette, and he has since recalled the pleasure he got from sitting in bed with a boombox in his lap, a foot away from his head.[12] This would influence the density of his recordings, in which all of the elements of a song compete with one another to cut through in the midrange spectrum.

In 2012, Shields shed some light on the different sound on the band's second Creation EP, *Feed Me With Your Kiss* (discussed in more detail in the following chapter) and the perception that it felt darker and more lo-fi, which was deliberate on his part. He was becoming more conscious of the full range of frequencies at his disposal, in part due to hip-hop's emphasis on midrange, and how most conventional 80s records made each element separate and bright. Compared to *You Made Me Realise*, this new EP felt more claustrophobic and blunted, but with a consistent feel across the song choices, the playing, and the mixing. 'You don't have to put all this top end on everything,' he later said.[13] The EP represented his changing aesthetic as he continued to better express himself—and it's perhaps no surprise that it marks the only time he wrote all the music and lyrics on an MBV release.

Later on, Shocklee would reciprocate Shields's appreciation of his work when he mentioned how much he liked 2013's *m b v*. 'I want to hear a really good Gang Of Four, but I don't want it to sound like Maroon 5,' he joked. 'I want to hear what they would do today, given the technology today. One of the records I thought was really cool recently was the My Bloody Valentine record. Dope. It stayed true to what it was. And it shows you don't have to be on this commercial timeline of putting out a record every year.'[14]

On first listen, MBV's Creation releases might sound like they would fit in with much of the American music distributed by Blast First. But these groundbreaking, fully realized recordings were the result of a set of random factors and creative inspirations that no one could orchestrate if they tried. At the time, a small percentage of music journalists, as well as the band's peers, opined that MBV had deliberately changed elements of their sound to follow the trends coming out of the USA. But listening to all of their recordings, it's abundantly clear that they were always being guided by their own vision. What other rock bands were using samples and hip-hop elements in 1988? No other indie guitar band of the era was making anything like 'Slow' or 'Instrumental No. 2.'

There's a profound distinction between being inspired by your peers and stealing another band's sound. And if you take a survey of American post-punk music and hip-hop and compare it to MBV's back catalog of recordings, their live performances prior to 1988, Shields's new guitar innovations, and the band's integration of hip-hop and dance music elements, the bigger picture is plain to see: MBV were always following their own muse.

chapter four

'In rock algebra, you might deduce that they'd worked out some new equation involving the barbed languor of the Mary Chain, the speed freak urgency of Sonic Youth, and a dash of The Vaselines' sauce—but none of that accounts for the savagely sensual results, it was as though a lovechild of some 1975 one-night stand between *Metal Machine Music* and *Another Green World* had finally come of age.'

STEPHEN TROUSSÉ ON *ISN'T ANYTHING*[1]

'[*Isn't Anything*] was the first time [Creation] had released a record by a band that sounded like the future, rather than a join-the-dots reworking of the past, however shambolic or elegant.'

RICHARD KING, *HOW SOON IS NOW?*[2]

As the summer of 1988 got underway, Kevin Shields and the other members of MBV were motivated and hungry. They were eager to record again after making two big leaps forward, through the addition of Butcher to the lineup followed by the creative freedom McGee had granted them. Shields's new, unconstrained outlook had led to a kind of sonic awakening in the studio and signaled good things to come. But the success of *You*

Made Me Realise and their growing reputation on the live circuit around Europe wouldn't mean much if they couldn't follow it up and build on it.

With financing from Creation, the band went to Foel Studio in Wales, around two hundred miles from London, likely because it was relatively inexpensive and offered them the chance to work without distraction. Dave Anderson, who owned Foel and was credited as one of several engineers for MBV's next recordings, would play a serendipitous role in helping Shields realize a sound he had discussed as far back as 1987, when talking to *Record Mirror* about the *Ecstasy* EP. 'Slow' was the first glimpse of it, even if Shields hadn't fully picked up on it.

Anderson's curiosity and amiable disposition paired well with Shields's unique abilities. His role as engineer and sounding board opened the floodgates for Shields, resulting in him making more inspired music than at any time in his life. And his experience enabled MBV to explore, expand, and then refine their sound more quickly than anyone else imaginable.

By the time Anderson had set up Foel in 1973, he was already a seasoned musician. Originally from Wales, he'd moved to Munich in 1970, staying there for over three years during one of the most exciting and innovative periods in modern music. Upon arriving, he was asked to join Amon Düül II as bass player, appearing on well-known albums like *Yeti* and *Dance Of The Lemmings*. He later played with Motörhead and The Groundhogs while continuing to run his own studio.

In preparation for the sessions with MBV, Shields asked Anderson to obtain an Alesis MidiVerb unit, which he wanted for its reverse reverb capabilities. Assuming the group would want the latest iteration of the device, Anderson instead ordered a MidiVerb II, which arrived in Wales on the same day as the band. It was the first digital device Anderson had ever used in his studio, so he sent the group off to have tea while he unpacked it and began investigating its capabilities.

While trying out the new equipment, Anderson ran some of Shield's first guitar recordings from earlier that day through the MidiVerb II and out of the studio speakers. Because he was unfamiliar with the device, he set the speakers to play only the 'wet' digital effect being created, in order to understand how it altered the sound. (Reverse reverb is usually applied with its default configuration, which contains both the 'dry' guitar track—the grounded part the musician actually plays—and the 'wet,' processed, more disembodied effect outputted by the unit.) Anderson realized he'd turned it up quite loud when Shields came running over, breathlessly, demanding to know, 'What's that sound? What are you doing?'

'Experimenting,' Anderson replied. 'I'm just seeing what the unit is capable of doing.'

'That's it!' Shields replied emphatically. 'That's my sound!'[3]

Anderson explained to Shields that what he was hearing was just the effect created by the MidiVerb II, not the complete mix of wet and dry sounds, and that it would change when he set the device correctly. But Shields was insistent that the isolated wet signal was what he'd been looking for. The reverse reverb digital effect, combined with his specific configuration of the whammy bar, utilizing the unique tremolo system on the Jazzmaster, was now *his* sound.

When an engineer comes attached to a studio, they aren't always open to new ideas, but Anderson was different. As Shields recalled thirty years later, 'In those days, a lot of studio people thought we were nuts and usually went into a kind of bubble and just did what we asked, kind of in a trance, everything sounded wrong to them. We were lucky in Wales, and they seemed to enjoy the trip we were on.'[4]

When Anderson first heard the results of Shields using just the wet signal, he thought it went 'completely against the rules on every level … [but] if you want to do something that's really different, that's the only way of doing it. … I wasn't sure what he was looking for, anyway, [but] if that's what he wanted, sod it, yeah, I'll give it to him … I've done enough mad music to know that what I think's right isn't necessarily correct.'[5]

By chance, Anderson had stumbled upon a series of settings on the MidiVerb II that produced a particular iteration of digital reverse reverb to which Shields felt preternaturally drawn. By using its unique percussive effect alongside the tremolo system he had set up, he could create a truly unique assortment of sonic landscapes simply by how he strummed the guitar. Those sounds could be altered even further in conjunction with alternate tunings and whatever other pedals and processors he put his guitar through. 'Several Girls Galore' and 'All I Need' are quintessential examples of the vast range of sound that was now possible. Even though both songs are derived from a similar setup—played through the MidiVerb II and with the tremolo arm raised, loosely held in his hand as he strummed—the sound of the wet guitar effects is very different.

This new lexicon of potential sounds represented another huge leap in the band's sonic capabilities and evolution, and it soon became Shields's mother tongue. While he was recording 'All I Need,' Shields remembered Anderson saying, 'This is really different. This is original.' To which Shields replied, 'I think this *is* original! I don't think anyone does this.'[6]

Although he remained open to suggestions, Shields was now taking on a much larger role in the studio, overseeing the equalization process and even the placement of microphones. But while Anderson was on board with recording whichever way Shields wanted, he was caught off guard when Shields came into the control room on the last day and said he wouldn't leave until Anderson had erased all the guitars—that is, the dry elements—to leave only the processed reverse reverb signal on the tapes.

Anderson was creative enough to understand that past methods shouldn't necessarily dictate how things should be done in the future, but as a professional engineer contracted by Creation, the idea of permanently erasing the original guitar parts concerned him; if he did what Shields was asking, there was no way to bring the tracks back, and he wasn't sure if he would ultimately have to answer to the label. What if McGee asked why the erased guitars simply weren't mixed down and left on the tape, just in case they were needed later? Erasing them was permanent.

Creation had given MBV complete artistic control over what they released, but Anderson didn't know the exact contours of Shields's relationship with the label, and he was worried. Nevertheless, he did as Shields asked. Fortunately, even though there were some initial questions about what had happened to the original guitar parts, Shields was able to convince Creation that this was the way forward.

This responsive and emotive new aesthetic—which can be heard on both *Isn't Anything* and the concurrently recorded *Feed Me With Your Kiss* EP—was something utterly new. It created individual sonic moments that stirred people's imaginations, but it also had the ability to generate the wide variety of sonic landscapes that were necessary to sustain a listener's attention over the course of an album. In interviews, Shields and countless others would try to describe the new sound succinctly, but it was difficult to capture just how disembodied yet powerful it was. It also seemed a little magical; Shields didn't perform the physical strumming motion you might expect to correspond to the sound being created. The motion, like the sound, was something ethereal; something nobody had ever seen or heard before.

•

After a week off following their stint in Wales, MBV resumed work on *Isn't Anything* and *Feed Me With Your Kiss* during an additional eleven days at the Greenhouse, a cheap basement studio back in London, where they recorded another six or seven songs. There were further noteworthy innovations during these sessions, including the use of a Roland delay unit as a primitive sampler. (Prior to that, they had used an even more primitive device, a Bel Delay unit, during the noise section of 'You Made Me Realise.')

Another memorable moment at the Greenhouse came during the tracking of the bass guitar for 'Feed Me With Your Kiss,' when Shields made the bass so heavy that the speaker popped off the wall. Instinctively, the engineer put his foot out to break its fall, breaking his ankle in the process. There were no hard feelings, according to Shields, and after having his foot treated, the engineer went back to reading *Lord Of The Rings*.

Though Shields had now perfected his signature 'glide guitar' sound, he did not rely on it for every song. In 'Feed Me with Your Kiss,' for example, he achieves a heavy, vicious, bass attack that meshes perfectly with the guitars and drums, demonstrating his ability to combine elements from the American bands he admired while upping the melodicism, noise, and drive to create something absolutely singular.

The band recorded at least nineteen tracks during the sessions in Wales and London. Twelve made it onto *Isn't Anything*, two instrumentals were released on a bonus seven-inch, and three more rounded out the *Feed Me With Your Kiss* EP. At least two other tracks were recorded during these sessions, though these didn't see the light of day until the release of *EP's 1988–1991* in 2012.

Some early reports erroneously stated that the sessions were completed in two weeks, but Deb Googe stated in interviews at the time that *Isn't Anything* took five weeks to record and mix, with the latter stage completed in London. In his autobiography, Alan McGee says the album took about six weeks to put together and cost £7,000. Shields seemed to confirm Googe's timeline when he noted that all of the recording was finished by the time the band played a show with the Pixies on October 2, 1988. Either way, it's clear that Shields remembered the experience as a time of unbridled discovery—the moment he found his voice as a guitarist and songwriter. That feeling was apparent to those around him as well. As Anderson put it, 'There was music coming out of his every orifice.'[7]

The initial excitement Shields chanced upon with the discovery of the Alesis MidiVerb II only grew as the band finished recording *Isn't Anything*, and the encouragement and goodwill they received from Dave Anderson had proven to be a real help. Yet one can't help but wonder what other elements Shields might have exploited, had he gone to another studio after Bark and never had his chance encounter with Anderson and the MidiVerb II. Ultimately, though, his innovations with sound weren't mere chance happenings. They reflect his inborn musicality and his intuitive ability to understand how things fit together in the aural world. When Anderson presented an opening, Shields jumped through it. He would look back at this era of his career and remember it as a time when creative ideas presented themselves effortlessly to him.

•

With their second EP and first long-playing record in the can, MBV began playing the occasional show about town, integrating their newly recorded but as yet unreleased songs into their set lists. A bootleg of the band's performance at Dingwalls in Camden on September 12, 1988, captures their new, raw energy and offers a window into how quickly the four of them were progressing as musicians. They were also playing songs they'd never attempted live before. The Dingwalls recording includes the band's first performances of 'Emptiness Inside,' 'Sueisfine,' and 'Slow,' and captures Shields castigating the venue after the sound person has walked off, leaving them with no monitors, completely unable to hear themselves, and prompting Shields to suggest that the patrons smash the place up. It's unclear whether the monitors were ever restored; an early attempt at 'Thorn' falls apart halfway through. Perhaps as a result of their treatment, the band close with a vicious take of 'You Made Me Realise' followed by an extreme, seventeen-minute version of 'Claire,' which they had previously used to vent their frustrations at other shows. ('Claire' and 'Please Lose Yourself In Me' were the only songs in the set from the band's Lazy releases.)

As October neared, there was every indication that MBV were finally making music that reflected their ambitions and capabilities. Two months on from the release of their first Creation EP, the closing months of 1988 signaled the fact that they were finally on their way. John Peel, the iconic BBC Radio 1 disc jockey, was a fan of *You Made Me Realise* and played tracks from it ten times during August and September—a clear measure of how he heard something special in it. He also invited the band to record a live session for his show—a rite of passage that involved a band spending a day recording four or five songs for later broadcast. The list of important and influential bands who have recorded Peel sessions could fill a small book, so it's not hard to understand why MBV jumped at the opportunity. On September 25, 1988, they went into Hippodrome Studio in London to record four songs that hadn't been released previously. Some bands would use a Peel session to try to surpass the studio version of a song or record a vastly different arrangement, but that's not the route MBV opted to take. The four recordings they made—'I Can See It (But I Can't Feel It),' 'Lose My Breath,' 'Colm's Song' (later retitled '(When You Wake) You're Still In A Dream'), and 'Feed Me With Your Kiss'—are mostly identical to how they are played on the versions that were eventually released. The results were first broadcast on BBC Radio 1 on October 5, several weeks before the release of the band's new EP.

The session has never been given an official release, perhaps due to its mediocre quality, but it can be found in various recesses of the internet. Looking back on it, Shields singled out 'Lose My Breath' as the weakest of the lot, saying that while the Peel session version was recorded using much more expensive equipment, the album version, cut in a cheap basement studio, is vastly superior. Cost of equipment, he noted, wasn't necessarily important to recording; what was more important was how one exploited the tools that were available.[8]

Like John Peel, *Melody Maker* journalist Simon Reynolds saw the band's transformation between 1987 and 1988, though he was measured in his praise of their set at the Creation Records all-day event 'Doing It For The Kids' on August 7, 1988, noting that they could not yet pull off many of their more delicate songs live.[9] His passionate three-page follow-up piece was nonetheless awarded the cover of the magazine's October 15 issue, which featured a striking close-up of Butcher looking right into the camera with her hair hanging over half her face, a large gold hoop earring exposed on the other side, and her slightly pursed lips on their way to a smile, all set against a crimson background. Shields can be seen off to her left, also bathed in red light, albeit out of focus.

The article itself featured some of the most flattering photographs of the four band members to date, accompanied by Reynolds's most impassioned writing about any group. By now, the coordinated haircuts and affected outfits had long given way to four musicians presenting themselves as they really were, which mirrored the original and unaffected music they had made since signing with Creation.

Reynolds was the first journalist to fully appreciate and understand how monumental and unique MBV's forthcoming record would be, and he correctly sensed the explosion that was about to go off. Entitled 'Suicide Kisses,' his article brimmed with a kind of love-at-first-sight excitement. 'They've become something I can barely live without,' he stated at the end of the first paragraph. 'Something *I die into*, on a regular basis.' Placing the band alongside Sonic Youth, Hüsker Du, Dinosaur Jr., and AR Kane, he concluded:

> Somewhere in between but decidedly of itself lies My Bloody Valentine's noise. Their guitars are rampant, clamorous, craving, grazed, engorged, honeyed, horny, somehow extremely *oral*, somehow obscurely *irritable*, they make me want to bite somebody. In 1988's rock pharmacopeia, My Bloody Valentine classify as a deliriant *and* a hallucinogen—they're hyped up *and* out-of-it, carnal *and* unbodied.[10]

Reynolds seemed genuinely taken, believing that nothing was going to stop the band from getting the attention and accolades they deserved after years of dead ends and false starts. Elsewhere, he would describe MBV as a 'departure from the traditional rock musculature of riff and power chord towards a new and private lexicon of sounds and effects—shapeless surges, swathes, plinths, precipices, vortices, wraiths, and detonations.'[11]

The *Melody Maker* cover feature made clear that the band's ascension to the top of the UK indie-guitar heap had begun. *Feed Me With Your Kiss* was released two weeks later, and *Isn't Anything* came out three weeks after that. (The EP's release was slightly delayed after running into 'manufacturing difficulties,' according to an unattributed blurb in *NME*. One has to believe Shields was determined not to lose any fidelity when pressing this record, as had happened with *Ecstasy*.)

The band's powerful live performances around this time also made it clear they could recreate the moving dynamics of their recordings. In a review of MBV's live show at the end of 1988, Reynolds's *Melody Maker* colleague Chris Roberts spoke about the group with much the same fervor, capturing just how timely the band's live sound felt:

> Right now, the Valentines are not so much crucial as a crux. . . . Suddenly My Bloody Valentine are all the answers, a trance, glancing

at romance, chancing menace, willing sacrificial lambs. Around now—what is it, autumn 1988?—this group is transcending the genre like it's shelling peas. We're talking historic. We're talking grandeur and grime.[12]

Of course, *NME* and *Melody Maker* were finding the 'next big thing' every few months, so writing like this can sometimes strain credulity. But the volume and sincerity of the acclaim MBV were receiving suggests the accolades were legitimate. Jeff Barrett, Creation's publicist at the time, has talked about how the band generated similar feelings when he accompanied them on tour in support of *Isn't Anything*. 'That's the point where everything started to go hazy,' he recalled. 'I remember a gig at Nottingham Trent Poly where the band were phenomenal. Nobody was prepared for it. *This was it now.* It was that exciting.' [13]

•

Issued in November 1988, *Isn't Anything* was MBV's third Creation release of the year. The response to the two preceding EPs helped position the album to get a great deal of exposure, both in the UK and on the continent. There was a significant number of feature articles about the band in the Spanish, French, Italian, and German music press, bringing more people out to their intimate live shows in 1989 for *Isn't Anything*, which received the widest distribution of the three releases. MBV had figured out how to recreate these songs in 1988, experimenting with a small number of pedals and processors. Live recordings and fan testimony attest to how powerful and in sync they had become.

The album sold forty thousand copies relatively quickly and soon went silver in the UK, which was quite impressive for a label as small as Creation. Sales remained steady in the intervening years. It was one of the best returns Creation had seen for any band up to that point, and the press coverage the band received raised the label's hipness quotient, eventually inducing other young, up-and-coming bands to sign with the label. The album was initially licensed to Relativity in the USA, while the first two

EPs remained imports for all other markets until they were remastered in 2012.*

Isn't Anything chronicles the band's lives at the time and the chaos around them. Reynolds's *Melody Maker* interview took place at the run-down squat Ó Cíosóig and Shields were living in, and his reporting made it clear that their world was not a simple place. Similarly, the album's lyrics are not about some fictional characters, and their focus is more specific and visceral than the two preceding EPs. That is not to say every song on the album is autobiographical, but they do reflect the band's lives and those of the people around them, letting you into their world in a genuinely immediate way, conveying their difficulties and desperation, the utter strangeness of human existence, but also the lust and excitement that can make it worthwhile. 'Everyone we know is just like us,' Shields said at the time. 'We don't know many happy, stable people. Or very confident, upfront people. We're not the Beastie Boys.'[14]

While Shields had written the majority of the lyrics on the band's two previous EPs, Butcher's contributions on *Isn't Anything* expand the group's range of emotions to match the unique sound of 'Lose My Breath,' 'Cupid Come,' 'No More Sorry,' and 'Several Girls Galore.' They are often highly sexually charged, and if some of them feel close to the bone, it's because they reflect her real life. Butcher has confirmed that the two songs about abuse ('No More Sorry' and 'Lose My Breath') are, in part, autobiographical. When she and Shields were asked on camera if they were obsessed with the sensual, Butcher, who most often deferred to her bandmate in interviews, spoke right up, saying, 'Sex is not just good things; it's all sorts of things.'[15]

The album begins with some of those 'good things' in the form of 'Soft As Snow (But Warm Inside),' a sequel of sorts to 'Slow' that also uses vocal phrasing inspired by rap's rhythmic delivery. The lyrics, by Ó Cíosóig and Shields, contain several evocative lines that are indicative of what's to come on the album—sentiments that are easy to relate to, often intimate, and carnal without being prurient.

---

* The lone exception to this was the Canadian release of a twelve-inch through Mercury that took three songs from each of the first two EPs.

One can't help but take note of the confidence and ambition that kicks off the album. This song, more than any other on the album, seemed to confuse some listeners with its inventive combination of elements, but once you're attuned to the guitar's rhythmic squawks and whoops, you begin to appreciate the perfect groove of the voice, bass, and drums. The final lyric gives way to a funky bass line break before the song closes out with some rhythmic guitar stabs and a loud splash.

Isn't Anything has more time to explore a larger range of emotions than the EPs that preceded it. The running order is well thought out, as the splash of 'Soft As Snow' gives way to the somber, hushed guitar and vocal of 'Lose My Breath,' itself followed by groupings of songs that each contrast with the dynamics of what came before. 'Cupid Come' picks things up with its mellow groove and sultry lyrics written by Butcher and sung by Shields, followed by the dynamic '(When You Wake) You're Still In A Dream.' Things slow down with 'No More Sorry' and 'All I Need,' which end side one calmly in preparation for the storm coming next. This last song on side one is particularly novel-sounding, even by the standards of MBV. It would inspire many while at the same time leaving them scratching their heads in their attempts to badly imitate its sounds with a mix of pedals and guesswork.

Side two kicks off with the album's intense fulcrum, 'Feed Me With Your Kiss,' which begins with an all-encompassing wall of noise that then makes some space for the subsequent swooning, suggestive dialogue between Shields and Butcher. As the chorus begins, leaving only the vocals and the snare drum, time begins to get exponentially slower, not unlike the moments before and during an orgasm, as Ó Cíosóig's perfectly drawn-out single stroke roll gets a little lower in the mix as Shields's and Butcher's chorus drags out each word.

SO FEED ME WITH YOURRRKISSSSSS

Just as their two voices are at their slowest, quietest, and most attenuated, the rumbling, undulating snare roll comes back up in the mix, setting off an attack by the perfectly synced guitar, bass, and drums that hit hard, over and over, thrashing you into submission before they resolve. Then the next set of verses does it all over again. Irregular beat counts and abrupt asymmetrical drum fills in the style of Keith Moon create more suspense and tension between the moments of resolution.

'Feed Me With Your Kiss' takes the classic form of a duet one might imagine from Dolly Parton and Porter Wagoner or Nancy Sinatra and Lee Hazlewood, though it's for a very different generation. Shields's somewhat indeterminate lyrics portray a dynamic in which the woman is in the dominant position.

This is followed by 'Sueisfine,' in which the chorus alternates between 'Sue is fine' and 'suicide.' The song isn't about actually killing yourself, however, as much as it is about the 'urge to exceed your identity,' as Reynolds put it when interviewing Shields, who described the song as having 'this jumbled-up, wanting, I-need-it feeling: it's about not knowing what you want, but wanting it desperately.'[16]

Butcher gives us her last set of lyrics on the album with 'Several Girls Galore,' asking, as she gets ready to go out for the night, which 'me' she should perform. The three-note chorus, in which each note seems to almost stop short and reverberate in place is another demonstration of Shields's unwillingness to repeat himself.

Prior to *Isn't Anything*, he'd shown he could make distinct, remarkably strong EPs, where specific themes came to the fore both audibly and lyrically. As listeners head toward the end of the album, he shows he has no problem sustaining a forty-minute journey, closing out the record with three more excellent songs, that, despite his comments to the contrary, show that he is more than up to the challenge of writing lyrics that never take you out of the song; actually, they often enhance it.

'You Never Should,' with its driving guitar leads and many rhythmic change-ups, keeps things lively and comes to a nice resolution during the final line of the chorus: 'You said the fault was mine, but you never should.' The album's penultimate song, 'Nothing Much To Lose,' throws a curveball, starting with the most abrupt and fitful drum fills on the record.

Ó Cíosóig somehow keeps them in time just as Shields's smooth guitar and vocals come up in the mix, as if from a totally different song. Toward the end, Shields dramatically asks, 'A soft salt taste, did you see me as a fool?' before the song's final chorus devolves into the noisy, busy drum fills again.

After that, you're left to enjoy the stark relief of Shields's laid-back rhythm playing on 'I Can See It (But I Can't Feel It),' which closes the album. The final sixty seconds of the song (and the album) consist of Shields and Butcher together, offering a wordless comfort in unison, until the final strum fades into the decaying ether.

Even before the accolades from the press came pouring in, Shields's comments, song choices, and production—along with his decision to force Dave Anderson to erase the dry reverse reverb parts—make it plain he wanted to cross the Rubicon with this record. 'Soft As Snow (But Warm Inside),' 'No More Sorry,' 'All I Need,' and 'Nothing Much To Lose' each have elements that were truly foreign to even open-minded indie music fans at the time. While *Isn't Anything* contains more input from the other members of MBV than anything that followed, fundamentally what it demonstrates is the breadth of Shields's unique vision. With that new confidence, his bold ambitions would play out over the next decade in ways that would make him a name for the ages—while also, ultimately, tearing the band apart.

chapter five

'Things started to become more and more like a business after we started selling some records. The two EPs that we recorded after we started to get somewhere sounded really uninspired, and at that point we decided that we had to work harder at it.'

KEVIN SHIELDS, 1991[1]

Shortly after the release of *Isn't Anything*, MBV entered a friend's studio to quickly work up the lo-fi track 'Sugar,' to be given away as a flexi-disc to accompany their interview in the February 1989 issue of *The Catalogue*. 'It was done in a cheap studio,' Shields said at the time, 'and we only spent £150 on it. It's completely weird—we just made it up in the studio because we didn't want to do an album track or acoustic version of a track like other bands. We wanted to do something different that we really liked.'[2]

Based on how quickly the band had worked in the past, Creation expected another single or EP to emerge around the same time, which the band could promote on the upcoming tour in support of *Isn't Anything*. In February, the label booked the band into Blackwing Studios in London for ten days. Five days into the session, Shields took a call from McGee, seemingly unhappy to have heard that the band hadn't gotten much work done. Several days later, he and Dick Green came down to the studio to find Shields was still unsure about what to do with the session. For the first time since signing with Creation, he and the band were showing little enthusiasm for the songs they were working on.

Shields ultimately decided that nothing they had recorded was good enough to merit being released as a single. 'We recorded four tracks which we don't really like that much,' he told the fanzine *Woosh!* 'There wasn't an A-side among them,' he added, though he indicated that some of the tracks from the session would eventually find their way out as B-sides.[3] (The one track they were actually pleased with, 'Moon Song,' would end up on the *Tremolo* EP in 1991; a few others from this and a second aborted EP session were finally released in 2012 and 2021, as bonus tracks on the digitally remastered *EP's* collection.)

Aside from 'Sugar,' MBV did not put out any new material in 1989. Fifteen months would pass between *Isn't Anything* and their next proper release.

•

From mid-February to early April of 1989, MBV played approximately thirty dates in the UK and Europe in support of *Isn't Anything*. A decent-quality video of their February 16 show at the University Of London Union is worth tracking down, as it contains some of the better footage of their live performances around this time, with cameras filming each of the four members at various points throughout the show.[*]

Although you can't see what processors or pedals Shields is using in the London footage, it's clear from statements he has made—and from the sound of various live bootlegs—just how straightforward the band's setup was on the tour. They performed eight of the twelve songs from *Isn't Anything* that night, plus six songs from the two preceding EPs, with Shields deploying much the same equipment as he'd used in the studio:

---

* Another bootleg recording exists of the band's show in Lyon, France, on February 21. It was recorded clumsily to two-track by the soundman without him really being able to hear the mix, but it is still worth seeking out, as discussed in further detail in the online appendix to this book.

Jazzmaster and Jaguar guitars, an Alesis MidiVerb II rack-mounted unit, and three pedals (a Roger Mayer Octavia, a Roger Mayer Axis Fuzz, and a Boss GE7). Photos taken prior to the tour show Shields using different setups to achieve similar results, and as he experimented with how best to recreate the songs in a live setting, various other pedals would be swapped in and out, including a Fender Blender.

With each successive tour, the band's PA system only grew larger, which would result in their rhythmic bite being toned down somewhat; the *Loveless* tour in 1991 and 1992 would offer the worst of all worlds. Various bootlegs from 1989 demonstrate just how dynamically their driving rhythms come across without being mediated by the additional equipment they would need post-*Glider*.

•

Having cut all ties with Lazy Records in 1987, MBV were caught off guard when Wayne Morris came back into their orbit in 1989. Noting the success of the Creation releases, he decided to repackage the 'Strawberry Wine' single and the *Ecstasy* mini album as a new ten-track LP that he retitled *Ecstasy And Wine*, releasing it in February 1989 on vinyl and CD, just as the band hit the road. The album spent five weeks on the UK indie charts, climbing as high as number two. Shields asserted Lazy had no legal ownership of the material or right to re-release it, however, as their contract merely stipulated that the label would pay for limited studio time and a small amount of promotion (which they didn't follow through with). Now, some fans were approaching the band on the tour to ask why it seemed they had regressed, as the 'new' Lazy LP didn't hold a candle to their work with Creation. Because *Ecstasy And Wine* had a 1989 copyright, there was every reason for fans to believe it was the band's next album, even though it was just Lazy taking advantage of their success.

Angry about listeners being conned into buying what they thought was new material, Shields decided to act. After returning from the first leg of the tour in April, he got together with one of Primal Scream's roadies, who went by the name 'Fatty,' and who in turn marshaled another fourteen toughs and descended upon Lazy's offices, where copies of *Ecstasy And Wine* were being stored. Shields went in by himself first and was told by a label employee that he could take whatever he could carry. With that, he motioned to the others to come in from outside. The employee's face turned white as Shields and his crew proceeded to liberate all ten thousand copies of *Ecstasy And Wine*. After all the records were confiscated, Shields popped back in with a simple warning: 'Leave us alone and we won't be back.'[4]

Even though the band hadn't wanted the Lazy recordings re-released, they decided it was better to keep the income from them than have the records destroyed. They proceeded to live off the sales of those albums for the next year or so, selling boxes of them to various distributors for £700 each. With that, they'd finally gotten some sort of return on the work they'd done with Lazy.[*]

•

There had been talk of MBV returning to the studio after the first leg of the *Isn't Anything* tour to make another attempt at recording a single or EP to promote their summer shows in the USA and Canada, but they wouldn't actually see the inside of a studio again until September. With no new material on the horizon, McGee asked them to consider releasing '(When You Wake) You're Still In A Dream' as a single. Shields wasn't even remotely open to the idea, though; he felt the band had already advanced a great deal in their thinking, and, in his mind, even *Isn't Anything* no longer represented where they were at creatively.

An idiosyncratic twelve-inch promotional record seems to have been the final upshot of McGee pestering the band to release something new. Released in North America by Relativity, who had also licensed *Isn't Anything*, to coincide with the American leg of the tour, the record

---

[*] Shields had nothing to do with mixing or mastering of *Ecstasy And Wine*, which is why it sounds noticeably subpar compared to the original vinyl releases of the single and mini-album. If you can spare the cash and want to hear them in all their glory, go for the 1987 versions and ignore the 1989 edition.

contained '(When You Wake) You're Still In A Dream,' 'Soft As Snow (But Warm Inside),' 'Feed Me With Your Kiss,' 'Slow,' and 'Instrumental No. 2.' In many ways, it was the perfect collection of tracks to demonstrate that Shields and company were on their own path.

As well as writing new songs, Shields was also making a major reassessment of how the band worked. Looking back on this period a couple of years later, he told *Melody Maker*, 'We made two EPs … that we just didn't feel were good enough, so they were never released. They weren't bad, it's just that they didn't excite us in the sense that they could make what we did before seem irrelevant. We made them like we'd made all our previous records, just went into the studio and wrote a lot of stuff really quickly, but that way of working wasn't working anymore.' The band's ambitions had outgrown their previous working methods. 'Basically we'd done everything we could working quickly,' Shields added, 'making songs up on the spot. We had to slow down, or we start repeating ourselves.'[5]

'Angel,' recorded during one of the aborted sessions of 1989, is a good example of what Shields was talking about. It could easily pass as an outtake from 1988, which meant it was no longer good enough. MBV knew that if they wanted to progress, they would have to fundamentally change their working methods. To explore new ideas and actually discover new sonic territories, they would need larger budgets, more time, and better equipment.

With their first three Creation releases, MBV had proven that they were creatively and financially viable. They had earned the right, they felt, to take more time in the studio—and, by extension, to run up more debt. (Here, it's important to remember that, as was typical musical industry practice, any costs a band incurred came out of their own pocket and had to be recouped before they would see any royalties from record sales.)

Even if they didn't release anything in 1989, MBV continued to pay dividends to Creation in less quantifiable ways due to the cachet they brought to the label. Creation signed a number of bands who had formed or found their voice thanks to *Isn't Anything* and who wanted to be on the same forward-looking label. Bands like Ride, Slowdive, Swervedriver, and The Boo Radleys would all help the growing demand for MBV-like products. As Creation record plugger James Kyllo later put it, while they couldn't say with any certainty if any of those groups broke even, they felt they were putting out the hippest records of the time.[6]

Eventually, the success of Ride, Primal Scream, Teenage Fanclub, and other groups would change Creation's calculus, but throughout 1989, MBV were still the label's top band. Other than The House Of Love—who were in the midst of falling apart after the departure of guitarist Terry Bickers—they were the only Creation band who seemed able to turn a profit. As such, McGee and his colleagues were willing to increase their investment in what the group wanted to pursue, without realizing it would be several years before they would actually begin to recoup any of their money.

The success of The House Of Love and MBV also improved Creation's standing in the industry, which led to a profitable publishing deal with EMI, giving Creation a percentage on every act they sent the major's way. Creation also expected to get better treatment from its distributor, Rough Trade, now that the label's combined sales put it in fifth or six position out of the fifty or so catalogs Rough Trade handled. Rough Trade refused to improve the terms of their deal, however, so Creation broke things off, eventually signing a new distribution agreement with Pinnacle.

While it has often been claimed that MBV's extended time in the studio working on the follow-up to *Isn't Anything* pushed Creation to the brink of bankruptcy, the label's financial problems actually started here, with the decision to switch distributors. Cashflow issues were already being felt *before* MBV started recording *Loveless*. 'The gist of it is that we had absolutely no money, Creation had absolutely no money, and neither of us expected to be in that position when we started the record,' Shields later recalled.[7] From the very start of the *Loveless* sessions, the label was regularly unable to pay the studio bills, and tapes were often confiscated. Things were off to an inauspicious start.

When MBV entered Elephant Studios in September 1989, McGee was hoping they would come up with something more akin to what he thought of as their 'live' sound—think 'You Made Me Realise' or '(When You Wake) You're Still In A Dream'—as opposed to the slower, weirder songs like 'Lose My Breath' or 'I Need No Trust.' He explained this to the in-house engineer, Nick Robbins, hoping Robbins would help him achieve this objective.

Based on MBV's live shows and the credits on their previous records, McGee was under the impression that they would be recording as a group. But that was just not the way they worked. While all four members had gone to Wales to make *Isn't Anything*, jamming was not in their repertoire, and it's not how they developed ideas nor how they recorded songs. When Ó Cíosóig arrived with the band's gear at Elephant Studios and heard from Robbins that McGee was expecting a live-sounding record, the drummer replied, 'Well that's not going to happen, because the girls don't come into the studio anyway.'[8]

Several months later, Robbins reported back to McGee that no recordings were close to completion—the only thing the band had accomplished was creating sampled drum parts for twenty-two songs that would eventually form the basis of their next three releases. As the sessions dragged on, Robbins began to think of Shields as some kind of conman; in turn, Shields and Ó Cíosóig would avoid recording when the engineer was present, so Robbins had no real inkling of how the band functioned.

This would not be the band's last clash with an in-house engineer. After three months at Elephant, they spent a month at Woodcray in Berkshire, where it appears the proprietors were less concerned with when Shields came and went but still puzzled by his working methods. The band picked up where they had left off, adding guitar overdubs and feedback to several of songs that would appear on *Glider*, but McGee had still yet to hear a note of new music.

New working patterns and a new relationship between MBV and Creation were forming. The band continued to keep the label in the dark as 1989 came to a close, but Creation continued to book different studios at Shields's request while he and Ó Cíosóig continued experimenting. Despite being slowed down by Creation's inconsistent finances, they worked steadily through September, October, and November of 1989 to try to finish *Glider*. Shields would end up subverting so many conventions with the EP—his use of sampled feedback, his use of midrange, his way of mixing the tracks to form one unique fusion of sound—that it would be well worth the wait. Problematically, however, he typically never let anyone hear the music until it was finished.

Tension truly rose as 1990 began. Shields had barred everyone outside of the band members from seeing what they were up to, and McGee was offended that they didn't embrace his presence or input. They would happily invite him to parties, but for Shields, the studio was something else entirely. 'Instead of us including him and bringing him in, we just sort of pushed him away,' he later explained. 'They thought it was strange that I wouldn't let them in the studio—like I was being overly artistic—but it was more because a studio, for us, was like home. . . . The way I saw it— because I was the producer and kind of in charge of everything—I was a bit of a tyrant. I would just really be strict.'[9]

Needing some reassurance that new songs were actually being recorded, McGee eventually convinced Shields to let him come to the studio and hear what they were working on. With the exception of 'Sugar,' no new music had been heard by Creation for close to a year. So, despite 'Soon' being unfinished, Shields gave in and let him hear it.

At this point, 'Soon' didn't have a vocal or a melody, but McGee was convinced of its qualities nonetheless. 'It was total genius,' he later said.[10] Elsewhere, he described the track as 'The Stooges meets the Mondays.'[11] Dance music, in the form of house, techno, and hip-hop, was already exerting an influence on guitar bands who were looking to be where the action was. That's certainly where McGee's thoughts were, and he and many others joined in with the dance revolution sweeping the UK during the second 'Summer Of Love' in 1989.* Together, he and Shields decided it

---

* He would even eventually start a sublabel, Infonet, specifically focused on dance music.

would be best to put out a stopgap EP, with 'Soon,' as the lead track before concentrating on finishing the full-length album. The four-song release would offer both a preview of the new album and a salve to fans hungry for new material. This preview would help a great deal to relieve tensions between the band and Creation through 1990 and into 1991—at which time the tension would begin to build like never before.

In the meantime, though, there were other concerns beyond McGee's need to get some idea of what the band were actually working on. For a host of reasons, as the band continued recording through 1989, Shields's relationships with engineers and studio owners grew more and more fraught. Anecdotes abound about the clashes during these sessions (and beyond), but they all play out in basically the same way: Shields and Ó Cíosóig would begin working, only to be told they were 'mad' and didn't know the 'proper' way to make recordings; studio staff would grow offended when the two musicians blew off their advice and told them they didn't require anyone else's input.

Ó Cíosóig believed in Shields's vision from the outset, but it was more difficult to convince others of it when equipment kept breaking down and other issues arose. In-house engineers would try to tell Shields and Ó Cíosóig what to do, freaking out over their unorthodox and sometimes incomprehensible methods. MBV were working in mid-priced studios that came with their own flaws and idiosyncrasies: a hum on the desk that interfered with the sound; a pot or knob that cut out at certain frequencies. Some musicians might not worry about or even notice these issues, but Shields did. Having decided to grant himself the time to make his recordings everything they could be (and incur the accompanying debt against future record sales), he no longer tolerated any issues that might compromise his work. He wasn't paying Abbey Road prices, but it seemed reasonable for him to expect things to work so the band could record as they intended to.

Shields's demands would lead to him being labeled as an irrational perfectionist, but he would argue otherwise. With the success he'd achieved in 1988, he felt he had every right to want to do things on his terms, with little concern for what the accepted conventions were. He possessed a confidence and vision beyond his years that most musicians and engineers couldn't really fathom.

How do we know Shields *wasn't* just being difficult? How can we be sure he wasn't just imagining sounds that weren't there? Alan Moulder and Guy Fixsen—both well-known producers today—were there at the time, and they both support Shields's version of events. They agree that his hearing was impeccable, confirming that nearly every time he spotted a problem, he would eventually be proven right. And while one can't help but feel some sympathy for the in-house engineers not used to working with someone like Shields, neither Moulder nor Fixsen would recall him making unreservedly irrational or unrealistic demands.

Moulder has pointed out another issue that might have complicated things further. The engineers MBV worked with at this time were often also the *owners* of their studios, and it's easy to see how this could create issues, from defensive attitudes to shoddy attempts to cover up faulty work or technology. Speaking to *Polymath Perspective* in 2013, Moulder recounted how Shields would ask an in-house engineer about, say, a microphone that was not working properly, only to be told everything *was* working properly. 'Kevin's comment was always, *I just want it to be decent*, so from his point of view, quite rightly, a faulty microphone isn't decent. He didn't want something out-of-this-world, he just wanted everything to do what it should do.'[12]

Regarding the use of mid-priced studios, Fixsen recalled McGee explaining to him that while he had other bands spending more money more quickly, MBV were a 'cheap date' by necessity, since Shields had begun to work so slowly.[13] This may have felt like a sensible compromise, but it could also cause Shields to become even slower, as he would lose momentum while battling with mediocre equipment. In fairness to the label and its limited funds, however, it's also easy to imagine Shields wasting time at a pricier studio, too, and costing Creation even more.

Partly by way of compromise, Moulder had been brought in as a conduit between Shields and the studio staff. He would deal with any equipment or recording issues—either resolving them or finding a workaround—which would then allow Shields to avoid further drawn-out confrontations. An experienced engineer who had worked with Depeche Mode and Eurythmics, Moulder had recently engineered The Jesus & Mary Chain's *Automatic*, and McGee and Green felt they could trust him to report back and assure them that Shields knew what he was doing and that their money wasn't being spent arbitrarily. Initially brought in to oversee 'Soon,' which was still missing vocals and a melody at this point, he was then tasked with helping to bring the *Glider* EP to completion, followed by an accompanying full-length album.

The original plan was to finish recording over three or four weeks in early 1990, though it's fair to say it didn't quite pan out like that. Over the coming year, Moulder would serve as a stalwart supporter of Shields while reassuring Creation that their investment was not in vain. Shields would later state that it was impossible to quantify the emotional and spiritual support he got from Moulder because of the legitimacy it gave him, adding that when Moulder was around—as he would be at various points over the next year—he would get much more accomplished.[14]

Moulder in turn would be credited as a significant contributor to the innovative sound of *Glider* on its release in April 1990, with some articles referring to him as the EP's producer. In the years to come, he would become busier than ever, working with Smashing Pumpkins, U2, Curve, Ride, The Boo Radleys, Swervedriver, and Shakespeares Sister, among others, and by his own admission, this newfound demand would be based in part on a misunderstanding of his role with MBV. 'The first thing I did with Kevin was mix the four-track *Glider* EP,' he later recalled, 'and when I say mix, I was doing what I was told! Kevin mixed and I was the engineer. That's how we got our trust and a working relationship that was good.'[15]

After discarding two EPs worth of material, Shields finally found his footing again. His recording experiments and techniques may have seemed esoteric at times, but *Glider* would be the first sign of the amazing things to come.

interlude two

glide guitar

Shields eventually settled on the name 'glide guitar' for his innovative way of generating sound with his instrument, but he didn't really talk at length about how he was able to accomplish it until after the making of *Isn't Anything*. Although he seemingly first used the term in jest, it's become a useful shorthand to describe one of the major components of MBV's sonic innovations.

Countless posts on Reddit and YouTube—featuring thousands of players comparing notes about their own instruments, pedals, processors, and tunings—have attempted to capture how Shields was able to accomplish a particular sound. Ultimately, though, the setup that has served as a starting point for most of MBV's songs since *Feed Me With Your Kiss* and *Isn't Anything* comes down to two major components: Shields's hack of the Fender Jazzmaster through a bespoke setup of the tremolo arm and bridge, and the particular type of reverse reverb he favors.*

The Jazzmaster was first introduced to the public in 1958. After the company's massive success with the Telecaster and Stratocaster earlier that decade, the Jazzmaster was supposed to be its next solid-body triumph. When it appeared, it was the best-made guitar Fender had ever produced, but the company eventually discontinued it when it was overlooked by the jazz artists it was specifically designed for. Fender next put out the

---

* There are other factors too, of course: Shields also uses a wide variety of open tunings, drone strings, and various pedals and processors. A deep dive into every last detail about the band's tech specs and studio innovations would be a book unto itself. But the most important elements to understand are the particulars of his guitar and his use of reverse reverb, which is why I've chosen to focus on those in more detail here.

Jaguar, which was designed as the Jazzmaster's musical 'cousin.' As with its predecessor, though, jazz players didn't like it, and because the neck radius wasn't ideal for the kind of soloing popular among guitar heroes of the 60s and 70s—think Hendrix, Clapton, Page—it didn't find a welcome audience with guitarists who played blues-influenced rock, either. Some models were picked up by surf-rock bands, but most of them were relegated to pawn shops and dusty stockrooms.

Demand for the Jazzmaster was so anemic that by 1973, Television frontman and songwriter Tom Verlaine was able to buy one for just $150. The success of his band's influential 1975 album *Marquee Moon* and Verlaine's unorthodox style with the instrument helped kick off the Jazzmaster's renaissance, and soon, other musicians would reinforce the guitar's modern capabilities and hip cachet. Elvis Costello can be seen holding one on the cover of 1977's *My Aim Is True*, and Robert Smith of The Cure would purchase one with his first record advance. Into the 80s, Jazzmasters and Jaguars became mainstays of influential guitarists in cult bands like The Birthday Party, Dinosaur Jr., and Sonic Youth—many of whom, like Verlaine, had to consider price when purchasing equipment. Not long after that, they became the first choice of guitars for alternative groups like Nirvana, Yo La Tengo, and Stereolab. As Johnny Marr explained, 'The funny thing is that vintage Jaguars are finally desirable because starving artists bought them, and they represent punk rock and holes in your Converse trainers. Now you can get one for £11,000.'[1]

Although the Jazzmaster is Shields's preferred guitar, he also appeared on *Mixdown* magazine's 2023 list of the ten most iconic Jaguar players of all time (alongside Verlaine, Marr, PJ Harvey, and Rowland S Howard, among others). 'Both Kevin Shields and Bilinda Butcher make extensive use of the Jazzmaster, Mustang, and Jaguar to create the band's atmospheric sound,' the magazine noted, 'and it's arguable that the group were a pivotal force in the renaissance of these said models throughout the 90s.'[2]

As noted earlier, Shields's friend and labelmate Bill Carey was the one who insisted Shields use his recently restored Jazzmaster (complete with tremolo arm) during his first recording sessions for Creation. Shields made further modifications, as others had done before him, by wrapping the arm with gaffer tape, which left it raised and very loose, giving him a wider range of motion. He also bent it slightly to make it easier to hold—in effect, lengthening it—while he was strumming vigorously.

Shields had used various types of tremolo systems before, but they hadn't done much for him, and he had never actually played a Jazzmaster in good shape with a tremolo arm until 1988. The guitar's innovative floating tremolo (as opposed to the Stratocaster's synchronized vibrato system) had several distinct advantages, and he soon learned how to exploit them to their fullest effect. The bar can be configured in a 'down-only' position, for example, which means that pulling back up on the bar brings the strings back in tune. Additionally, the tremolo arm can swing all the way into a strumming position, which meant Shields was able to keep it in his hand as he strummed—something a Bigsby or Gibson tremolo does not allow for.

Rather than use the tremolo arm for vibrato or for Eddie Van Halen–style 'dive-bomb' effects, Shields bends the strings downward a little bit each time he strums, and then, at the end of each strum, he allows them to relax back into their normal position. He integrates pitch bending into a natural motion as if the loosely configured tremolo bar were an organic extension of his right hand. 'That sound is purely physical,' he said in 1992. 'It's a movement, a manual moving of the strings: the short travel for the Jazzmaster and Jaguar trem[olo] that gives it that characteristic sort of upward drone to the chord.'[3] With this setup, Shields can put as much or as little pressure on the tremolo arm as he decides is called for to obtain the needed sound.

Shields's playing affects both pitch (the frequency of a sound wave, as measured in hertz) and tone (the quality or timbre of the sound). 'Essentially, when you use a tremolo arm on a guitar the way I use it, it's not only pitch bending, it's also tone bending,' he has explained. 'You get a totally different tonal response as the guitar is changing. Each string has a different tension so you're not getting uniform tone change.'[4] When he adds distortion, it creates a kind of reverb, blurring the distinction between chords and adding even more depth. When the bar is set up with a lot of slack or 'give,' it's possible to strum away aggressively and still get that subtle, slight bend of pitch that is the essence of glide guitar.

Shields strums dynamically, with a pick held between his thumb and index finger, while the tremolo bar rests against the palm of his hand, moving effortlessly as he plays. In photos of him performing, you can see the end of the bar sticking out through the gap between his thumb and index finger. It's a relatively simple concept—a product of the instrument itself and Shields's acuity with it. 'All the parts that sound like the guitar is speeding up and slowing down are just the tremolo arm,' he explained.[5]

Shields's Jazzmaster is then run through a particular kind of digital reverse reverb, something he discovered (as noted earlier) with the help of Dave Anderson. The term 'reverse reverb' was first used in the 1960s to refer to what was essentially backward reverb on analog equipment, but with changes in technology over the years, it has come to mean many very different things depending on who is talking, as more digital devices have offered many more ways to process input signals.

Some of the earlier digital reverbs—including the Yamaha SPX90 and the Alesis MidiVerb II, Shields's preferred processors—offered a workaround by simply replaying short samples of the original sound in a crescendo or swell, giving the impression of a reverse effect but with a much shorter delay. Today, most modern digital reverse reverb units (essentially a recorded reverb played backward) actually simulate the same process as 1960s analog tape reverse reverb. This process typically begins with a noticeable delay between the dry source and the wet playback as it waits for enough music to play before it can start to reverse the reverb, making for a smoother sound. But Shields has stuck with the SPX90 and MidiVerb II and its more percussive workaround.

In interviews, Shields has noted the 'percussive elements' these types of delays create, while offering a visual description of the resulting sound:

> You have the sound, and then what it does is, it takes little samples of the sound, little squares, and then, to make it sound reversed, it just repeats them getting louder. So it's a little box and then a

slightly bigger box in a slightly bigger box. . . . It sounds reversed, but it is, in fact, still forward. It's not turned around. It's just the velocity is reversed, for want of a better word.[6]

Los Angeles musician Joe Kennedy, who has met Shields on more than one occasion, offers a more technical explanation:

> It takes the initial attack by the guitar which the algorithm processes in milliseconds using computational power to create the reflections we know as reverb—and with it the sense that the listener is in a specific acoustic space. The reverse reverb simply plays the results back in reverse (without reversing the envelope). With the dry attack removed, the most distinct effect of reverse reverb is that it tends to soften the attack of certain sounds. Instead of a note ringing and then decaying, the process is reversed; notes seem to bloom instead of fade. The wet reverse reverb signal can be manipulated to get a limitless number of interesting rhythmic effects, something that Kevin Shields first recognized and then exploited beautifully.

Shields largely relied on two rack-mounted processors, the SPX90 and MidiVerb II, to create his various iterations of reverse reverb. The former was ubiquitous in the late 80s and early 90s and was frequently spotted at project studios and in commercial recording spaces, as well as in live mixing rigs. Both boxes were far less costly and glamorous than the classic Lexicon units that were staples of high-end studios.*

In 2001, *Tape Op* magazine ran an instructive interview with Shields that revealed how, while many of the recordings on *Isn't Anything* were

---

* Thinking back on the session, Bark's longtime owner/engineer Brian O'Shaughnessy concluded that Shields used an even more basic device for his initial experiments with reverse reverb on 'Thorn' and 'Slow.' The sub-£350 Yamaha REX50 was marketed as a 'budget' version of the SPX90. Photos of his live setup from 2018 seem to confirm this, showing the GEP50 (essentially a rack-mounted REX50) still among his gear, with names and codes for those exact songs attached. O'Shaughnessy was certain that the studio would not have been able to afford the Yamaha SPX90 when it was introduced at £600 in 1987.

highly sophisticated, they didn't require any particularly expensive or obscure equipment. Listing the tracks that make up 'All I Need,' for example, Shields noted that it is primarily made up of a heartbeat effect made using a drum machine, plus an acoustic guitar played over it with reverse reverb applied. The whole track was then put through some other high-frequency processor, but there are no other guitars and no bass—his point being that if you took out the four to five tracks of vocals, it could have been done on an eight-track.

The reverse reverb, he noted, 'creates a sort of simulated effect—you get kind of a rhythmic effect out of it if you have any transients, anything with attack, the attack comes back slightly but you wouldn't know it from listening to the record.'[7] Having stated elsewhere that he lacked the technical gifts of a Jimi Hendrix or a Bert Jansch, he explained, 'The reason I loved [reverse reverb] was because it allowed you to be expressive. If I play softer or louder, it's super affected by how you play. Things like chorus and flanger and things like that are put on top of what you are playing; it's hard to interact with.'[8]

Shields's style of musicianship requires a specific, almost unconscious type of concentration. In a sense, he is no longer playing the guitar but has instead become a part of the sound. Thurston Moore, who has his own signature line of Jazzmaster guitars, has described it as 'a bit like Zen—it's not like he's trying to be sacred, but he's simply merged into the sound. He's listening and feeling the sound. Also he's really calm but at the same time he's making this extreme sound … Kevin reaches some sort of altered state of mind while playing.'[9]

Of course, there's more to Shields's sound than simply getting a Fender Jazzmaster, putting tape on the tremolo arm, plugging it into a Yamaha SPX90, and strumming. 'If someone else plugged into my guitar rig, it would just sound like a mess—it would just feed back,' he has said. 'It's the way you play it and control it that becomes the thing.'[10] At its heart, it's about physical motion and musical technique; those elements, combined with Shields's understanding of songwriting, sound, and sound processing, are what ultimately make it so evocative.

Shields had limited time and equipment when he recorded *Isn't Anything*. But the sound he created when this direct line between his mind and his tremolo arm—a tenuous and uninterrupted communication he discovered with the help of Dave Anderson—triggered a tsunami of creativity. He would go so far as to say that, when making *Isn't Anything*, 'It was like meeting the love of my life for the first time. You know how it feels like in the first three or four months of being together with a new love interest? It was like that the mixture of everything feeling brand new and exciting.'[11]

With his discovery of how the Jazzmaster's tremolo system could uniquely interact with the particular kinds of digital reverse reverb he favored, Shields had found a more direct and unmediated way to express himself that could be used in both subtle and forceful ways. It had never happened before, and it was something he could truly call his own. He said simply. 'You just do it, get into it, listen to it when you play it, in the same way that happens when you do anything a lot—you don't think about it anymore.'[12]

chapter six

within: *glider* and the zeitgeist •

huw price • radical equalization •

lyrical leaps forward • angus

cameron and a visual analog •

the cost of quality control

'*Glider* is breathtaking. . . . *Glider* comes out at us from deep in a dream, a nether world where everything is clouded, ambiguous, deliciously ambivalent. It could be the sound of the cosmos shifting on an imaginary axis. . . . All our hopes have been realized.'

IAN GITTINS, MELODY MAKER, 1990[1]

'Once again, MBV are leading the way forward. If they weren't such lazy-ass slug-a-beds, who knows where they might have got to by now?'

'1990: SYMPHONIC CHAOS,' MELODY MAKER[2]

Released in April 1990, the *Glider* EP marked a significant leap forward in the band's evolution, continuing their upward trajectory, winning them new fans, and setting them even further apart from their closest peers. Upon its release, it was almost as if someone put a bubble over MBV and labeled them 'ZEITGEIST.'

Though there were some snarky comments from *Melody Maker* about the group's working habits, MBV had spent a good deal of their time in the studio productively, breaking barriers other guitar bands wouldn't consider for years. The ultimate result was a new EP that was impossible to mistake for something by Sonic Youth or Dinosaur Jr. The record's opening track,

'Soon,' which integrated indie rock with the fast-approaching revolution in electronic dance music, would handsomely reward Alan McGee's patience and faith. Once again *the* band of the moment, MBV seemed to be showing listeners what the future of music would look like.

Alongside his forays into sampling, Shields's passion for exploring new sonic possibilities meant he was making other changes to his working methods as well. Creation had given him free rein to explore, but that would take time; some paths led to dead ends, and on more than one occasion, weeks of work in the studio were totally disregarded. But 'Soon,' which offered an astounding glimpse of what could happen when everything came together, was the ultimate payoff.

Huw Price, a staff engineer at the Garden Studio, worked with Shields on 'Soon' in January 1990. His recollection of that time is consistent with other engineers who collaborated with the band. He remembers that Butcher, Googe, and Ó Cíosóig would show up at various points, only to all head out to a pub while Shields worked solo with an engineer to help place mics and do other rote tasks. He also noted that while Shields was pleasant and interesting to talk to, when work on music began, 'He focused like nobody else I ever worked with.'[3]

Price's recollection of how Shields mic'd up his guitars is pretty typical of the guitarist's methods around this time, though some songs would diverge from this setup. First, Price recalled, he would set up an array of microphones on the best cone of each amp, giving each its own channel. Then, he would hunch over the desk, pushing faders up and back, listening to the sound coming through each feed. Eventually, he would find an amp and microphone balance that 'didn't traumatize him'—a customary setup would use four or five mics—at which point he would record the guitar and typically he would get it in one take.

No equalization, compression, or generic effects peddles were used during the session, according to Price, just gated reverse reverb from an SPX90 or Alesis QuadraVerb. 'Kevin also manipulated the whammy bar continually as he was playing. When the various takes and tones were combined, there was a randomness to the whammy bar effect, with guitar tracks changing pitch together and independently. The result was a massive composite guitar sound that was greater than the sum of its parts,' Price recalled, while also acknowledging Shields's 'outstanding accuracy and feel.'[4]

'Soon' was initially recorded and released with one main guitar performance, using its clean and dirty guitar sections played through a combination of Marshall and Vox amps. He turned to his much-beloved Tone Bender fuzz pedal to get the dirty tone and would also run the bass guitar through it. Explaining the two main guitar tones on the track, Shields would later describe 'Soon' as 'literally a drum track, a bass track, and it's just one guitar part that goes from the beginning to the end, starting with the Vox guitar part, and then I kick in the Marshall, as well. And that's it.'[5] Well, not exactly. In this same 2009 interview, after running through the basic setup, Shields went on to mention double-tracked vocals by Butcher, as well as keyboard parts and guitar loops consisting of sampled feedback. The 'flute' chorus is particularly hard to pin down, with various loops going in and out of phase behind the melody in a manner reminiscent of the minimalist composer Steve Reich. I suspect his point, though, was that while the band would not be able to exactly replicate the studio version onstage, they could get the major elements and dynamics when playing live with the addition of just a few sequenced parts.[*]

Some listeners mistook the use of open tunings and chord inversions on 'Soon' for additional guitars that simply weren't there. As Shields has explained, they can create a 'heightened effect.'[6] On 'Soon,' he was able to find a harmonically rich and dense guitar tone that was still able to carry through all the subtleties of his playing.[†]

---

[*] Shields would later clarify the band did not use backing tracks onstage but did deploy sequenced parts in a few places for 'To Here Knows When,' 'I Only Said,' and 'Soon' during their 1991 tour.

[†] Although Shields was happy with the initial version of 'Soon,' it had to be remixed for the brighter sound of *Loveless* later that year, at which point he added a second guitar. Not completely satisfied with how the guitar sat in the mix, he redid the second guitar in 2007 for the version that would surface on the 2012 CD releases. Finally, new technology allowed him to remake the second guitar to his satisfaction for the 2018 vinyl reissue. That brings us to four distinct mixes of the track.

According to Price, the 'flute' part was a late addition. On the band's final day at the Garden Studio, they were tasked with finishing specific elements so the basic tracks of 'Soon' could be made available to Andrew Weatherall, who had been asked to remix it.* With another band waiting to use the studio, Shields had a flash of inspiration and asked for another few minutes. He quickly set up a Yamaha DX802 to a guitar amp, pulled up a preset, and laid down the flute-like hook at the heart of the wordless chorus in under ten minutes.

•

Up until 1988, MBV's lead vocals typically comprised one track sung by either Shields or Butcher, without any reverb or double tracking. That changed with *Glider*. Huw Price recalled as impressed as he was with the guitar on 'Soon,' the vocal track was even more astonishing, with Shields improvising his parts and adding more without going back to listen to what he'd previously recorded. 'These vocals shifted arbitrarily between harmony and dissonance. When Kevin processed them with radical equalization and reverb, he created something akin to whales performing Gregorian chants in a canyon.'[7]

Contrasting the band's new approach to vocals to what they had done in the past, Shields himself described them as 'purposefully raw.'[8] This stemmed in part from the sometimes torturous effort it took for him and Butcher to put together the lyrics to their songs. Back in early 1989, he had self-effacingly noted, 'I have absolutely no talent for writing lyrics … it's really difficult for me. It takes me half an hour for a song; it will take me a whole, terrible, sleepless night at the studio for the lyrics.'[9] In a pragmatic sense, by making the words of the song harder to decipher, Shields felt he

---

* Weatherall's remix is worth seeking out, as it's a good place to hear some of the isolated vocal, guitar, and synth tracks and get a better understanding of what Shields created on the original recording. Shields had volunteered the song to be remixed mainly for the opportunity to watch Weatherall work in the studio, although the results were not among the latter's best efforts. Though he was already a respected DJ at this point, 'Soon' was only his third remix. Nonetheless, he would go on to become known as a true musical innovator, in particular for the key role he played in making Primal Scream's *Screamadelica*.

no longer had to worry whether or not every single combination of words made literal or conventional sense.*

It wasn't as simple as burying the vocals low in the mix or singing softly; Shields would maintain that his vocals were as loud as those of most other bands if you compared them, decibel for decibel.[10] But because of the way he recorded and mixed the songs, it doesn't always sound that way. 'One thing that tends to make the vocals sound submerged is that, EQ-wise, I tend to use a lot of the noise end of a guitar amp,' he told *Guitar World* in 1992. 'From that, you get this airy kind of hissy sound all around a lot of the music. Because that's there, I have a tendency not to make the vocals overly bright, so they don't seem to stick out.'[11] Instead, they are in the same stereo image as the guitar, and share the same frequencies, giving the perception that they are low in the mix, though Shields maintained that there would be a marked drop in the level of the track if the vocal were removed.

Shields's lyrics and vocals also had a renewed focus on the use of 'imaginative imagery,' whereby the words don't get in the way of the overall sense of the song. Beginning with *Glider*, he would grow to rely on more common words and vowel sounds—familiar enough and drained of meaning—to create an effect where, in some cases, you don't notice the words at all, or you assign your own meaning to them when you hear them in the context of the song. By making the vocals another instrument in the mix, he wanted to draw listeners in, forcing them to take in the whole song and hopefully expand their horizons in the process.

•

Because 'Soon' appeared on the national charts in the UK, MBV ended up being interviewed by *Number One*, a mainstream teen-pop magazine that

---

* While he may have found the process difficult, the final products show he was certainly up to the task. 'Emptiness Inside,' for example, is a perfect union of music and words, climaxing with a final line ('I'm coming round') that artfully resolves both lyrics and melody. In fact, it's hard to find fault with any of Shields's lyrics, but there was no doubt that writing lyrics took a lot of effort, and he and Butcher often needed a lot of time to put them together.

typically featured acts like Kylie Minogue and New Kids On The Block. Nonetheless, editor Sara Lawrence noted how the track's rhythm defied easy categorization, remarking that it was 'dancey' but 'isn't really house, is it?'

'It's not house,' Shields replied. 'That's the thing about that beat we have—I know it sounds silly, but it's actually original. I would bet anyone £50 that they couldn't find a beat that is the same as that. It's just making a rhythm out of all the instruments together, the drums themselves don't add up to very much. With house music, it's the rhythm alone that carries it, with little hooks you stick on top of it—which is all fine, but that's not what we're about, we're about the whole thing.'[12]

When 'Soon' was released, it had an immediate impact on almost everyone who heard it. The EP garnered glowing reviews and then found its way back into the news when Brian Eno singled out 'Soon' during a Q&A following a lecture he delivered at the Museum Of Modern Art entitled 'Speaking High And Low: Modern Art And Popular Culture,' in which he remarked:

> It's a fantastic piece, it's a wall of distortion with a few motifs arising like icebergs out of it here and there. It's probably, I guess, the vaguest piece of music ever to become a hit; it's hard to hear the beat, it's very hard to hear the key, there are no lyrics as far as I know (though there are voices sort of waving around). It's really set a new standard actually for pop music.

The MOMA exhibition dealt with the many ways 'high' art appropriated 'low' art, and vice-versa. And though the exhibition dealt with visual arts rather than music, Eno's comments could not have been more germane, as MBV, ostensibly a 'pop group,' had created something that most certainly blurred the lines between high and low art. Eno went on to say that, had the song been created by Glenn Branca or Steve Reich, the classical music establishment would have recognized it accordingly. In 2016, he again praised the track—and in particular its vocals—when he named it as one of his favorite recordings in a 'Baker's Dozen' piece for *The Quietus*.

The fact that Shields was able to turn these totally amorphous guitar tones with heavily abstracted vocals into a modern dance tune that very nearly became a top 40 hit in the UK and aired on MTV's *120 Minutes* in the USA speaks to the fact that he believed listeners could handle music that wasn't spoon-fed to them if done well. As a musician, Shields has never been interested in anything self-consciously avant-garde. In 1996, in an extensive interview with the journalist Ned Raggett, he offered an amusing take on some of the more pretentious and convoluted writing about his work:

> The amount of people that have given names to what we do—I'm not talking about the indie/underground scene. Even in the avant-garde world or the jazz world, they've taken us on, to some degree, and created theories about what we do. I think they decided it was something to do with music that was expressing a state of nothing. I was like, 'Yeah yeah, nothing to do with me!'[13]

Later in the interview, discussing a cover song MBV had recorded for a Wire tribute album, Shields noted that the way bands like Wire and The Velvet Underground made music was in tune with what MBV were trying to achieve as a pop group: 'Not a pop group with an intent to be pop stars, but a pop group in a sense that you're writing music that's essentially pop music, easy, instinctive music, but you're also doing other stuff, because that comes the same way, as opposed to placing limits [on yourself].' Of the Velvets, he added, 'They were into what was good, and I don't think they put a big distinction between what John Coltrane was doing and what the Beach Boys would be doing. I think that's the key.'[14]

At their core, Shields very much wanted MBV to be seen as a pop group. 'Soon' even led to comparisons with seminal 60s songs like 'Good Vibrations' and 'Strawberry Fields Forever'—a sign that MBV were capable of making music as forward-looking as that of pop music's most innovative standard-bearers. 'Soon' is exactly what he'd always said he wanted to create. It was instinctive but also entirely new—an inspired mix of disparate elements that made it cutting-edge while also able to connect with a large audience at the same time.[*]

With *Glider*, Shields went against the grain in terms of what was typically expected of bands on a label like Creation, and it led people to wonder: what could MBV accomplish with their next full-length album, if they were allowed to continue working without the pressure of arbitrary deadlines? Asked years later if he took so long because he was a perfectionist, Shields disputed the notion.

> I just know the difference between achieving what I want to achieve and not achieving it. You know? Most of that early Creation stuff from '88, for example, was done very cheaply and done very quickly. It wasn't about being a perfectionist. It was about doing what you can do in the time you've got. ... I decided that I wasn't going to finish things off based on the fact that there was no more money left. I decided I would only allow things to be released when I was happy with it.[15]

•

MBV went on a short promotional tour of *Glider*, playing shows in the UK and Ireland between April 25 and May 4. The promotion of the EP was also helped by a new video, which received airplay in the USA on *120 Minutes* and on various alternative music shows throughout Europe, often interspersed with generic interview clips from their press kits or with footage of them talking to the shows' hosts.

MBV had made their first two videos in 1988 with Douglas Hart, the bass player for The Jesus & Mary Chain. His clips for 'You Made Me

---

[*] The smiles on the faces of the band members on the cover of this book are very real, as that great shot by Matt Anker was taken soon after *Glider* made them the toast of the town. While financial and critical success would come further down the line, this was the greatest, simplest, unbridled success they would ever know.

Realise' and 'Feed Me With Your Kiss' used a primitive aesthetic (limited to some degree by the minuscule video budget), intercutting random images with shots of the band members playing in the squatter milieu in which they lived and rehearsed. Now, however, wanting to capitalize on the success of 'Soon' and come up with a unique visual signature that reflected the group's evolving sound, Shields decided to go in a different direction.

The aspiring young director Angus Cameron first came into the Creation fold when a video he had created on spec fell into the hands of The House Of Love, who passed it along to Alan McGee. McGee was impressed, and although he had almost no budget for videos, he offered Cameron the opportunity to direct a virtually no-budget clip for 'Chelsea Girl' by Ride, a band McGee assured him would be the next big thing. Pleased with the results, the label asked Cameron to create a video for Primal Scream's 'Loaded,' a clip which he made in collaboration with Sam Montague and Nigel Simpkiss (at the time a trainee on-line editor). Working out of hours, Simpkiss initially treated all of Cameron and Montague's footage using a Charisma digital video effect (DVE) device. The other part of the team, Sam Montague, would shoot all four of the videos that Cameron directed for MBV in 1990 and 1991. Simpkiss too stayed on after playing such a vital role in the look of 'Loaded' and was actually at the controls when it came time to edit the first three MBV videos.

Not much has been written about Cameron's collaborations with MBV, but the videos he created for the band were an important step in helping reframe the band for an audience that was increasingly listening to more and more music on television. Up to this point, videos for bands like MBV, Sonic Youth, and Dinosaur Jr. tended to be lo-fi, black-and-white affairs. By contrast, 'Soon' uses a white, washed-out aesthetic with colored highlights and digital effects that were more commonly used in graphics for local television stations or sports coverage. (For example, during the broadcast of a tennis match, a DVE might be used to fly in graphics for each score change, along with a separate window in the corner offering a preview of the show scheduled to air after the match.)

This mundane technology was a utilitarian Swiss Army knife for video production, not a tool people generally used for more artistic endeavors. Imagine trying to make graphic art using Microsoft Paint rather than Adobe Photoshop—that's an apt analogy for the challenges Cameron faced, and the level of creativity he had to muster to overcome them. Much like Shields's repurposing of the Jazzmaster's tremolo setup, Cameron and the ever-inventive Simpkiss exploited the technology of the Charisma DVE and Grass Valley mixer in increasingly novel ways. It was a fitting collaboration. Cameron would run ideas by Shields, who would 'highlight certain sounds in the mix that he thought were important and I would reflect them in the edit.'[16] At other points, Shields might speak about his ideas in more abstract terms, leaving it up to Cameron to figure out how to best reflect what he wanted.

According to Cameron, upon seeing 'Soon' for the first time, Bobby Gillespie reportedly remarked, 'It's like the camera is on acid.' The video also grabs one's attention with its footage of Butcher dancing, which is made that much more otherworldly through the Charisma DVE's blurring effects. Her flowing movements—done at Cameron's suggestion, with a little liquid courage—were completely unrehearsed. When edited together with more static clips of the band members, her graceful dancing would demarcate different parts of the song and supply visual cues to make it easier to take in the music.

'Soon' clocks in at around seven minutes on vinyl but was cut in half for the video—an obvious commercial concession that helped ensure it would receive airtime on MTV and other outlets. The video edit was never released in audio formats, however, leading one to believe that Shields didn't see it as a 'real' version of the song.*

---

* An alternate edit from September 1990, clocking in at 4:30, would eventually turn up in the Warners archives. Was this the original video edit Shields had in mind before being advised to take another minute off the song, or was it simply another edit Warner might have wanted for a promotional single? Some years later, another official video for the unedited 'Soon' would appear, created for a few dollars using a basic audio visualizer. The fact that Shields put it up on YouTube while the video edit went unreleased either as a single or for radio suggests that he felt the cut-down version infringed on some of his values as an artist.

•

Broadly speaking, Shields wanted to offer his songs up as pop(ular) music for the general public while also maintaining the luxury of time and ample budgets he associated with bands like The Beatles or Pink Floyd. In the years to come, acts like Radiohead and others of their stature would want this same kind of freedom.

Shields's desire to record only when he was in a good frame of mind, and to sell his work on his terms and on his schedule, allowed him to maintain a particularly high level of quality control. But this was not without cost. His growing unwillingness to compromise would cause problems with Creation while the band continued work on their next full-length album, and it would eventually lead to even more dire consequences after they eventually signed to Island. After it was all over, he would come out in a good place, but his deliberateness in the studio and his uncompromising vision would put him and his bandmates under stresses they had never known before.

chapter seven

within: colm's breakdown • sampling

drums • the *glider* tour • hitting

a virtual standstill • the great lost

period • *tremolo* • more videos

'It was just a funny world. I can't describe it. They're really nice people, but the way they lived, it was like performance art or something, the way they were, the torture of making it. Whether it felt right or it wasn't. I didn't even know what was going on half the time.'

ANJALI DUTT, ENGINEER, 2022[1]

In the months leading up to *Glider*'s release, as Shields continued to embrace his new working process in the studio, a great deal of drama had begun to unfold with another member of MBV. Toward the end of 1989, Colm Ó Cíosóig experienced a personal breakdown that made it impossible for him to record with the band. Speaking about it in 2008, he explained, 'I went through a bad year—squatting in various places and getting evicted all the time ... I was essentially homeless. After every day in the studio, I'd walk down the street until I'd find an empty house to live in.'[2]

Colm's girlfriend was deported around the same time, which only added to his isolation and misery. With Creation unable to provide him with even the £300 he needed to put down a deposit on an apartment, he would wander aimlessly between sessions in the cold November air. It was all getting too much, and although he still had all his cognitive faculties, he found that he was losing his 'brain-to-arm muscle control.'[3]

The band had made cassette demos of around twenty-five tracks that they planned to record over the next year, which now required them to invent a workaround to accommodate Ó Cíosóig's inability to play. Things were made easier due to the fact that MBV were no longer going for the Who-style drums that had marked *Isn't Anything* but now sought something 'more simplistic, more pure.'[4] To that end, they first tried several unorthodox configurations, including trying to record Ó Cíosóig playing using just his arms, but these efforts failed when they tried to integrate them with the other instruments. They decided instead to break the drum rhythms down into smaller constituent parts that could be sampled and combined later.

Engineer Harold Burgon, who replaced Nick Robbins in the fall of 1989, helped teach Shields and Ó Cíosóig how to program drums on a computer, first at Elephant Studios and then at Woodcray. The new method proved more than serviceable under the challenging circumstances, and Shields would later say that he had taken such care with the sampling that Ó Cíosóig's physical absence behind the kit didn't make a major difference. Nonetheless, learning how to do so from scratch only added to the time the band were spending in the studio.

Despite the difficulties Ó Cíosóig was going through, he and Shields managed to piece together drum parts for twenty-two of the twenty-five songs from the demo cassette using this new method. Over time, they had taken between ten and fifteen of these songs further, although they were still missing vocals, and a number of particularly difficult guitar parts still had to be recorded. These recordings would eventually serve as the foundation for most of the tracks on *Glider*, *Tremolo*, and *Loveless*. For now, however, the band had decided to pause their efforts to finish their new album and instead make another EP. They would not return to what would become *Loveless* until around March 1991.

•

Things might have worked out differently had the band had a bit more financial support. But they had chosen to sign with a small label, for all the creative freedom that would entail, and working within a budget was all part of the package. At one point, *Select* magazine offered a bleak report on the band's progress:

> Homeless, skint, and stymied by Creation's unwillingness to give them any more money for equipment, the Valentines sulked, squatted, and eventually slowed to a standstill as 1989 ended. The 'positive environment' Kevin cites as essential for him to catch his flashes of genius in the studio had evaporated… 'You're expected to make this great new record and you're sitting there thinking, well, my guitar doesn't even work properly. So, yes, that's exactly what we did. We just went into slow motion.'[5]

The group lost even more time when they began preparations for a tour in support of *Glider*, and then, once they had returned from the road, as they tried to get back into the swing of things. When they finally returned to the studio, the pace was slower than ever, and it was increasingly evident that Creation's attitude toward the band had begun to sour.

As discussed elsewhere, Creation had been in the red since changing distributors, and everyone on the inside knew about all the drama with MBV. Pat Fish, who put out various albums on Creation as The Jazz Butcher during this period, would sneer that the Creation staff were struggling to make payroll because Shields's project had gone on so long. While MBV used relatively inexpensive, midrange studios, the label's finances were increasingly strained (even as McGee freely admits that he was still spending significant sums on drugs and travel). Creation would achieve unprecedented chart success in 1990 with Ride's *Nowhere*, but the label nevertheless seemed to be permanently on the verge of bankruptcy until 1992. MBV, in turn, were now receiving only £70 per week from the label, and they were always strapped for cash. Living hand to mouth was yet another thing that slowed the pace of their work in the studio.

Even so, Shields was insistent on pursuing his new approach to recording, and he refused to budge, however long his experiments might take. The band would spend hours sampling and editing guitar feedback with primitive equipment (they didn't get their first proper Akai sampler until late in 1990), exploring every path that presented itself. Shields would refer to the summer of 1990 as 'our great lost period'—three months of very slow progress with 'loads and loads of weird stuff with drums and feedback,' much of it in an attempt to complete 'To Here Knows When.'[6]

These extended stints in the studio involved a long line of engineers and countless studios. They eventually settled on Protocol in North London, where they would spend approximately 250 days between 1990 and 1991. This studio, at least, was in relatively good shape. More importantly, it came with a twenty-one-year-old staff engineer named Guy Fixsen.

Already a fan of MBV when he started working with the group in May 1990, Fixsen immediately had the sense that the band were working on something truly groundbreaking, and he had the patience to work at whatever pace Shields dictated. Together, they would spend months investigating various ideas, some of which were discarded, while others—specifically with regard to 'To Here Knows When'—were buried so deep in the mix that they'd almost be forgotten about.

'I thought it was going to be a very minimal song,' Shields said in 1991. 'I did the one guitar thing very quickly, and I thought, *That was easy. I'll just put the vocal down and we'll be finished.* Then I got this picture in my head, and I knew I had to pursue it. And the song was responsible for an excessive amount of wasted money on this record [and] time spent pursuing this idea of textural rhythm.'[7]

•

My Bloody Valentine handed in their new EP in November 1990. If *Loveless* is the group's great long-playing masterpiece and go-to work, then *Tremolo*, released in February 1991, is their most overlooked and underrated release. It features seven tracks, but because the UK's Official Charts Company decreed that an EP contain a maximum of four songs to be eligible for the charts, the three linking, interstitial pieces were not listed on the sleeve. Seven tracks or four; either way, it was an undisputed masterpiece that sounds like nothing that had come before it.

Over the years, Shields has given some particularly astute observations about the differences between traditional commercial music and the sound MBV were pursuing in response. 'Most people have got used to really bright, bright music because that's the kind of music that initially comes across best on radio and TV,' he explained, noting that what they were trying to achieve, 'the overall picture of the music ... fits in itself ... *in a way, you have to look into it, as opposed to it comes out to you. Most music's made, constructed, to come out, kind of, to attack you.*'[8]

This description could be applied to a great deal of MBV's music, but when *Tremolo* was released, this 'blunted' approach was even more heightened, and it could sometimes feel downright disorienting. When promotional tapes of the EP were being run off at the Creation office to be sent to the press, radio stations, and other outlets, Shields closely monitored the dubbing process, listening to each individual copy to ensure quality control.* It was time well spent, as Creation received more than a few calls from recipients asking for replacements because they thought their tapes had arrived warped or damaged in some way. Creation's employees would then have to try and convince them that what they were hearing was the intended sound. Even Alan McGee initially failed to comprehend the EP's lead track, 'To Here Knows When,' insisting to Shields over the phone that there was something wrong with his tape. Shields assured him there was nothing wrong—that was the record. In disbelief, McGee insisted even more emphatically that something was up. 'I can't deal with this,' Shields replied angrily, and then he hung up.[9]

'To Here Knows When' consumed the most studio time, energy, and experimentation of any of the tracks that eventually ended up on *Loveless*. It is disorienting for a host of reasons, from the amorphous guitar track that seems to have no point of origin or attack to the challenging rhythmic

---

* *Glider* and *Tremolo* mark the end of Shields's journey with this type of tonality, requiring 'To Here Knows When' and 'Soon' to be remixed to fit the brighter sound of *Loveless* (which he attributed to the band now sleeping more regularly).

ideas that came as a result of months of studio experimentation. 'There's lots of things going on,' Shields told an interviewer. 'We really wanted people to check their stereos with this one. There's things in there that even the engineers barely remember doing, tons of really subtle inflections. And yet it's just one guitar.'[10]

The original intention for the track may have been relatively simple, but it grew into the most conceptual piece of music MBV had made to date. Initially, Shields thought it would all be easy once the guitar was recorded. All that remained was the vocal. Then, out of nowhere, he had a vision that he couldn't not pursue—one that involved numerous experiments, many of which didn't come off, and, in turn, wasting a 'pathetically ridiculous amount of time' in an arena where time is synonymous with money.[11]

As with many of the band's other songs, recording the guitar part was fairly straightforward, once Shields figured out what he wanted to do. But what the song does with synthesizers, samplers, and other sound processors is extremely sophisticated. 'This nice little ten-minute idea took six weeks of work on the rhythms,' he said, 'all of which were scrapped in the end and replaced by this rumble.' Attempting to explain the ideas he was pursuing, he added, 'The idea was to make you feel that the rhythm had gone off one way or another while it stayed perfectly in time.'[12] In other words, he was using textures and sounds distinct from those you associate with percussion (much like he did with 'Soon'), but this time also creating a second rhythm distinct from the pulse of the bass drum, then having those two rhythms converge and diverge at various points in the track.

Both Alan Moulder and Guy Fixsen could see that Shields's first priority was quality; he was not going to be pushed around by anyone if he wasn't ready. Both engineers have noted the care and discipline he put into his recordings, and how intense, extremely detailed, and complex his process could be. Shields may have recorded the entire *You Made Me Realise* EP in five days, but when it came to 'To Here Knows When,' he spent a week working on just the tambourine track. The final product demonstrates how even the most seemingly mundane elements can elevate a whole song, however, yielding results that justify the time and cost.

Recalling that tambourine part, Fixsen explained most groups might play a few bars of it, loop it, and be done with it in five minutes. Not Shields. First, there was the matter of selecting the right tambourine, and then they had to combine it with the right mic to get the tone they were after. Next, in Fixsen's words, 'It had to be played with a really nice feel. From that, a bunch of candidates were selected. Then a lot of time was spent treating them in such a way, moving them ahead or behind the beat, trying to get it exactly right. When I tell them that story, people ask, Can you even hear it, at the end of the day? And I tell them, It really, really feels nice. It has, like, a perfect groove.'[13]

Not everyone who collaborated with Shields in the studio had Fixsen's level of patience and understanding. Anjali Dutt, the other engineer hired by Creation in addition to Moulder, had a different memory of those days and how they dragged out, and what she felt was an awful lot of wasted time. Describing a typical studio session to Creation biographer David Cavanagh, she recalled how Shields would arrive at eight in the evening; they would eat, hang out, and watch television for a few hours; and then finally, at two in the morning, they would start. Perhaps exaggerating for effect, she mentioned with particular disdain the tambourine part taking three weeks to get right.[14]

It seems pretty clear Shields's methods and the pace of working didn't agree with Dutt, though in more recent years her attitude has become more sympathetic. Speaking to Reverb.com in 2022, she noted, 'I think one of the hardest things in the world is to write in the studio. Kevin just had this vision. I wouldn't say he had a complete vision, but he had something, and he had to kind of motivate himself to do it.'

•

Though things were moving at a glacial pace during the summer of 1990, there were moments when music seemed to pour out of Shields in quick flashes of inspiration and amaze those around. Fixsen mentioned another event, seeming out of the blue without warming up, Shields played the (sampled) flute part for 'Swallow,' in one take saying, 'He sat down at the keyboard and played this totally evocative flute part that really used the whole nuance of the sample. Me and Anjali sat there going, *Wow*. Can't believe he just did that.'[15]

The flute part was typical of Shields's methodology. Instead of using a pre-existing sample, he seems to have merged it with a sample of Butcher's voice, creating something more otherworldly, more exotic than a real instrument or voice. Also interesting is the way he fractures the main flute sample at various parts, playing notes on a keyboard that would be impossible on an actual flute. He plays a stuttering series of different notes before coming around to the melody, which sounds like an organic yet exotic reference to the Clavioline on The Beatles' 'Baby, You're A Rich Man.' The sample runs through the entire song and perfectly complements the lyrics, at times devouring and almost overwhelming the rest of the song. It ends with some more stuttering and stammering as it transitions into the short nameless interstitial piece that links 'Swallow' to the next track, 'Honey Power.'

The EP's third named track is noteworthy for the fact that Shields doesn't play the guitar chords in his typical way. He's clearly holding the tremolo arm in his hand, but you can follow the notes he fingers as the chorus progresses. Instead of strummed chords, the chorus is made up of two single-note patterns layered over one another while the bass guitar defines the chord changes.

Tremolo ends with the wistful 'Moon Song,' a track that owes something to 'Caroline, No,' the final track on *Pet Sounds*, which closes with the forlorn sound of a train passing and dogs barking in the distance. Recorded in early 1989, it was the only song from the sessions at Blackwing Studios that would see the light of day before 2012.

The EP's three interstitial tracks haven't received the attention they deserve from critics. The segue at the end of 'To Here Knows When' begins as the song proper fades out around the 4:40 mark. It is built around a rolling guitar figure in an ambiguous time signature, while the elements in the palette include a horn-like sound playing a single-note melody along with some sustained atmospheric sounds, likely guitars playing a melody in reverse. Sixty-six seconds long, it is a very effective palate cleanser, creating a seamless transition.

This next interstitial piece emerges as 'Swallow' fades out. This one is more tense, with a chugging guitar figure that creates the main rhythm, which is almost atonal in nature, and a sustained drone element that sits on top of the rhythmic guitar and adds further suspense. This drone sound also has a stereo panning effect that rapidly flutters right and left in the stereo spectrum.

By contrast, the segue at the end of 'Honey Power' has a more plaintive, serene feel to it, featuring Butcher singing an airy, wordless melody over a compelling chord sequence played on a gently strummed electric guitar with gauzy atmospherics shimmering in the background. It's a highly consonant piece that almost plays as a full, proper song.

Taken together, these three tracks add a lot to the overall immersive nature of the record. The other four tracks just wouldn't flow into each other as well without them. The seven pieces cohere into a unified whole—a fully fledged work of art that serves as a bona fide companion to *Loveless*.

·

Creation once again engaged Angus Cameron to make a video to coincide with *Tremolo*'s release. The band wanted to make one for 'To Here Knows When,' but the label wanted 'Swallow.' Cameron came to the rescue, proposing that he would make both videos for the £10,000 figure that the label had budgeted for, virtually guaranteeing that he wouldn't see any money at the end of the day.* As a result, we have two more videos that continue the white, washed-out aesthetic of 'Soon.' Because Cameron continued to push the available technology to the limit—he created the two new videos using the same low-budget equipment he had used earlier—a great deal of time was spent making the videos look their best. It was time

---

* Cameron has emphasized that he can't remember what any of the videos he made for MBV cost, though he's sure he ended up donating his salary for all of them so he could continue working with the band.

well invested. Both videos are filled with constantly changing images, and much like when one looks at moving clouds in the sky, various shapes surface and swirl into one another. They hold up after multiple viewings, allowing your mind to run wild with whatever your subconscious happens to be fixated on.

In a sense, MBV's music was mixed to allow listeners to interact with and hear different things each time it was played. Expanding on an earlier explanation as to why the vocals often sound as if they are low in the mix, Shields has explained, 'If you mix things in a way that they share a lot of frequencies, your brain plays a role.'[16] Your imagination, he noted, can fill in fifty percent of what's happening, particularly when you can't tell where one sound begins or ends. The listener plays a large role in this by allowing their mind to be open. You also hear things differently each time because the pitch bending makes the actual sounds harder to recall. The videos engage with these ideas, creating the perfect visual analogs to the songs.

Though McGee didn't understand 'To Here Knows When' when he first heard it on tape, he changed his tune when he saw Cameron's video. 'I get that track now, you know?' he told the director. 'I understand it. I like it now.'[17] The video uses as many as thirty-six different visual layers, bringing the film to a point where it is close to coming undone. It is based on a shot of Butcher pirouetting, which was then duplicated multiple times, each time manually tinted a different color. These looped shots were then laid over themselves, creating an evocative, kaleidoscope effect. Look closely toward the end of the video and you'll see Butcher cracking a smile, on the edge of losing her balance and composure, dizzy after performing so many revolutions.

The video offers a visual cue for the moment when the two rhythms in the song diverge to the greatest degree when, at 3:09, the visual of Butcher rotating becomes two mirror images, expanding to fill the whole screen. At that moment, one rhythm track speeds up while the other, the delicate pulse of the bass drum, stays at the same pace. The song then achieves another level of transcendence as the bubbling rhythm surges and leaps forward in time, as each of its successive pulsations crisscross through the many layers that bend and twist in and out of focus and in and out of tune, all while the main rhythm stays in place, continuing its gentle journey. This concept of 'textural rhythm' is likely the aspect it took Shields so much time to achieve.

The video for 'Swallow' offers yet another take on this heavily looped and layered technology, but it is sufficiently different and original that one would still never guess how little money went into making it. It's all the more remarkable considering Cameron was still very new to directing and editing, having only made three other videos before he began working with MBV.

•

The staff at Creation were not overly enamored with *Tremolo*. Some of them felt panicked while others were shellshocked, unable to say anything to Shields for a week after he handed it in. Eventually, he got the message, which seemed to be: *We give you another six months, and this is what you come up with?* Undeterred, Shields told the label, 'It's my ambition to make music that makes present-day music sound like scratchy old 78s made in the early 20s sounds today.'[18]

Though the new EP might have scared Creation, the label soon realized the band's fans were into it. And even if it didn't bring the same kind of monetary returns *Isn't Anything* had in 1988, they hoped Shields's ambitions would translate into significant sales for the band's next full-length album.

The often-fickle British music press did not see *Tremolo* as much of a leap forward for the group, and as such did not give it a great deal of attention. It probably didn't help that almost a year had passed since the release of *Glider*, or that the new EP was denser and more esoteric and lacked the direct popular appeal of 'Soon,' which had immediately caught the attention of both the indie scene and the dance floor. It would take much longer for listeners and reviewers to truly appreciate *Tremolo*. In fact, it wasn't until the EP was digitally remastered for CD in 2012 that critics would begin to reflect on just how timeless it was in its own right, rather than just as an adjunct to *Loveless*. But while it may have seemed at the time like a relatively minor release, it was another major demarcation point for Shields—a definite step forward in his pursuit of a particular sound.

The band dutifully made the rounds in the UK and Europe after *Tremolo*'s release, although the press campaign itself was relatively modest, with a bigger publicity push planned once their new album was finished. By then, however, the stress on Shields and Creation to finish it—and the comments he would begin to make about the label in the press—would put the final nail in an already difficult relationship.

interlude three

mbv & gender

In the sometimes-esoteric discussions of sexual dynamics in rock music, guitar playing can be seen to embody a certain kind of power dynamic, which makes Shields's unique technique with the Jazzmaster and its tremolo system particularly noteworthy. This also opens up a broader discussion about the gender and sexual dynamics in MBV, and how they played a pivotal role in shaping the band's sound.

Shields has noted how everything began to change for the group when Bilinda Butcher joined, giving them a gender balance they hadn't had previously. And as Butcher began contributing more lead vocals and lyrics, the makeup of the band began to draw attention. Few groups at the time—especially those who played indie rock—had both male and female members whose influence was equally felt. Even fewer were able to genuinely encompass the huge spectrum of emotions MBV captured on their records of the late 80s and early 90s. And even now, perhaps even fewer bands are able to evoke feelings we typically associate with *both* men and women in a single song in the way that MBV seemed to be able to seamlessly achieve.

As early as 1990, journalist Ben Fulton had noted in a piece for *Option* magazine that many people perceived MBV as a band that wrote songs that transcended gender. Shields thought that the equal proportion of men and women in the band was essential to how people viewed them and their music, which in turn either obscured the line between masculine and feminine or erased it altogether. 'There's a different feel with women, definitely,' he said. 'There are so many things that fall into the category of *guys in the band.* When you get two women in the band, things come from a more general point of view. We get approached more as people.' He also understood and valued the freedom the gender balance granted, noting that with a higher level of gender parity, he could get away with things an all-male band couldn't conceive of.[1]

Part of what makes MBV's songs so unique and affecting is that their songs explore intimacy and lust within the context of monogamy. Speaking to *The Quietus* in 2012, Shields drew a comparison with Led Zeppelin, noting, 'Their sex songs were about wanting it. We were doing it! It's from the inside out, rather than the outside in.'[2] In a sense, bands like Zeppelin were selling an unattainable male trope to draw in female fans; their particular brand of fantasy-world lyrics isn't sexy in a grown-up, real-world sense. Shields saw conventionally masculine rock posturing for what it was:

> It's a cliché but it comes down to the fact that most music is dehumanizing, it's sanitized. Heavy Metal bands and disco music, it's *Dallas* sex. No real person can relate to it when some rock singer is going on about giving you his 'lurve.' Our records are about the feelings that ordinary people have and the language they might use with each other.[3]

'Cupid Come' from *Isn't Anything*, for example, perfectly encapsulates MBV's unconventional approach to sex. The lyrics were written by Butcher within the first year or so of her relationship with Shields. They are carnal yet still reflect the intimacy of a monogamous relationship. '*Swallow me into your bed / With glimpses of your thighs,*' he sings. '*Forget your vanity / Come cupid come.*'* The allure of Butcher's lyrics grew out of genuine sentiment. She and Shields were among a small fraternity of artists who

---

* The second line of 'Cupid Come' is often erroneously transcribed online as '*sickly heavy heart.*' The first and second lines are actually '*Cupid come from coffee cup / Sickly heavy high.*' Butcher was clearly playing with the idea of something heavily intoxicating, in the same way the band's earlier 'Strawberry Wine' was something you ingest and also an altered state of mind. Butcher was not referring to a real cocktail, however; as later revealed by the band during Tim Burgess's Twitter listening party for *Isn't Anything*, the song grew out of a story involving Birthday Party guitar player Rowland S Howard and a coffee cup of sexual fluid.

were able to put it all out there, documenting the pleasures of intimacy in a way most bands couldn't even begin to articulate.

Simon Reynolds has written extensively about sexual dynamics in popular music, and he has noted MBV's integration of what is typically the preserve of either male or female performers. In his book *Blissed Out*, he writes, 'My Bloody Valentine are remarkable for reconciling the two great pleasures in rock today, apparently at odds with each other: the masculine pleasure of the oppressive, spine-crushing arse quake, and the feminine bliss of the border-dissolving, spine-melting oceanic wash. But then both are forms of surrender to sound.'[4]

Another prominent critic, Jon Savage, has also touched upon the band's unique fusion, which he has described as an aural way out of today's problems: 'They suggest not only a fusion of apparent opposites but a way through the chaos that is today's emotional and physical reality . . . they make a different future conceivable.'[5] Savage recognized that their music reflects the masculine and feminine within each of us, whether we recognize it or not, and shows it on the spectrum it exists upon, as opposed to reducing it to something binary.

Writing for Popmatters.com, Joseph Fisher focused on the way the group 'offers a gender-bending sonic style—a style that severed the entrenched connections between the electric guitar and masculine phallic power.' He went on to reference Steve Waksman's *Instruments Of Desire: The Electric Guitar And The Shaping Of Musical Experience*, noting that MBV's sound and intimate lyrics are the polar opposite of the 'cock rock, pure and simple' of Led Zeppelin, in which Jimmy Page's guitar becomes a 'technophallus' used to 'accentuate the phallic dimensions of the performing male body.' By using the tremolo arm throughout his entire performance, Kevin Shields effectively renders his own guitar flaccid. But to Fisher, flaccid isn't the same thing as impotent. 'By liberating the electric guitar from its ties to masculine sexuality,' he concluded, 'the band, through its blurry, woozy aesthetic, ultimately eradicates the stagnant gender constructions that are so often employed to categorize and pigeonhole performers of any kind.'[6]

MBV's records with Creation certainly feel like they were ahead of the curve when we consider the changes and expectations surrounding gender dynamics that have become more prominent over the last decade or so. In addition to Shields's unique use of the guitar, he and Butcher combined their voices in a myriad of ways that often make it unclear who is singing—or, by extension, which gender the song's protagonist is supposed to be. Songs like 'When You Sleep,' 'Soon,' and 'Who Sees You' are quintessential examples of this aesthetic. 'It isn't like they're harmonizing in the truest sense of the word,' Google has explained. 'It's as if their voices simply just glide into one another. You know there are two different people, yet at the same time it's quite genderless.'[7]

It seems clear that Shields's lyrics—and the band's potential—changed when Butcher joined the group. MBV had had female members going back to when Tina Durkin played with them, and it's evident that Shields and Ó Cíosóig always saw women as equals. But with Butcher's contributions to both vocals and lyrics, Shields seemed to grow freer than ever before to assume any point of view—both musically and lyrically—and explore all the different sides of himself. Even when Butcher contributed relatively little to a particular release, like the *Feed Me With Your Kiss* EP, it's clear she opened a door for Shields that would never close again.

It's noteworthy that MBV's synthesis and blurring of gender wasn't part of some political agenda or some aspirational hope to change society. It was more just that, as a group, they naturally gravitated toward the blurring of boundaries—male/female, loud/soft, east/west, mind/body—in their overall attempt to articulate what it means to be human.

chapter eight

within: creative entropy • going
grey • emotional blackmail • knowing
when the switch is on or off • not
pulling the plug • technological
transition • pushing back

'We recorded *Isn't Anything* really quickly in Wales. With *Loveless*, it took a much longer time, and no one enjoyed it. … All four of us were losing it in our own ways … we had no money. Colm was homeless and Kevin's and my relationship was cracking. Quite frankly we were driving each other insane. The reason the album was called *Loveless* is because it all was when we made it.'

BILINDA BUTCHER, 2004[1]

Shields has said that *Loveless* earned its name from the general sense of isolation he felt while making the album. The band's previous full-length, *Isn't Anything*, had involved all four members working together to craft it at studios in Wales and London. Many of the stories that have been told about the follow-up, however, portray it as a Kevin Shields solo project—a labor of love that he created in almost total isolation. At some points, it may have felt that way to Shields himself, though ultimately this description oversimplifies what really happened.

The obstacles to completing *Loveless*—both personal and professional— were legion. Over the twenty-six months in which the album came together, pretty much everything with the band was in flux. Shields, either directly or indirectly, brought some of this on himself. Eventually, all of the challenges added up, producing a kind of creative entropy that was extremely difficult to overcome. The band faced problems at every turn: subpar studios and instruments, Creation's inability to manage its money and pay for studio time, and MBV's own deteriorating relationship with McGee and the label. Today, it seems a minor miracle that *Loveless* was finished at all, not to mention that it became the record that is widely considered to be Shields's supreme artistic achievement.

Shields has also spoken about the various personal difficulties that dogged the band throughout this period, which made their professional worries seem unimportant by comparison. At one point in February 1991, while doing press for *Tremolo*, he explained:

> Our lives have been too real to talk about. Not glamorous stuff like getting arrested for drugs or whatever, it's more mundane domestic shit that really fucks you up, personal things that are totally beyond the experience of the average student. Bilinda happened to bring up a kid under bad circumstances, it's very real, we don't really talk about it. That's why we often think we might break up because the band seems too trivial sometimes.[2]

Shields has also noted how his own rocky relationship with Butcher was putting a creative strain on the band. Although they were living together, they rarely saw each other due to their different schedules and different priorities. (Butcher had to take care of her son while also fulfilling her role as a member of the band.) For Butcher, the name *Loveless* represented their relationship coming apart and served as a description of the whole process of making the record.

All of these issues put additional stress on the group as they tried to cobble together new work that matched the level of innovation and newness they'd accomplished before. In his own explanation for why the album took so long to complete, Shields has given several different versions of the same story, making clear that despite everything, he was intent on doing whatever was necessary to see his creative vision to completion. In 2009, he explained:

During the *Loveless* process, I was completely under the spell of that. I had no choice but to do it and there was no other way to do it … I didn't care what anyone else said. There was zero outside influence in that respect because only I knew what I had to do. … It was just like a feeling, a mood—I was in a certain state or frame of mind. I always knew what was right. If you allow yourself to really go in a certain direction, without any outside influences, then it has a purity to it. In a way, it never gets diluted.[3]

Shields is not the first musician to indulge every impulse and whim while trying out a large number of ideas. Brian Wilson moved between three studios over six months under the spell of 'Good Vibrations.' It's also easy to forget all the time and effort that went into Beatles songs like 'Tomorrow Never Knows' and 'Strawberry Fields Forever'—tracks that ultimately became masterpieces because John Lennon could spend whatever time he needed at Abbey Road. Unlike Shields, however, Lennon was well capitalized, and he also had three other bandmates who played on the tracks, created loops, and generated other ideas. He also benefited from inspired input from producers and engineers who made contributions both during the sessions and on their own time.

Shields looked to these iconic musicians to guide his own expectations about what MBV's music should aspire to. 'To me, all the financial details seemed to overshadow the record's artistic qualities,' he later said. 'Why is that an issue? Do you know how much The Beatles' and Pink Floyd's records cost? You'd be shocked.'[4]

Another major theme of the *Loveless* narrative that has been repeated endlessly is the depiction of Shields as some kind of irrational perfectionist who spent countless hours of studio time doing take after take, making minuscule adjustments no one else could hear. In actuality, the true reason for the extended time the band took to complete the record was much more prosaic: Shields's mental state on any given day was the key to whether or not he would be productive.[5]

Basically, I know when the switch is on or off. When the switch is on, everything's fine, everything's good, and when the switch is off, everything's pointless. I would go, *Okay, I'm not trying, I'll watch television, I'll read magazines.* That's why *Loveless* became this seemingly long, drawn-out process, because I discovered pretty quickly that when circumstances around me turn the switch off, I just feel like it's a labour, or I feel too much emotional and psychological uncomfortableness around me to be doing music in a way that's pure, the way everyone should be doing music.[6]

Alan Moulder has recalled how some of band's studio setups were extremely time-intensive, but he has never described Shields's process as overly fastidious. 'Each song had a different approach,' he explained. 'Kevin would have an idea for different amp and pedal setups, and we'd try them out.'[7] Once Shields figured out what he wanted, he would perform three takes at the most. He clearly knew when everything in his mind and body was aligned, which allowed him to arrange difficult parts in his head and record them in just one or two attempts. At one point, he compared the act of recording to playing a gig that you've spent weeks preparing for.

Shields found it difficult to get excited about making music when he was dealing with so much adversity, which could change from week to week. The chaos around him, and the band's financial hardships, laid bare one of the major disadvantages of being signed to an independent label that didn't have the same monetary resources the majors did. The upside, of course, was the freedom he enjoyed with regard to what he recorded. At this stage in his career, this was the trade-off he opted for, and he was counting on the fact that when all was said and done, Creation fundamentally cared about the music.

At various points, McGee thought it might be useful to use third parties, including Moulder and Guy Fixsen, to try to motivate Shields to get *Loveless* done more quickly. Moulder finally explained to McGee that this was counterproductive; if Shields felt pressured, he would only slow things down further. He had a vision for the album, and it was clear he wasn't going to allow it to be compromised, no matter how long it took. But McGee was anxious for the drama to end, and in a frank discussion at Protocol Studios at the beginning of 1991, he warned Shields that Creation might become insolvent if the band took too much longer.

It's debatable how legitimate a threat this was. Although McGee was concerned that Creation might go under at any moment, he also had major labels wining and dining him on a regular basis. He had traveled to Los Angeles a number of times to discuss proposed investment deals. He was torn about entering an arrangement with a bigger company, however; even if he and his partners technically remained in control of the material Creation put out, he felt everything he'd built at the label would go down the drain if he got in bed with a major. But if the label needed to take that step to survive, perhaps it was the only viable option.

A few months into 1991, Creation co-owner Dick Green's hair was going grey—literally—and both he and McGee were nearing a breaking point. It's hard to stress just how agitated they were, with Green reportedly quivering in fear as he opened each piece of mail. According to McGee, he had invested every penny he had, including from his personal savings, to help MBV finish the album. At one point, he called Shields, practically in tears, and told him, 'You have to deliver this record.'[8] Whether or not the tears were real depends on the telling, but regardless of what happened in that one moment, McGee and Green were on a tightrope they could fall off at any moment.

The threat of Creation going bankrupt may ultimately have helped push Shields to finally finish *Loveless*. In hindsight, McGee has admitted he felt that he had emotionally blackmailed Shields; either way, the pace of work did speed up, even if finishing the album would still require several more injections of capital.

In May 1991, the band began working on vocals, which they finished the following month. Recording them in almost complete privacy over sessions lasting as long as ten hours, Shields and Butcher would cover the window of the control room and have the monitors turned off so the tape operator couldn't hear or see anything, only pulling back the sheets to tell them if a take was good or bad or whether to keep it or record over it. While some of the lyrics were written out in advance, others were made up on the spot. Butcher has since said that she often had to guess what Shields was singing, writing down her best guesses at the lyrics if he wasn't around or didn't make a point of revealing them. Some of the songs contain between ten and twenty-four vocal tracks, layered in such a way as to get a unique effect distinct from ADT (artificial double tracking), with Shields moving up the best take in the mix so that the vowels were a bit more defined.

Mixing the album required yet another injection of money because Shields wanted to utilize one of the best facilities available, insisting he needed the kind of advanced equipment typically used to mix a movie's complete soundtrack of dialogue, music, and sound effects (as opposed to just the musical score) in order to perfectly crossfade the main tracks with the short interstitial numbers.

By September, with the help of Dick Meany at the Church, the album was mixed, which meant that all that remained was to master it. And then came a demand for £22,000 to release the tapes. According to McGee, Shields berated him to find the money, which was a step too far. 'I'll tell you why that really got to me,' he later recalled. 'It was the insurance money my dad had got from my mum's death. I borrowed it to finish a record.'⁹

Mastering an album typically takes one or two days. Shields took thirteen days to master *Loveless*—an unheard-of amount of time to put the finished touches to a record.* McGee has a specific memory attached to the thirteenth, final day, when the album was finally handed over. His accountant called him that day to let him know that, actually, the label was not £700,000 adrift but in fact in debt to the tune of £1,700,000. He had somehow missed the one at the front.

After two years of false starts, personal troubles, and acrimonious exchanges with the label, Shields finally delivered *Loveless* to Creation in

---

* In his defense, it's been reported that the computer crashed midway through the mastering sessions, and that Shields had to reassemble the album from memory.

September 1991. The label scheduled it for release in November. All that remained was to create the cover art, for which Shields chose an image of a Jazzmaster from the 'Swallow' video. He and Cameron tinkered with it, tinting it a dark shade of red. The name of the band, also in red, was placed across the bottom.

•

Nothing on *Loveless* was done without forethought. A great deal of consideration and experimentation went into every element of every song. According to Guy Fixsen, 'Shields exploited every resource of the studio to make each song distinct yet still fit within his larger vision of the whole album.'[10] And as Alan Di Perna pointed out an excellent profile of Shields for *Guitar World*, he wasn't simply a guitar player: he jacked into the 'biggest box anyone's ever invented: the recording studio.'[11]

It's important to understand the pivotal point in time—especially with regard to the new types of recording technologies—in which *Loveless* was made. The album was recorded before the revolution of Pro Tools and other digital devices that are ubiquitous today, though some digital technology was available. Fixsen, who lived through the technological transition, explained it by saying, '[*Loveless*] was recorded on analog tape but with sequencers and samplers synchronized to it—the old world of commitment to ideas and working within constraints versus the new world of cut and paste and working within the equally constraining framework of too many options. It was a hybridization.'[12]

The feel of the drums, like everything else at this point in time, had to sound right. Even as the drums became more functional, they were never quantized, with Shields using a wide variety of samples of each drum sound to construct sequences that have a more utilitarian feel than Ó Cíosóig's playing on *Isn't Anything*. 'We put movement into it,' Shields has said, meaning that the sequenced parts have all the hallmarks of an actual human playing the drums.[13] As such, many listeners did not realize they weren't hearing live drum parts. Eric Tischler of *Tape Op*, who knows as much as anyone about recording, was positive 'What You Want' featured

Ó Cíosóig's live playing. He was one of many journalists and musicians who got it wrong.

Perhaps the most conventional element on the album is the bass guitar. For those tracks, Shields used a Steinberger bass—the distinctive trapezoid-shaped guitar with no tuning pegs at its head—because he liked how the notes ring out at a consistent volume up and down the neck.* Moulder remembered the Steinberger being used with a Vox Tone Bender fuzz pedal fed through a vintage SVT Ampeg amp. Shortly after the *Glider* EP was finished, Shields spent five days nimbly putting down all the bass lines for the twenty or so songs that were still in the running for the band's full-length album (and the *Tremolo* EP). By all accounts, he didn't use any reference tapes or notes; it was all done from memory.

The guitar parts, of course, took far longer. Most tracks have between one and three guitar parts, with one of them proving particularly challenging to bring into existence for each song. For *Loveless*, his go-to starting point would involve reverse reverb from the SPX90 (as opposed to the MidiVerb II), alongside an array of different amp and mic setups. He would take the wet sound from the SPX90 and 'feed that into a Marshall amp, and that created the kind of distortion essentially.'[14] Alan Moulder has also recalled seeing a Jim Dunlop fuzz pedal and a Digitech Whammy (a harmonizer), and he has mentioned how he often saw the Roger Mayer Octavia and Axis Fuzz pedals connected together to create a specific gating effect Shields often used with reverse reverb. That aside, it is difficult to identify the specific processing, effects, or pedals Shields uses on each track beyond what he has since revealed himself. So much more time went into each one that it's impossible to say for sure what he did on any particular song.

When listening to the album, it's instructive to know that like most of Shields's recordings, *Loveless* was created to be a monaural experience, although about half the tracks have stereo elements, most obviously the guitar in 'Loomer' and some of the segues. 'I just think in real life you don't

---

* Prior to this, the band had used a German Warwick bass on their recordings. The last time they used it was most likely during the *Glider* sessions, as engineer Huw Price remembers it from a session for 'Soon.'

hear in stereo, you've just got two mono ears that make up the stereo,' he would later explain.[15] He elaborated further in another interview, saying, 'Everything I do is mostly in mono . . . there's no set area of separation. The sense of bigness comes from the depth of perception.'[16] For Shields, EQ and the balance of frequencies were much more important to creating depth than stereo effects. So, while the album wasn't strictly recorded in mono, its overall effect hearkens back to a more straightforward live sound, guided by Shields's own sense of how best to create a sense of space.[17]

The album's opening track, 'Only Shallow,' immediately hits the listener with the kinds of sound only Shields could dream up. 'The first song is so fucking straightforward it's like a real garage song,' he told *Lime Lizard* magazine.[18] When he later broke the track down in more detail for *Sound On Sound*, however, he revealed its true complexity, beginning with two distinctive brands of amplifiers facing each other, with a microphone dropped in between, to create a basic sound where the tremolos were going at different rates. He then did a second overdub, making for four different tremolo rates. 'Then I sampled it in the Akai and played it backward, so it was backward and forwards at the same time.'[19] Or, as he told *Guitar World*, 'I did a couple of overdubs of that, then I reversed it and played it backward into a sampler. I put them on top of each other so they kind of merged in.'[20] Whichever is the more accurate explanation, it is not nearly as straightforward as Shields first made it out to be.

The next track, 'Loomer,' stands out in much the same way as 'To Here Knows When' and 'Soon.' All three are songs that conform to pop's primary purpose once you adapt your ears and expectations to the way they radically reformulate a well-worn template. One critical element of the song's sound comes from the unique guitar Shields used: a Stratocaster neck attached to a Jaguar body with EMG pickups, giving it a denser sound than your typical Jazzmaster. Another element that makes it so distinct is the way the guitar sound and the drums are compressed together in such a way as to make you feel as if you are moving in some sleek vehicle, be it an underground train, jet, or spaceship. It's one of the most unusual songs in the MBV canon.

'When You Sleep,' by contrast, is in keeping with the conventions of the album's other tracks in many ways, with one relatively straightforward guitar riff created through the physical motion of the tremolo arm and reverse reverb. The many vocal takes are all just Shields's voice sped up and slowed down, while the keyboard part used in the chorus combines samples of Butcher's voice with feedback and synthesized flute and oboe.

Shields got into some specifics of 'I Only Said' with Alan Di Perna, revealing that this particular song was run through Duncan amplifier (as opposed to his usual Marshall/Vox combo) with a built-in graphic equalizer preamp, which he used to overdrive the sound to tape. He bounced that track through a parametric equalizer—which offers significantly more flexibility than a traditional equalizer—adjusting the signal in real time to give the track its utterly distinctive sound.

'Come In Alone' was one of the easier songs to record, according to Shields, and it might be most notable for its use of extreme varispeed processing on the vocals. Shields's voice sounds significantly higher here than on any of his other vocals on the record.

'Sometimes,' which was one of the last songs recorded for the album, is also something of an anomaly due to its seven acoustic guitar tracks, which Shields would later note are 'panned like a fan left to right so it sounds like one track.'[21] He added yet another wrinkle by setting two Boss tremolo pan pedals at slightly different speeds; a Vox fuzz pedal was also used to achieve the distorted guitar sound.

The overall sound of 'Blown A Wish' has often been compared to the Cocteau Twins, though Shields didn't use any of Robin Guthrie's go-to effects to create the main guitar part. The affinity has more to do with the kind of melodic sensibility expressed by the singer Liz Fraser. To create the wobbly chorus/vibrato sound in the bridge, Shields used a Jim Dunlop Rotovibe pedal.[*]

'Soon' closes out the album with an utterly brilliant fade out, highlighting Shields's ability to take advantage of all the illusions and

---

[*] While Shields does have a huge collection of guitar pedals, they play a much larger role in his live setup, particularly since 2008. In the studio, however, he used them very sparingly.

paradoxes inherent in sound. Six minutes and thirty-nine seconds in, almost everything drops out, leaving behind a sort of phantom version of the song for another twenty seconds as a jewel-like sound bounces around in the last moments before everything disappears into the ether. Hearing both the song and its fadeout, one wonders if the whole thing was just a well-constructed illusion.

Loveless also features four prominent segues. 'Only Shallow' has a hard ending rather than a fadeout, and after the last chord rings out, a thirty-seven-second piece fades in, its warm and fuzzy sequence of chords creating a little bit of an oasis between the squall of 'Only Shallow' and the tense intro to 'Loomer.'

The segue that appears at the end of the *Loveless* version of 'To Here Knows When' is entirely different from the one on the *Tremolo* EP, and it creates a very different effect. On the full-length record, it comprises a reverse guitar figure that sounds like a repeating two-bar phrase, though like most of the band's interstitial tracks from this period, it is ambiguous in nature—it can be counted out as two bars of four/four time, but really it feels unbound from any conventional time signature. What is perhaps more interesting is how it is mixed very low, compared to the majority of 'To Here Knows When,' so when the next track, 'When You Sleep,' kicks in, the effect is loud and dramatic—just one of the many almost imperceptible details that make *Loveless* such a compelling listen.

'When You Sleep' is another song that has a hard ending, with the band landing on an echoing chord. As the last notes reverberate, a shimmering, bubbling chord crossfades in for thirteen seconds before the dramatic opening of the next track, 'I Only Said.' Once again, this small detail provides a little bit of additional space so that the intro of the subsequent track really pops.

The segue at the end of 'What You Want,' ushering the listener into 'Soon,' feels almost like a false ending to the album. Seventy-four seconds long, it is built around flute sounds that appear to be repeating in an ambiguous loop with no clear rhythmic center. Underneath those sounds is a pulsing, blinking tone that implies a steady rhythm. Added together, the effect is beautiful and beguiling, making it feel as if the album is gently floating away before the deliberately stilted intro of 'Soon' pulls you back in for one last ride.

In his review of the album, Simon Reynolds referred to the segues as 'ear-baffling studio sorcery.'[22] Each one requires repeated listens before you get your bearings, and even then you may never truly figure out everything that's going on. They reflect Shields's truly intuitive grasp of music's many dimensions, often making you feel as if your ears might be playing tricks on you.[*] I tend to think of them as music from the quantum realm, where nothing obeys the rules in a way you'd normally expect.

•

Shields was clearly happy with what he achieved with *Loveless*. In his own uncompromising way, he had been able to distill his artistic vision into something that listeners connected with, and he was able to accomplish that both with something as radical as 'Loomer' and something as straightforward as 'Sometimes.' It didn't really enter his mind to pursue the unconventional for its own sake, as he would note in interviews:

> I kept going, 'I'm not trying to make a weird record, this isn't supposed to be weird, it's something organic.' That was my big catchphrase back then, 'organicness.' And how this is part of something natural, do you know what I mean? It isn't weird, the bending had a quality that is universal. It's in all cultures, and it's something that just got a little bit wiped out of Western music for a while.[23]

For Shields, there was nothing to gain from simply disorienting the listener or being weird for the sake of weirdness. If the music doesn't ultimately connect with listeners, what's the point?

---

[*] Emeritus Professor Diane Deutsch at the University of California at San Diego has written extensively on the paradoxes and illusions of sound and music perception. Her book *Musical Illusions And Phantom Words: How Music And Speech Unlock Mysteries Of The Brain* details a few examples of the paradoxes in the human brain that Shields exploits.

Loveless would eventually be deservedly recognized as one of the best rock albums ever made. Two decades after its initial release, Mark Beaumont captured the record's staying power in his history of Creation Records for *NME*, closely echoing the ways numerous other critics have come to see the album as an almost mythical work of art, a piece of music almost etched in stone:

> At times, it's the operatic mourning wails of creatures mutated in nuclear winter ('Touched'). At times it's a blissed-out pagan sacrificial dance at sunrise . . . ('Come In Alone'). At times it's an angel's rave in the pleasure domes of Coleridge's Kubla Khan ('Soon,' 'I Only Said,' 'Blown A Wish'). Most of the time it warps and stretches music through dimensions you never knew it had.[24]

The album's seemingly bottomless moments of artistic discovery were a product of Shields's own musical genius, but they also came about through the support and fortitude of the band's label. Even after finishing it, though, Shields clearly felt an immense strain. In an interview that ran in the January 1992 issue of *Les Inrockuptibles*—most likely conducted just weeks after he handed in the album—his responses were expansive, forthright, and pessimistic. At one point, he claimed that MBV hadn't taken new promotional photographs because he couldn't say with confidence that the group even existed anymore.[25] More than any other interview Shields gave around this time, the exchange gives us insight into his state of mind following the completion of *Loveless*. The record was done, but the process of finishing it had left him feeling bleak, aggrieved, and cynical.

chapter nine

within: release and overexposure •

playing catch up • the sound

of the future • razor-sharp

edits • mutual craziness •

dividends for all involved

'Our records always make a lot more sense years later.'

KEVIN SHIELDS, 1991[1]

'It was him or me.'

ALAN MCGEE, 2010[2]

NME put My Bloody Valentine on the cover of its November 9 issue, which hit newsstands the week *Loveless* was released. The UK's other main music newspaper, *Melody Maker*, went with Nirvana for the cover of its November 2 issue, which coincided with the release of *Nevermind*, although it did include a small photo of MBV in the bottom left corner. *Q* magazine gave MBV a two-page spread in January, and *Select* ran a substantial piece about the album and the group's US tour the following month. But *Guitar Player* was the only prominent monthly magazine to put the band on its cover, with Shields and Butcher sharing the space with Jim and William Reed of The Jesus & Mary Chain as a way to promote their joint Rollercoaster tour of early 1992. (Each band received their own profile inside the magazine.)

Simon Reynolds's *Melody Maker* review of *Loveless* was a quarter-page long, and that was one of the more substantial reviews to appear in the UK periodicals. Most critics initially saw the album merely as a consolidation of the innovations the band had explored previously on *Glider* and *Tremolo*. There just wasn't the same excitement that had accompanied MBV's earlier releases.

It was clear that the additional time MBV had needed to innovate and experiment had a very specific downside. For a UK press that was always on the hunt for the next big thing, the band soon became old news. In 1988, just four months passed between MBV's first and second Creation EPs and *Isn't Anything*. By contrast, the lead-up to *Loveless*, which began with *Glider*, took over nineteen months. If one were to add in the previous aborted sessions as well, it had been nearly three years. And yet, when *Loveless* finally came out, the initial anticlimactic reception reflected the biggest issue facing the band in the UK as they saw it—overexposure. MBV had garnered a great deal of press for *Isn't Anything* and *Glider*, and they had become constant topics of conversation in the larger narrative about shoegaze. Even before *Loveless* was released, Shields was predicting that the band's new album would be panned, sensing that MBV had received so much attention from the UK press already that the expectations for each successive release had grown completely unrealistic.

Writing in *Lime Lizard*, Jon Selzer understood the ridiculous expectations attached to anything the band put out around this time, noting that those who first heard *Loveless* thought it 'surprisingly conventional'— even if that was very much a relative term when it came to MBV. 'If it doesn't stretch their capacities,' he added of the album, 'it surely dissolves them ... all you can do is give in.'[3] Even Simon Reynolds, previously one of the band's biggest boosters, felt that despite its clear moments of genius, the new full-length missed certain opportunities. In his largely positive review, he still pondered whether the band could have changed their focus and made an entire album where each track was as radically revolutionary as 'Soon' or 'To Here Knows When' or 'Loomer.' That's quite a tall order, especially when one considers Shields's intention to make a pop record that would actually connect with listeners.

The critical response was somewhat different on the other side of the Atlantic. Although MBV had received copious amounts of coverage in the UK after *Isn't Anything,* the album had received just a fraction of that coverage in the USA, leaving the American press to play catch-up when *Loveless* was released. They compensated by dedicating more coverage to the new record, including several major feature articles. *Alternative Press* and *Option* both put MBV on their covers when the band came to the States to tour in early 1992. Michael Azerrad also gave the band a prominent writeup—which took up two-thirds of a page—in *Rolling Stone.* Beneath the provocative headline 'The Sound Of The Future' was a subheading stating, 'With its first two albums, My Bloody Valentine has redefined rock.' It was clear that Azerrad understood what the band were up to. '*Loveless* can be as ethereal as the Cocteau Twins and as grindingly discordant as Sonic Youth,' he wrote, 'yet it's a quantum leap past both bands. Excepting perhaps The Beatles' wildest sonic flights and the work of minimalist composers Steve Reich and Philip Glass, it simply doesn't sound like anything else.'[4]

MBV's US distributor, Sire/Warner Bros, tried to capitalize on the increased coverage by promoting 'Only Shallow' with a video and a promotional single sent out to radio stations and other outlets. The label commissioned a straightforward performance video of the band miming along to the song and initially requested that they use a prominent director, but MBV stood by Cameron, and eventually Warners relented.

The resulting video has a beautiful sheen, with the band members all cleaned up and dressed up to one degree or another. It is the only depiction of them on camera in their prime, looking their best, perhaps suggesting they had allowed a stylist to do some very basic work with them. Cameron had to manually synchronize the edits to match up with the dramatic surges in sound, much as he did for his three previous videos for the band, although the visual aesthetic this time is completely different. Using razor-sharp edits to match the crystal-clear look, he deftly captures the rhythms and feel of the song—especially during the chorus—and follows some of other the various sonic elements competing in the mix. Though he was working with a bigger budget this time, he and producer Fiona Adams nonetheless found themselves once again having to make a late-night decision to contribute their entire fees to pay for additional time at what was one of the UK's first all-digital facilities.[*]

After the album's release, the band played eight shows in Australia, followed by four in Japan. By the end of November, they were back in the UK for the first of thirteen performances. But as 1991 was coming to a close and the album was finally in stores, Alan McGee was growing more and more eager to part ways with the group. Although *Loveless* sold decently by normal standards, it was not getting the kind of blockbuster sales that were necessary to recoup Creation's investment right away. It sold a respectable fifty thousand copies in a relatively short period (and has sold steadily ever since), but by comparison, Teenage Fanclub's *Bandwagonesque*, released two weeks later, sold more than four hundred thousand copies during a similar timespan, with sales split evenly between Europe and the USA.

The birth of the album had, of course, been extremely stressful, and from Creation's point of view, there was little point in going all out promoting the record if MBV weren't going to lend a hand. Among other things, the label felt the cover's amorphous design made it hard to make out the band's name, while the name of the album wasn't there at all. More importantly, the band wouldn't allow Creation to release another single in the UK to coincide with *Loveless*. As such, McGee didn't want to put any more money into the band's upcoming North American tour.

On a personal level, too, the relationship between the two men had

---

* Though he was unable to remember the precise budget for 'Only Shallow,' Cameron surmised that it was probably five or six times more than he'd been given to make 'Soon.' He made some twenty-odd videos for the label between 1989 and 1993—some of which, including four for MBV, a pitch-perfect take on Primal Scream's 'Loaded,' and two for Ride, appear on the 1992 Sire VHS release *The Story Of Creation*—but finally decided he had to turn down McGee's 'next big thing' band after being skipped for some of the more plum assignments for bands with lucrative American distribution deals. That 'next big thing' was none other than Oasis. Nevertheless, he has parlayed his video work and experience into a successful directing career, earning a BAFTA Scotland nomination in 2005. And though his and other Creation videos of the time were difficult to obtain before the internet era, 'To Here Knows When' has since been recognized as one of two hundred landmark music videos by the British Film Institute.

run its course. By now, the two men were no longer on speaking terms. McGee has since portrayed Shields as being more than a little passive-aggressive and callous around this time. Instead of thanking McGee and Creation for their belief in the band and their financial support as collaborators or brothers in arms, Shields ended up portraying them as inept. In a prominent interview that coincided with the album's release, he told *NME*, 'We know more about how the record industry works than our record company half the time!'[5]

This must have been particularly galling to McGee and Green, after all the sacrifices and effort they'd put forth, most recently by way of several large cash outlays to finish the mixing and mastering. Even when Creation dropped the band, however, the label engineered it in such a way as to make the transition as easy as possible. In early January 1992, McGee called Shields to inform him that Creation would be dropping the band, adding that he felt it was time to part ways. He has since portrayed Shields as being shocked at the news; Shields has said he was totally unfazed and simply headed off to bed. He would later say various hurtful things about McGee and Creation, some of which may have been the result of the label boss's flamboyant personality rubbing him up the wrong way. Yet there was more to it than that, and it would all play out again, in a similar fashion but on a grander scale, a decade later.

•

Whatever else we know about *Loveless*, we can say with certainty that it didn't bankrupt Creation Records. The label would still have been in the red after dropping Rough Trade as its distributor in 1989, with or without MBV, and there were other bands on the roster—Primal Scream among them—who were spending more in a month than MBV did during the entire time they were recording *Glider*, *Tremolo*, and *Loveless*. Furthermore, the label never actually filed for bankruptcy at any point during this time.

The bankruptcy myth that followed MBV for years began as a series of unsubstantiated rumors. Even before *Tremolo* was released, *Sounds* printed a blind item about how 'the band have been in the studio on and off since

June and have reputedly racked up a bill far in excess of £100,000.' A similar piece in *Melody Maker* in September 1991 claimed that *Loveless* was the cause of Creation's insolvency, citing recording costs of £250,000.* But while Creation's financial problems were real, and *Loveless* was a major focus of the label's neuroses at this time, finishing the record wouldn't do anything other than slow the bleeding.[6]

McGee has said in no uncertain terms that Creation came very close to going under three times in their first decade primarily because they had no professional accounting structure in place. Neither he nor Green had any kind of background in finance, and while the label had experienced some success early on, there were no controls in place to help manage the label's finances. 'To be fair, our business acumen around that time was fuckin' shocking,' he said in 2011. 'We were still trading like we were selling out of a cardboard box. . . . True, Kevin Shields spent too much money . . . but he never bankrupted me. It's down to me and Dick [Green] being a couple of chancers.'[7]

Dave Cavanagh's exhaustive history of Creation, *My Magpie Eyes Are Hungry For The Prize*, includes extensive details of every accounting shortfall and bookkeeping error, so much so that McGee has referred to the book as 'the accountant's tale.'[8] Between the lines of coke and money pissed away randomly flying to Paris for dinner, one gets the sense that McGee's priority was to just keep the label afloat for a bit longer so *Loveless* and the other amazing albums that were then in the pipeline could be finished. He truly believed that, like *Screamadelica*, *Loveless* would be another groundbreaking album, and he wanted to see it through to the end. But the rumors about MBV's outsized role in the label's solvency issues stuck, and for the next fifteen years, interviews and reviews continued to speculate about how much *Loveless* cost and how close Creation came to

---

* According to Shields, the actual amount of money Creation spent on *Loveless* was between £140,000 to £160,000; in some interviews, he would state that Sire ponied up an additional £50,000, bringing the total to around £200,000. By 1994, he would note that the band only owed £20,000 of that, adding that they could quickly recoup it by putting out a greatest-hits compilation.

collapsing because of it. In the process, these stories came to overshadow the album's musical innovations and unique vision.

In some ways, it seems irrational that *Loveless* became the whipping boy for all the cash flow issues Creation was dealing with around this time. Despite getting amazing reviews for *Screamadelica* and *Bandwagonesque*, the label was learning quickly that it didn't have the distribution network to sell records commensurate with what those sales should or could be. *Screamadelica* was a cultural touchstone in the UK and sold five hundred thousand units worldwide, but it's hard to know if the demand for the album outside the country was satisfied simply because of Creation's poor distribution arrangements. McGee certainly thought that it and *Bandwagonesque* could have been even bigger, had Creation's distribution setup been better. But even with great bands and touchstone albums, the label's whole model was hamstrung without the infrastructure of a major at its disposal.

Creation was in a difficult position, and it's reflective of just how much risk-taking was involved in running the label. As Cavanagh explains in his book, 'By extracting from US labels considerable advances that would immediately be swallowed up by Creation before it was even clear if the band was going to recoup or not, McGee was swimming in dangerous waters.'[9] The label had unintentionally created the premise of Mel Brooks's *The Producers*, wherein a huge hit might have sunk the company completely. At one point in 1990, the label owed Ride £75,000 solely for the band's domestic sales in the UK—a figure that dwarfs the £6–12,000 MBV were spending every month. Had Ride achieved a huge hit in America (on Sire), it would have been disastrous.

The return on investment and cash flow that MBV brought to Creation in 1988 was one of the reasons McGee and Green were initially so eager for the band to begin recording a follow-up to *Isn't Anything*. But by 1991, their outlook had changed dramatically, and their main concern was to stop spending so much cash every month, even if MBV's use of more affordable studios meant they were, in McGee's words, a 'cheap date' compared to some other bands on the roster. Not having to put up six to twelve thousand pounds in studio fees every month would bring some measure of psychological relief for McGee and Green, but it wasn't going to fundamentally change the label's overall financial position.

Green ceded the public face of Creation to McGee and rarely appeared in the press over the years. Speaking in 2008, however, he was quite categorical about MBV:

> I certainly don't think *Loveless* was the only cause of the troubles at Creation. It was an ongoing struggle for survival financially, constantly pushing for what we could and couldn't achieve, waiting for that golden egg always just beyond reach at that point. I think My Bloody Valentine did become the focus of all the tension because the recording was just going on and on with no end in sight.[10]

Some sources have stated that Green wanted to pull the plug on *Loveless*, and the 2021 film *Creation Stories* contains several scenes that dramatize the debate within the label's brain trust concerning what to do about Shields. Green has denied this, however, noting that he remortgaged his house to contribute funds toward completing *Loveless*.[11] And given how *Glider* and *Tremolo* had made it plain that something special was brewing with the band, it's hard to see how abandoning the album after 1990 would have made sense, especially after so much money had been invested in it already. The losses needed to be minimized, but there was still a great deal of value that could be realized—and that would only happen if *Loveless* was completed.

While MBV continued to work on *Loveless*, McGee and Green began entertaining offers to sell minority stakes in the label. True bankruptcy was no longer a real threat, so long as they were willing to let a major label invest in the company. But it was becoming abundantly clear to McGee and Green that they were going to have to sell a *large* minority share of their baby unless *Screamadelica*, *Bandwagonesque*, and/or *Loveless* sold in the millions. When they finally did negotiate a deal in 1992, the transaction itself was easy, but psychologically, getting to that point and reconciling it with their values was no easy task.

In the end, after sufficient due diligence, Sony bought a 49 percent stake in Creation for £2.5 million, in addition to a £1 million advance. Sony got almost half of a nearly bankrupt company, a worthwhile back catalog, and the A&R acumen of Alan McGee, which would prove as prescient and valuable as ever when he signed Oasis the following year.

Looking at the wider picture, it's clear that in many ways, Shields and McGee were simply two men at cross-purposes. One was concerned with stopping the ongoing financial hemorrhaging of his company, the other was completely set on finishing the album without letting outside influences distract him or corrupt the pure vision he held in his mind. In hindsight, both have admitted to 'mutual craziness' during this period, in addition to numerous misunderstandings.[12] Shields has acknowledged that he put McGee through much more trauma than he realized at the time, and McGee has conceded many times that his unhinged, unsustainable, drug-fueled lifestyle was not the ideal way to run a record label.

In the end, MBV weren't ever going to sell that many records—or at least, not quickly enough—to justify Creation's outlay. And there was no way for Shields to repair the damage done. McGee thought MBV were so talented that they might have crossed over had they released *Loveless* sooner and done more to promote it. David Geffen made a similar bet with Sonic Youth and *Goo*. But for any number of reasons and matters of cultural happenstance, it was Nirvana's *Nevermind* that broke through instead.

Throughout the early 2000s, Shields and McGee would make amends, only for some comment by the former would set the latter off again, leading him to respond with similar vitriol. In 2007, perhaps taken aback by Shields's latest comments about Creation, McGee noted, 'My Bloody Valentine were a joke, my way of seeing how far I could push hype.'[13] Considering all he had done for the band and the esteem in which he held Shields, it's not hard to understand why he felt unappreciated.

Prior to that, at one point in 2004, Shields revealed that he'd apologized to McGee for the stress he put him under and explained that it was never intentional. McGee, in retrospect, has always been unequivocal in his opinion that Shields is a genius, driven by a certain kind of obsessive nature over his music that even he can't control, and Shields, too, has said on more than one occasion that MBV got away with murder, so great was their indulgence with how they used their studio time. Asked if he was glad to have been on Creation, he replied, 'It cuts both ways. ... For us it was an honour to be on the label, but we did them a favour too.'[14]

Ultimately, in spite of the strains each put on their relationship, MBV and McGee could not have been better positioned to help one another. Shields was responsible for one of the truly groundbreaking albums of the 1990s, and *Loveless* will always be associated with Creation and McGee. It seems fitting that the best A&R person of the era came up against the most maddening musical genius of their generation, and that it bolstered both their fortunes.

With each passing year, the question of what *Loveless* cost has become less and less important. Over thirty years after its release, the album now stands on its own as an iconic record, venerated and separated to a degree from the drama that went into its making. But what if Creation had pulled the plug earlier? Without McGee's backing support and patience, the record may very well have gone the way of Brian Wilson's *Smile*, becoming one of rock's great lost, incomplete albums—a 'what if' record. As such, the role McGee played in the story of MBV is a momentous one, because he allowed Shields to finish *Loveless* the way Shields wanted to finish it. He was electrified upon hearing an early unfinished version of 'Soon'—a song he has said reminded him of why he'd started a label in the first place—and he recognized immediately what Shields could be capable of if he were given the necessary time and money to create. There might not have been anyone else in the world who had such abiding faith in Shields's abilities. In spite of everything, McGee put the music first.

In a 1994 *NME* feature on the history of Creation, Shields explained the many things that made the label so special, first noting that it was the least sinister or cynical company the band could have worked with.

Creation allowed him the freedom to go as far as possible with the only caveat being not to be too pedestrian. He looked back on his time on the label as a good experience, noting that even when money became tight, it was there to be spent on music:

> The reason why we're not on Creation anymore is simply a case of a relationship separation. We were off Creation the best way a band could be dropped off a label, it was less than an eight-hour gap between not being on Creation and having nine other companies phoning and that was overnight, so I slept through it. Again, Creation orchestrated that. They let us off easily, they could have made our lives difficult but they didn't so I have zero complaints.[15]

•

After severing ties with McGee in January 1992, MBV spent much of the next six months on the road, with the majority of the shows taking place in the USA. With no label support to draw on, they used publishing money to pay for the tour. Shields considered the £20,000 Creation had initially spent on equipment in 1991 as woefully inadequate for conveying *Loveless*'s distinct sound, featuring Marshall and Vox amplifiers. Not having the funds to purchase Vox amps to present the much more diverse songs on *Glider*, *Tremolo*, and *Loveless* made this their most onerous tour. Some songs simply didn't translate well onstage; live recordings of the choruses for 'Only Shallow' and 'Honey Power,' for example, demonstrate the group's inability to recreate the guitar timbres with the same force or fidelity as the studio recordings.

Despite these shortcomings, however, Shields was intent on using the equipment that was available to him to recreate the band's recent studio work for live performance. Doing so required an immense amount of work at each venue, necessitating that different guitars, along with specific combinations of equipment, be dialed in for each song. Long, painstaking soundchecks were required to make sure everything was working properly and that there could be smooth transitions during the show itself. Although

Dinosaur Jr. were headlining these shows, J Mascis's most prominent memory was how MBV's pre-show preparations required a larger crew and more monitors than his own band's.* 'Their sound check seemed to go on forever,' he recalled. 'We would come in, play for five minutes, and be done; theirs would go for hours and it seemed very emotionally draining.'[16]

After completing a run of around twenty-five dates in the US, MBV returned to the UK for a dozen shows, eleven of which were part of the Rollercoaster tour, which was organized by The Jesus & Mary Chain and also featured Blur and Dinosaur Jr. The tour ran from March 24 to April 7 and was noteworthy for the control MBV had to give up as far as their sound was concerned; they had to share a PA with three other bands, which Shields bristled against. 'The actual playing part is good, like having all the bands,' he told MTV's *120 Minutes UK*. 'I like that, and that's why we did it. The other side of it, the control side, isn't so good.'

Even the communal spirit of the Rollercoaster tour couldn't keep MBV from trying to reassert control when they could. Shields recounted one example, explaining that on large tours there are typically two sound units for the PA. One is the crew that travels with you, the other is specific to the venue. At one point, the PA crew for one of the venues went on strike, offended that MBV had turned their monitor speakers toward the middle of the crowd to ensure that the people at the very front (who were too close to the stage to be in the sound path of the main amplifiers) got the full impact of the sound. 'We can't have that!' said Shields. 'And there were all these little girls at the shows, and the PA people thought it was cruel to

---

* Besides serving as a means for MBV to establish a stronger foothold in the US, these shows and the subsequent Rollercoaster tour cemented a long-lasting friendship between Shields and J Mascis. Mascis would visit with Shields and Butcher at their Streatham home studio to record some of 1997's *Hand It Over*, and Shields would reciprocate and visit Mascis in Massachusetts for seven weeks around 2000 to work on *More Light*, which Mascis recorded under the moniker J Mascis + The Fog. 'He's one of the only people that I can think of that I care about or trust his opinion about my music,' Mascis said. 'He would get different guitar sounds and bass sounds.' Shields also helped produce and engineer Mascis's BBC sessions, which saw a proper release in 2003.

have all this huge noise in their faces, 'cos they were squashed up front and couldn't get away from it.'[17]

After the UK dates, the band headed to Europe for seven dates in France, three in Germany, and a handful of other dates across the continent. This was followed by thirteen more dates back in North America. But despite their active touring schedule, MBV were becoming concerned about their growing reputation as a dysfunctional band. The narrative that had been building up over the last three years had clearly gotten inside their heads. Speaking in March 1992, Shields said, 'I think the only way we can break a certain kind of reputation we have, or break a cycle we've gotten into, is to bring a record out in a relatively short time.'[18]

First, however, they wanted to demonstrate they were competent enough to tour and promote *Loveless*, even if they had to do so on a shoestring budget. The tour wasn't a moneymaker, but it was part of the group's long-term goal to raise their profile. They also hoped it would send a message to labels who might be interested in signing them—namely, that they could be trusted to get the work done when it mattered. They believed this would lend them credibility when they eventually negotiated a new contract.

If they played their cards right, the band could end up with a significant advance from a new label—which they could potentially use to build their own studio—while still retaining the complete control they had known up to this point. But would any major labels offer them the kind of money and control they really desired? Could they navigate the catch-22 that dogged so many bands who sign to a major—that of trying to keep both their integrity *and* their shirt? The drama that would unfold over the next fifteen years would see Shields learn a great deal about his own capabilities and limitations, about how much control he could exert over himself, and about his value to the music industry.

Read any history of shoegaze music and My Bloody Valentine are guaranteed to be included as the genre's primary practitioners. Search Google or YouTube with the term and their name will invariably show up at the top of any list cataloging the best bands or albums. *Loveless* routinely takes the number one spot in most of these articles and polls, even though it was still just a vision in Shields's head when shoegaze took off in 1989 and 1990. And, like so much else that critics have gotten wrong about MBV, it's a label that's never sat well with the way Shields thinks about the band's music.

The truth of the matter is that MBV inadvertently created a new genre that they themselves didn't want to be associated with. It's clear, though, that shoegaze wouldn't exist without the excitement, innovation, and new life that *Isn't Anything* brought to guitar playing and the British indie scene in 1988. The closest parallel might be The Beatles' impact on the ways the British Invasion coalesced into a discrete movement after their arrival on the scene. But unlike The Beatles, MBV weren't really party to the movement that formed in their wake.

In an effort to convey the radical new sound found on MBV's records from 1988 onward, writers began searching for ways to combine words like 'ethereal,' 'hallucinatory,' 'heavy,' 'ambient,' 'lust,' 'bliss,' 'androgynous,' and 'dislocation.' By 1990, journalists in the UK had created various narratives around a nebulous genre from a new generation of bands who had been inspired by MBV. But it was Simon Reynolds who introduced the term 'shoegaze' to American readers with his first draft of its history in a December 1991 report for the *New York Times*:

> This year, the most happening phenomenon in British alternative rock has been a wave of hazy neo-psychedelic guitar groups, for which the UK rock press has yet to settle on a label. Some critics call them 'shoe-gazers.' . . . But perhaps the most useful term is 'dream pop,' as it evokes these groups' blurry, blissful sound and 'out of this world' aura. Currently, the key dream-pop groups (My Bloody Valentine, Slowdive, Lush, Chapterhouse, Ride, Swervedriver) have US major label records already released or in the pipeline.[1]

Initially, several other terms were batted around for this new genre (including 'miasma music' and 'the scene that celebrates itself'), but 'shoegaze'—first used as a pejorative, noting the tendencies of band members out in front to look down at their guitar pedals and away from the audience—was ultimately the one that stuck.

Regardless of how later histories may have framed it, it was *Isn't Anything*, not *Loveless*, that got everyone's attention in the UK and catalyzed the musical movement—if that's what you want to call it—that followed. As Corey Dubrowa put it in *Magnet* in 2002, 'Perhaps the single most important tipping point for this scene was the 1988 release of My Bloody Valentine's *Isn't Anything* … if it's shoegazing ground zero you seek, your quest begins and ends here.'[2]

After that, MBV found themselves in the unenviable position of being at the center of a 'new' genre of younger bands who name-checked them while utilizing techniques and making aesthetic choices that Shields shunned. But despite the many laudatory reviews, very few writers actually got into any of the mechanics of *why* MBV's recordings sounded so different.

To take one example, Dave Segal's cover story about the band for *Alternative Press* is indicative of both the gushing coverage MBV received in America in 1992 and the way many writers seemed to *feel* the band's influence without necessarily understanding the techniques and aesthetics at the heart of their recordings. 'At once ethereal and sexual, oceanic and astral, blissed-out and fucked up, beautiful and noisy, the sonic innovations on *Isn't Anything* infiltrated the atmosphere of guitar-centric indie music and birthed dozens of disciples,' he wrote, before citing 'androgynous, sleepy vocals under layers of honey-dripping melodies' as the key tenets of bands influenced by MBV. He also tried re-labeling the genre 'Wombadelia,' but for some reason that new name didn't ever take.[3]

Writing in *Artforum*, a journal largely concerned with contemporary visual art, Lena Relyea also sensed something new was taking place, astutely describing the band's music as 'dismantling the opposition between noise and melody.' She went on to describe the music as 'following the logic of dreams, generat[ing] disorientation through compression, as the high and low ends are sucked into a dense, undifferentiated middle. The effect is like a whirlpool, the music's center feeling at once charged and collapsed, all distinct identities lost as everything melds together—the players and their instruments, the instruments with each other.'[4] In so doing, Relyea managed to touch upon several of MBV's specific aesthetic characteristics—including their use of midrange, Shield's glide-guitar technique, and the band's desire to try to make everything blend, rather than using effects to make each element stick out or sound distinct in the mix—despite perhaps not knowing how this translated into the actual techniques used in the studio.

Ride, Slowdive, Chapterhouse, and The Boo Radleys all released their first singles in 1989 and 1990, and they all specifically cited MBV as a major inspiration and influence. Yet they too evidently had no real idea of *why* the band's 1988 releases sounded so different than what had come before. Their own recordings all utilized a certain aesthetic, using well-worn modulation-type pedals featuring reverb, echo, chorus, flanging, phasing, and other common effects of modern music, all applied in a typically top-down way.

This was all the press needed to group these bands together. A specious narrative took hold suggesting that all of these groups, including MBV, were somehow of a piece—each of them members of a generation reflecting larger trends such as the banality of middle-class values, twelve years of conservative rule in the UK, or a desire for escape. On the eve of

Loveless's release, Andrew Collins called it out in the *NME*: 'This loose-fitting taxonomic heading now embraces any and every sort of indie guitar band who neither jangle nor groove . . . and it's all My Bloody Valentine's fault. They have spawned a thousand pale imitators, and boy do we need them back.'[5]

Shields was bewildered that people couldn't hear just how different these other groups were in almost every way. The production values, their attitudes—almost everything, as he saw it, was in direct opposition to the original way MBV went about things. Perhaps in an effort to help others discern what separated MBV from their growing roster of disciples, Shields started to reveal more details about his own methods. 'People think it's all pedals,' he told Collins, 'but all my pedals are graphic equalizers and tone controls. It's all in the tone.'[6] In another interview, he explained, 'Ninety percent of what we do is just a guitar straight into an amp.'[7]

Shields was trying to make clear that, as he saw it, MBV's sound was fundamentally based on the way he played, as opposed to how he could manipulate a sound if he ran it through pedals or processors anyone could buy and plug into. He didn't nullify that feel by laying modulation pedals over his playing, but he enhanced its sensitivity in ways that brought out its subtleties. It was a unique, bottom-up way of applying electronics to his guitar playing, making it intrinsic to the songs. It baffled him to be associated with these other bands merely because of arbitrary factors like being on Creation, playing guitar, or being from the UK and of the same approximate age range. He thought it truly strange to be linked to all these bands that were, in many ways, the exact opposite of what he was all about.

Despite seeming like logical jumping-off points, no one actually experimented with the central innovation at the heart of *Isn't Anything*—namely, Shields's unique combination of reverse reverb and the Jazzmaster's tremolo system. Nor did any of the younger shoegaze bands concentrate on midrange to push their sound together. Eventually, however, one band would distinguish themselves both by copying MBV's sound and by refusing to acknowledge their debt to Shields. He didn't seem particularly threatened by them, though he was keen to set the record straight.

'There's this one band around at the moment who I think definitely owe their sound to us, The Boo Radleys,' he said in 1992. 'They're friends of ours... but they're sort of deliberately playing us down... I say, if they don't want to sound like us then they should stop using the exact same studio techniques that we taught the engineers who did their record![8] Indeed, Alan Moulder, Guy Fixsen, and Andy Wilkinson had each engineered sessions for Shields and then worked with The Boo Radleys in 1990 and 1991, with some of the resulting material bearing the unmistakable stamp of MBV's sound. 'Foster's Van' is just one of many obvious examples. However, unless you actually worked with Shields, as these three engineers had, it would be difficult if not impossible to recreate the MBV guitar sound.*

A perfect example of just how reductive the shoegaze sound could be is Chapterhouse's 'Pearl,' which seemed directly inspired by 'Soon.' To a casual listener, the two songs may seem similar, but if you listen a bit more closely, you can notice how all the elements in 'Soon' join to form a profoundly beautiful and amorphous blur, only to have most everything dramatically drop out as the song fades into the ether; 'Pearl,' by contrast, is utterly conventional, taking no chances. And it manages to include everything Shields avoided: blurry modulated guitars from pedals, a sampled Led Zeppelin beat in place of something novel, and unintelligible vocals sung softly and set low in the mix. It lacks the creativity and revelation that came together to make 'Soon' sound like a dance tune transmitted from the future.

Shields saw this new wave of groups as following a set of rote rules, using the same effects bands had been using for years. Meanwhile, he continued to experiment, creating new techniques by, for example, sampling guitar feedback in a way that had never done before. As his budgets grew, he continued to explore new sonic territory, allowing him to harness the studio in ways that continued to reveal new levels and nuances of emotion.

---

* The exception that proves the rule is 'Crystal Eyes' by The Nightblooms. When MTV's *120 Minutes* showed the video of the single to Shields, he seemed bemused by it.

As much as he didn't like being lumped in with other shoegaze acts, Shields showed genuine sympathy for these younger acts, appreciating the attendant difficulties that were a part of starting out and admitting that, for a while, MBV had been the number one Jesus & Mary Chain knockoff band. Many of the bands who were lumped together as shoegaze acts were going through the rites of passage that were necessary to progress and eventually develop their own voice, and as Shields put it, 'I genuinely believe that unless you're a genius, you have to be derivative first to get to know how to be original.'[9] He regularly mentioned that he liked the other musicians as people and occasionally even singled out particular songs he enjoyed. The only band he ever dissed by name was Chapterhouse, remarking that 'something's not right with them,' although it's unclear if it that had to do with their bizarre pronouncements or their cynical music.[10]

By 2018, Shields had grown philosophical about how things unfolded:

If we had been able to release *Loveless* just a little sooner, I think perhaps we would not have been referred to as a shoegaze band. That said, the press at the time wanted to write various things, but we didn't have any particular rivalry with [these other bands]. I listen to their music and liked it, and on a human level they were all appealing people.[11]

Even if *Loveless* had come out in 1990, say, it's still likely that MBV would have been seen as shoegazing's leading light. The impact of *Isn't Anything* was so seismic that nothing was going to stop the press from writing about the influence it had, even if the younger bands who wanted to emulate its sound didn't really understand what Shields was up to. That would still have happened regardless of when the follow-up album was released.

By 1993 and 1994, bands like Ride, Slowdive, and The Boo Radleys had begun to mature and move in other directions. Britpop became the next big trend in the UK, with Oasis and Blur dominating the headlines for the remainder of the 1990s. Meanwhile, in America, it was still all about grunge.

Shoegaze would fall to the peripheries of the music scene, but it wasn't gone for good. The story of the genre took on a life of its own, with each new history of it including more bands that existed both before and after *Isn't Anything*. The Jesus & Mary Chain and Cocteau Twins—two bands who first released records in the early and mid 80s—were the most prominent acts to be retconned into the story. At the time, however, these bands were not yet seen as revolutionaries ushering in a new genre of pop. It was only after 1988—MBV's banner year at Creation—that anyone and everyone became part of some broader 'dream pop' grouping, including bands that had preceded MBV.

In 2016, Cherry Red Records released a box set, *Still In A Dream: 1988–1995: A Story Of Shoegaze*, featuring no less than eighty-seven bands and a half-baked accompanying essay that posits, 'It certainly can't be debated by any rational person that The House Of Love, The Stone Roses, My Bloody Valentine, The Jesus & Mary Chain, and Cocteau Twins guided this scene from day one and shepherded it into existence which changed modern music as we know it today.' Even considering how ridiculously broad the 'genre' has become, anyone remotely familiar with The Stone Roses and The House Of Love will wonder how they fit under the same umbrella as the other acts here.

This contrived and confused narrative has continued unabated. In October 2020, *Vice* ran an article entitled 'Autumn Is Shoegaze Season,' offering the usual tropes and the obligatory mention of *Loveless* as the blueprint for the genre. A month later, Vinylfactory.com defined shoegaze as 'a genre that came to prominence during the 1980s, beginning in the UK before expanding globally. Also known as dream pop and fueled by groups like Cocteau Twins and My Bloody Valentine, it combined experimental effects and sampling, washed-out vocals, and hazy guitar riffs with a DIY spirit.' The definitions and examples may vary, but they all share one main idea—that despite having little or nothing to do with the aesthetics or recording techniques of the other bands listed, MBV are central to the genre.

In theory, there's no reason a band can't start a genre and remain its leading light. And as new information becomes available and a bigger picture emerges, history can be rewritten. But the truth is, MBV simply don't belong in the same category as any of these bands. Listen to *Isn't Anything* or *Loveless* and then listen to any other 'shoegaze' band. The latter groups' efforts are often akin to artists using primitive computer graphics programs to put together a picture, while MBV's albums stand like impressionist paintings in which everything comes together to form one coherent vision.

chapter ten

within: time as a non-issue •

maintaining good contact •

ann-marie shields • living in la-la

land • skyscraper music • free

time • torturous circumstances

'We'd like to come out from the shadow of the greatest things ever done.'

KEVIN SHIELDS, 1992[1]

'One of the things I always dread, in a way, about bands that I really like becoming hugely famous, is they seem to stop doing anything, really. I mean, obviously, a lot of them get into kind of serious drug abuse and disappear, by and large. But the bands that you care for, as I say, it's distressing when they become famous and don't make records anymore. Whatever became of My Bloody Valentine. Are they still out there somewhere?'

JOHN PEEL, 1993[2]

MBV played about sixty-five shows over seven months in support of *Loveless* in 1992. Once they were back home, the plan was to record another full-length album for release the following summer, though the band still hadn't signed with a new label. Shields began fielding calls, laying out the group's strategy going forward.

'We're going to get our own recording setup to cut out the concept of recording costs,' he said. 'Time will be a non-issue because no one will know when we started or finished. We'll cut all that out and just work on music and definitely release records when they're good.'[3] Despite Shields's sincere ambitions and best intentions, however, putting together another album in a year was completely beyond the realms of what the group was capable of.

Over the past few years, MBV had fielded offers from a number of major labels. At one point between the release of *Isn't Anything* and the completion of *Loveless*, for example, they had passed on an offer of $150,000 to leave Creation and sign with Sire. Instead, they accepted $15,000 and the promise of retaining artistic control from Creation, though Sire remained the band's North American distributor. It was clear the money was there for a group of MBV's caliber, but they opted instead to maintain their creative freedom, even if that decision came with other sacrifices. Even when Creation struggled to cover the band's most basic living expenses, Shields would have never seriously considered turning to a major if it meant having to give up the ability to make the record he wanted to make.

The Virgin Prunes had once faced a similar dilemma—commercial viability or artistic freedom? As Shields explained, in choosing the latter, the Prunes 'lost something that they had. They were once free—they once could do anything. It's one of the most difficult things for bands to have that freedom and be successful enough to have the freedom.'[4]

It's clear from Shields's comments in interviews on a plethora of topics—from drug addiction to groupies to managers to contracts—that he was deeply cognizant of the history of the music industry's most obvious pitfalls and determined to avoid them. He was also aware that times could change, and that MBV might have to face a different set of obstacles and opportunities than the ones The Virgin Prunes had been forced to navigate. By this point in his career, he had leveraged his talent and knowledge—along with a great deal of patience—to get both the full financial backing he was after *and* the ability to freely explore his own creative whims, wherever they might lead him. And now that *Loveless* had been released to wide acclaim, he was in a position to negotiate a contract that would guarantee him both a comfortable lifestyle and full artistic control.

According to Shields, within twenty-four hours of the band parting ways with Creation, nine labels reached out to him. While he was talking with various companies—at one point, MBV were rumored to be close to signing with MCA—he explained their main priorities, making sure to include another dig at how difficult things had been with Creation. 'We just want the control we've had to date,' he said. 'And one thing that would be nice would be to actually have some money, hopefully to be able to do something a bit creative like buy a guitar when we need it.'[5]

At the time, Marc Marot was the managing director of Island Records UK, having previously run the label's publishing arm. Island founder Chris Blackwell had personally chosen him for the position. Blackwell's interest in Island had begun to wane after he sold the label to Polygram in 1989, and after Marot took over as managing director in 1990 at the ripe age of twenty-nine, he successfully saw Island through several other mergers and acquisitions. He also smartly recruited Nigel Coxon from the Polygram tape library after noting his preternatural ability to spot promising talent. Coxon started out as an A&R scout before eventually taking over as the company's head of talent.

Like Blackwell, Marot firmly believed that if Island focused on releasing high-quality music, the money would follow. He and Coxon were devoted to developing only the most unique and talented artists, which quickly made Island stand out among other labels of its size. It also reaped enormous profits. The label enjoyed a very successful relaunch of U2, whose 1991 album *Achtung Baby* (which incidentally was heavily influenced by MBV) put the Irish quartet back at the forefront of modern music; achieved great success with Pulp and the twenty-one-million-selling Cranberries; and also signed PJ Harvey, Tricky, PM Dawn, N.W.A., Stereo MCs, Nine Inch Nails, the Orb, and Talvin Singh—a truly impressive roster.

In October 1992, Marot and Coxon outbid other competitors and worked out a deal with MBV for all territories except the US (where the band would remain with Sire). The deal reportedly provided the group with an initial £250,000, which they intended to use to secure a place where Shields and Butcher could live and the band could write and record their next album. It was just what Shields wanted—a massive payout that didn't require the band to sacrifice any creative control.

Upon announcing the deal in October, an Island spokesman noted, 'The immediate plans of the group consist of finding the right site for the studio that they intend to put together. This would give them full control over their recording environment for the first time, hopefully giving them room to continue to turn pop music inside out and create some new sonic delights. Island's commitment to the future of innovative music is demonstrated by this new signing.' The band's next record was tentatively scheduled for release the following October.

Before they started setting up their new studio, MBV made their first recording for Island: a cover of the 1969 James Bond theme 'We Have All The Time In The World,' originally recorded by Louis Armstrong, for the charity album *Peace Together*. Released in July 1993, with Butcher's warm, sinuous singing at the fore, the cover was a seamless fit in with the MBV aesthetic while also fully realizing the original's romantic sentiments.

This quick first release for the new label may have led the public to believe that the delays involved in making *Loveless* were a thing of the past, but it wasn't long before worrying signs began to appear again. Marot was particularly concerned with Shields's plan to obtain a home in which to construct his own studio. After signing The Orb, Marot had watched the duo waste an inordinate amount of time building and maintaining their own recording space instead of actually making music. He was keenly aware of how much time the upkeep of a studio involved, and he wanted Shields to be able to devote his energy to writing new material.

Marot warned Shields about the potential pitfalls, but Shields was set on his decision, and once it became clear that he had made up his mind to construct his own studio space, Island supported him in doing so. Speaking to Marot today, it's clear that he's always been sincere in his interest in helping artists find their way without imposing his vision, even when he can see them going down a dead end—as he has witnessed many times.

In March 1993, Shields used the Island advance to buy a seven-room house in Streatham, South London. He had installed a new recording desk by June, and at that point, everything seemed to be going according to plan. Soon, however, he ran into problems with how the console was wired into the house. It can be difficult to run commercial stereo equipment without interference in a conventional residence—Ó Cíosóig would later note the difficulties that can arise with electricity, tones, and frequencies when wiring a studio—and with Shields's keen sense of hearing, one can only imagine the problems he heard coming from the new setup.

The band brought in other engineers to try to resolve the problems, but for the most part, they too were puzzled. After several months, most of the problems had been ironed out, but one unresolved issue remained: a hum could be heard through one of the speakers, and Shields found it intolerable. Marot and Coxon visited the house to see for themselves what was going on, with the former recalling that, to his mind, none of the issues were significant enough that they should have prevented the band from recording. He compared it to refusing to drive a new vehicle because one of the windshield wipers was defective.

Once all of the wiring issues were fixed, Shields began to notice problems with the board itself. Some of the pots were already failing to maintain good contact after very little use, meaning the signal would cut out at times. He came to believe that the manufacturer had rushed the product to market without doing enough testing.

Whatever the cause, the band's relationship with Island was not off to an auspicious start. As Christmas rolled around, the band had spent their entire advance and still had no way to record. Short of money, Googe and Ó Cíosóig were forced to move into the band's 'cramped commune' to cut costs, even though the original plan was for just Shields and Butcher to live there. The band also had to resort to selling off equipment to raise money. The irony that their home studio had been conceived as a cost-cutting measure was not lost on anyone.

Marot has had only positive things to say about his working relationship with Kevin's sister, Ann-Marie Shields, who began managing the band and communicating Shields's needs starting around 1990. In contrast, Creation would single her out for the many demands she made on behalf of her brother and her preternatural ability to ask at the worst possible moment.

But this could not have been more of a different situation. Through Ann-Marie, Marot found out about the dire straits the group was in, and in a show of unconditional support, he offered them another significant injection of funds, followed by a monthly stipend of £5,000. This was above and beyond what they were due from their contract, and it came with no new conditions attached. With the new funds and a newfound sense of confidence, they were eventually able to purchase a new, more reliable analogue recording console with an established track record: a DDA AMR24, commonly seen at midrange studios at the time.

Marot came to regret the stipend, however. He soon grew concerned about how much money the band were spending on marijuana and about how isolated they had become as a result, and in hindsight, he felt the regular influx of cash was counterproductive. Though Shields has sometimes portrayed this period as a time of difficult negotiations during which Island tried to stop him from building his own studio, his version of events only confirmed Marot's worst fears. (In 2004, Shields glibly recalled of the label's monthly allowance of £5,000, 'When you're getting that much money a month for so long, it allows you to live in the la-la land that I was in.'[6])

With the studio built and continued funding squared away, Shields and Ó Cíosóig devoted the next year to exploring concepts involving guitars combined with drum & bass/jungle rhythms, which Shields later referred to as 'skyscraper music.' It was clear he was looking to make an artistic leap that was just as radical as the one from *Isn't Anything* to *Loveless*, and jungle, he decided, pointed the way. After beginning his initial experiments with the form, he felt confident he could pull it off, telling Jim DeRogatis, the pop critic at the *Chicago Sun-Times*:

> I'm trying to prove that you can make genuinely interesting music and come out with new ideas without an emotional drain to the point where you break down. I could make another record that would top the other we've made—I've been ready to for a while now—but to me, it's extremely important to make that record in

such a way that I'll be able to make another one. For lots of small, petty, human reasons that I won't go into, I'd like to be around in five years' time, making better and better records.[7]

Drum & bass was widely considered the most relevant and innovative music of the time, and Shields shared similar sentiments.* Discussing his hopes of integrating jungle into MBV's songs in much the same way he had previously incorporated hip-hop and house music, he noted, 'When I first listened to jungle, it seemed full of possibilities in a way I hadn't encountered since hip-hop. Raw, yet as out there as you can get. Hip hop's re-educated us about rhythm; now jungle's re-educating everyone again.'[8]

The more you learn about the kinds of music that inspired Shields, the more you understand what attracted him to this latest underground scene. Whether it was jungle, 60s garage rock, or American country blues from the twenties and thirties, the common thread tended to be rhythms that don't adhere to strict, traditional time signatures. Speaking to *The Wire* in 1999, Shields noted how drum & bass paralleled the energy and freedom of music from the past: 'I'd been influenced by . . . this whole concept of free time, where things just kind of drifted along. That's why I like a lot of folk-blues stuff, because I was into the way that, when they do the finger pickin', it's actually a type of jam, a freeform picking style.'[9] Elsewhere, he observed:

Someone wrote that black American music, being born of oppression, is downbeat even when it's meant to be lifting your spirit, but that African music is always stepping off the ground. I think that's what jungle rhythms do, and there's so much room for making the music air-borne, it really fits what I do with guitar on a track like 'Soon.' But the point is not to have jungle beats with guitars over the top, it's got to be more oblique, just letting that influence seep in like hip hop did with tracks like 'Slow.'[10]

---

* See for example Greg Tate's 1996 article for *Pulse Magazine*, 'Jungle Boogie: London's Drum & Bass Music Is Taking Hip-Hop Back To The Future.'

In 2001, Shields further clarified his idea of 'free time' when he compiled a mixtape for *Select* magazine, choosing eighteen tracks from the 1920s to the 1970s and offering some insight into why each one interested him in the accompanying notes. The most prominent idea running through his commentary was a lack of concern with time signatures or what might 'technically' be correct. 'All the songs I've picked make me wonder what happened with music, how it became so straight and predictable after being so free.'

At various points throughout 1995–97, Shields continued to give the impression that things were on track and that his skyscraper music would eventually see the light of day, but the numerous difficulties and setbacks cataloged in the press told a different story. In April 1995, for example, Keith Cameron of the *NME* noted the rumored difficulties the band had encountered with their new studio setup and wondered if they were doomed—either by circumstance or their own 'singular personal chemistry—to make records under the most torturous of circumstances.' Nigel Coxon was interviewed for Cameron's article but would state only that he hoped to hear results 'shortly,' without elaborating any further.[11]

In another interview Shields gave that year, he admitted that while he was busy writing and recording, the material he was working on wasn't conducive to the type of music he had originally planned to make. 'I was coming up with loads of songs,' he explained, 'unusually complicated melodies—I have about ten hours' worth now—but few of them were the sort of songs that facilitate the ideas I wanted to explore.'[12] He also states that the band had just returned from a three-month break but were now ready to put out an EP before starting on a proper album, much as they had done before *Loveless*.*

Perhaps Shields felt more confident now because the band had enlisted several people to school them on how drum & bass tracks were created from the ground up. As with their early experiments with sampling, Ó

---

* This interview resulted in erroneous reports that Shields had handed in ten hours of music to Island, when in fact he had merely mentioned that had accrued about ten hours of loosely sketched out songs on tape but that the melodies didn't fit the skyscraper project.

Cíosóig and Shields had initially tried to master the new technology completely on their own. 'We wouldn't use the benefit of other people's experience; we'd just muddle through everything,' Shields later admitted.[13] Now, however, they had brought in Alex Buess of Swiss jazzcore outfit 16/17 to help with programming, followed by Mads Bjerke, the engineer for Spring Heel Jack. Bjerke showed Shields that programming could be a much simpler undertaking once you knew a few basics, and that in fact there was a fairly small number of samples that drum & bass musicians regularly used as the foundational building blocks for their tracks.

Neither Buess nor Bjerke was able to solve the more fundamental issues holding the band back, however; later, Shields would lament just how 'unmusical' most of the equipment they were using was and the difficulties he had in actually getting his ideas recorded while he was still in the throes of inspiration. Speaking to Ned Raggett, he ran through some of the struggles that came with such a heavy reliance on technology in the studio:

> Basically I don't like shying away from technology on principle, but after all this time I've come to a certain conclusion on technology and where it's not worth dealing with. Some of it is not worth dealing with because it seems to pull people in a certain area, and that area is slightly cold. Technology is capable of producing a human, warm music. Whatever you can imagine, technology can do it. But the methods in which you have to use the stuff, all the computers and stuff, it's so unmusical it's unreal.[14]

Though MBV were at a standstill, Island remained steadfast—in public, at least—about a forthcoming record. According to a small *NME* write-up in February 1996, 'The head of A&R [Nigel Coxon] at MBV's label, Island, stated categorically that there would be an album released in 1996.'[15] But the year came and went, and by the following April, when asked by the same publication about the status of MBV's work, a label spokesperson sounded rather more agnostic. 'They're just recording and writing at the moment with no specific plans to release anything as yet. There's nothing on the schedule. That's about all we can say at the moment.'[16]

All the while, Shields continued to feed the narrative that things were on track. In July 1997, in a short article entitled 'About Bloody Time Too!' he insisted, 'We could put an album out by the end of this year. We've done tons of stuff. It just doesn't always turn out the way we want! But we've definitely got enough for an EP.'[17] By now, however, it had been almost five years since the band had signed to Island, and no one was putting much stock in his assurances anymore.

chapter eleven

'We were like the Partridge Family on acid.'

DEB GOOGE, 2018[1]

In February 1996, *NME* announced the upcoming release of a new MBV recording: a cover of 'Map Ref 41° N93° W' for the Wire tribute album *Whore*. The article also mentioned rumors that the band had scrapped their new album 'and decided to start again from scratch,' while speculating that some members of the group had either gone back to Ireland or were driving taxis to make ends meet.[2]

This wasn't far from the truth. Though Ó Cíosóig hadn't returned to Dublin, he had left the house in Streatham in June of 1995 and moved to another place in London. He continued to help Shields with digital programming for another few months, but he had had enough of the negative atmosphere. He could see that things were not going to get better anytime soon, and he knew that the only rational thing to do was leave. In the 2014 documentary *Beautiful Noise*, he explains, 'We just imploded. We kinda just went a little crazy on ourselves … we had gotten very psychedelic on ourselves in our minds. We had a psychedelic meltdown, pretty much.'[3]

Googe followed in November and began driving a taxi to earn some money. 'We were absolutely, completely dysfunctional as a band, as people,' she admits in the same documentary. 'And it got worse after *Loveless*. I mean, after *Loveless*, we signed to Island and we built our own studio and didn't do anything and went completely and absolutely AWOL.'[4] With the departure of Colm and the loss of their morning catch-up over coffee, Googe felt even more lost. One Friday night, after dropping off the tape for the Wire cover at Island's offices, she reached a tipping point and decided she simply couldn't return to the house in Streatham. She called Kevin and told him she was out.

Googe had been in the band for a decade, but for her, the last three years had been entirely unproductive. They were cloistered in their own unhinged world, and there was nothing on the horizon. It was clear to her that she needed to look after herself, which meant quitting the band and moving out of the house.

Shields talked about this fraught moment in the band's history as it was happening, and his responses in an April 1996 interview seem tinged with hostility:

> It's just me and Bilinda, really. Debbie has been in the band for years, but she stopped playing on the records in '88. She only played on one song in 1988. To tell the truth, she only played on one whole record in 1985 . . . she didn't have anything to do with making the records. Colm had something to do with making the records, but not that much. It was always more of a closed thing between me and Bilinda, because we were together at the time. When we went through this long, long period of not being too sure of what we were going to do, that's when they decided to take the chance to do something else, because it wasn't really their thing, if you know what I mean.[5]

Shields would also suggest that this new two-person setup had its advantages—one being the fact that, as a duo, he and Butcher could better recreate the spirit of creative adventure he remembered from 1988. As he saw it, the stripped-down group would have a better chance of capturing that elusive and experimental energy. 'I always wrote for the whole band before,' he said, doing his best to rationalize things. 'In a way, I'm a lot more free now.'[6] He even floated the idea of assembling a new group, making another subtle dig at Ó Cíosóig and Googe in the process:

> It's been an idea or dream of mine I've got, to get a group of people who can play in their own way but are really into it. Put it this way ... me and Bilinda could always rely on each other to deliver what we were going to do. Everyone else in our organization around us weren't like that. We would feel left out. I suppose what we want to do, now that me and Bilinda are the only two that are left, is to bring in people who are just as committed, very driven about just trying to do something past what's comfortable, what gives them a comfortable lifestyle.[7]

Shields again mentioned the idea of assembling a new band in an interview with AOL in early 1997, which was ostensibly published in support of a solo album that was scheduled to come out later that year. Asked if he enjoyed working with others, he responded, 'I'd rather work with others in the next few years, but I'm finishing this record by myself ... music-wise, I am going to try and make a semi-international band ... around May, I'm going to try and put a band together or WILL put a band together.'[8] Given everything the foursome had been through together, and the fact that Shields never again mentioned the potential of assembling another band, these somewhat bitter comments seem to reflect ephemeral, momentary feelings that didn't truly capture the deep connection and affection he felt for everyone in the group.

•

Shields and Butcher tried to soldier on after the departures of Googe and Ó Cíosóig. Shields had abandoned his experiments with drum & bass and started a new album from scratch in a style inspired by Brian Wilson's *Smile*, challenging himself to write songs in discrete sections without having a completed composition in mind. But though he was adamant that he and Butcher were still recording, albeit slowly, and had every intention of finishing a follow-up to *Loveless*, in actuality, he felt that little of value was being recorded in Streatham. He would only change his mind when he revisited the work about a decade later; it was at that point that he realized some of the material he'd recorded over a six-month period in 1996 and 1997, after aborting his drum & bass odyssey, was worth pursuing.

All of these conflicting details are important to keep in mind when attempting to sort out the differing accounts of everything that happened while MBV were signed with Island, as well as how Shields portrayed the label's treatment of him when their relationship ultimately fell apart. Part of what makes it hard to accurately reconstruct this era of Shields's career are the few public pronouncements Island made about their relationship and the way Shields himself would later completely alter the narrative. He stuck to one distinct narrative until about 1999, but after Island released him from his contract in 2003—a charitable act, all things considered— his portrayal of the label's treatment of him did a complete 180.

To a large degree, it's understandable why his story changed; this was an extremely difficult time for him, both creatively and personally. Who do you blame when you're given everything you ask for but fail to live up to the potential that's been assigned to you, and which you've assigned to yourself by signing a deal with a major label for a very large amount of money? Shields has grappled with this question over the years, changing his assessment of that time in his life multiple times, at times rationalizing or exaggerating what occurred to try and make sense of things. These inconsistencies make clear what an upsetting and challenging time it was for him.

•

As 1997 wore on, Shields gave fewer and fewer interviews. One of the last was an 'Invisible Jukebox' feature for *The Wire*, for which interviewees are played clips of music and asked to identify them. His hesitance to discuss his own current work seems logical, though, considering how fraught things were for him at this point. One journalist who did speak to Shields during this time, John Robb, would later describe 'a man who was lost in a fug of creativity, every single drum loop was analyzed over and over as the relentless search for perfection engulfed him.'[9]

During the internet boom of the 90s, one of the first sites set up to keep track of all things MBV was ExpectDelay.com.* According to rumors published there in 1997 and 1998, various friends and acquaintances—including engineer Andy Wilkinson and members of Swervedriver and Mercury Rev—dropped in on Shields and found that he had somewhere between eight and nine songs recorded—enough material for a full-length album. Shields would later confirm this to be true but added that he ultimately felt this material wasn't worth pursuing, concluding that the melodies weren't memorable enough.[10] (It's likely that he was referring here to his jungle-inspired experiments rather than the music he created with Butcher in the style of Brian Wilson's *Smile*.)

In 1997, Shields gave one of his last formal interviews for several years as part of an open forum with AOL. He seemed as committed as ever to releasing new music with Island, stating, 'The truth is you can't expect anything but, I really am dead if I don't get my record out this year. Nobody's threatening me, BTW, I just have to.'[11] No new music appeared, however, and Shields would not give any more interviews until 2003. At that point, a new narrative began to take shape as he claimed that Island had put him in a difficult position financially and then interfered with his creative process. He described attending a formal meeting at Island's Hammersmith offices in early 1996 and being told that he was one of three acts on the label, alongside The Orb and Stereo MCs, who had run up costs of nearly £500,000 without releasing any new music, and that whoever reached that figure first would be cut off. According to Marc Marot, however, there is no way the label would done anything so crass as

---

* The name was actually a reference to the growing pains involved with the first years of the internet's development, not the fact that the band's follow-up to *Loveless* kept getting pushed back, though it only became more apt in that regard over the coming years

to stage a 'debt race' between acts. 'It is absolutely untrue,' he said, without a moment's hesitation.[12] (Shields has also claimed that at one point, Island suggested he register for state support payments, though in a very brief chat with the *NME* in 1999, he had said, 'I'm just glad that I've not had to be on the dole for ten years.'[13])

What should we make of this discrepancy? It's likely that Shields conflated these other Island acts into his fanciful narrative in the knowledge that they too had received money from the label to build their own studios. But Stereo MCs were very cognizant of how much money they were borrowing, and band member Nick Hallam confirmed that they did not come close to accruing £500,000 in debt, nor did they receive any threats of being cut off.[14] And both they and The Orb had found out the hard way that the unfettered freedom that came with owning your own recording space was much more complicated than it first seemed.

Regardless of any other issues Shields might have faced, he has never been accused by Alan McGee or anyone else of deliberately inventing things. In this case, however, it's likely that his memories were shaped by his general disdain for the record industry and for anyone who has tried to exert any form of control on his music—plus the massive amounts of pot he was smoking at the time, which does not lend itself to clear recollections. But there was clearly no deception or subterfuge about what he was getting himself into when he signed his contract with Island.

We don't know for sure exactly how much money Shields went through during his time on Island Records, and it's possible that the amount of money he actually spent between 1992 and 1997 was more than what the label contributed. Alan McGee, who is privy to inside information but also prone to hyperbole, said in 2000 that Shields had taken '£500,000, I think, off Island; approximately a quarter of a million off EMI publishing; and approximately a quarter of a million off Warner Bros in America. And none of them have heard one piece of music. And the best bit is—he thinks *it's their fault*. Which I love.'[15]

We will likely never know how much Island, EMI, and Warners (Sire's parent company) cumulatively invested in Shields and the follow-up to

Loveless, but it's clear that he never got close to completing an album he deemed worthy of release during this period. He seemed to be experiencing some sort of cognitive dissonance, which drove him to continue with a narrative wherein he fully believed new music would be forthcoming while simultaneously sensing that everything he recorded was worthless and should be scrapped. It's also possible that even when things weren't going well, Shields could convince himself that everything would eventually fall into place and he would soon have enough songs that were good enough to release. With his previous records, everything came together in the end, and perhaps now, even as he felt himself sliding deeper into a creative slump and his relationship with Island grew more strained, he continued to tell himself that it would all turn out fine in the end.

In the meantime, rumors continued to circulate. In 1997, another small, unattributed notice in the *NME* made it seem as though the new record was still on track:

> Late last year, Kevin emerged from his south London studio to take three vocal-less tracks into Island, when the label threatened to cut off his money in an attempt to spur him into action. According to the few who've heard them, they're 'amazing,' and though Kevin wanted to release them as an EP, Island boss Marc Marot elected to wait, presuming that to put anything else out would distract Kevin from finishing the album, which is apparently closer than it has been for some time. It's currently thought that there are about seven finished tracks.

Both Marot and Coxon confirm that this rumor had some basis in fact. Shields had, in fact, asked Marot to meet and was excited to play him some new tracks. Since Shields had initiated the get-together, Marot came to the meeting with high expectations. But when he heard the new material, the tracks were so underdeveloped that, as he put it, they couldn't have even served as background music for a film soundtrack. 'It wasn't the score for a movie. It was the atmospherics for a movie. So I was hearing sounds rather than compositions, and I could see what might get him excited, but they need to be articulated into a composition. And what I was hearing was a whole series of sounds.'[16] Coxon had a similar memory of a CD from 1996 containing five backing tracks but nothing to convey chords or melody. They weren't anywhere close to being proper songs.

At some point around late 1997, Marot made clear that Island couldn't continue to fund Shields's work indefinitely. Shields, in turn, decided that no matter the consequences, he wouldn't release any of the material he'd recorded over the last four years. Whatever he was going through at that time, he knew the music he was creating just wasn't good enough for the world to hear. Or, perhaps, he couldn't tell if it had any value or not and simply didn't want to release work he might regret later.

The two men were at an impasse, and Marot had no choice but to cut off all monetary support. This didn't mean the label refused to work with Shields entirely, however. Marot volunteered to pay for an engineer or producer if Shields wanted to demo any new tracks or move forward in a different way, but Shields made it clear he would never work within these kinds of restrictions. He'd never demoed tracks or worked with engineers or producers he didn't specifically choose or sanction in the past, and he would later note that there was specific language in his contract forbidding such an idea. Of course, Marot had given MBV an initial advance, as well as an additional stipend (beyond the contract terms) when their recording desk died, so this new request doesn't seem particularly diabolical. In Shield's mind, however, Island were no longer patrons or collaborators in any sense. He saw the situation as an echo of how he had been treated by Creation.*

In truth, Shields might also have realized that no matter who intervened or whatever help he received, he just wasn't in the right frame of mind to

---

* A lifetime away in early 2008, a month after the reunion concerts were announced for later that year, MBV's nominal manager, Vinita Joshi, was asked about future recording plans. Without hesitation, she asserted to *Mojo*, 'We're not talking to any record companies at the moment. The band got fucked over financially by every label they were signed to, so we'll probably release it on our own label.' For good measure, she added, 'Kevin doesn't want people breathing down his neck, saying, Where's our album?'

make new music. Perhaps he realized the moment had passed and didn't see the point in continuing to try. Years later, he justified his hesitation toward working with outside collaborators by suggesting that Island had interfered with his creative process. 'I had to be controlling because otherwise it would have diluted what was happening. If you've painted a picture, you can't have people going, *That's great, but that red you've used? Can we use a different red, because that's easier for us to do?* And that's what happens all the time. The music world is full of that.'[17]

This analogy isn't particularly convincing, however, especially considering how Marot and Island tended to operate. It's hard to imagine anyone at the label telling Shields what to record any more than Alan McGee had. Talking to Marot now, one can't help but come away with the impression that he and his team were sincerely trying to create a long-term home for Shields, eager to nurture his talent for everyone's benefit. Why would he have signed MBV in the first place if the label was going to micromanage what their recordings sounded like?

Instead of working with Island, however, Shields put them off. He kept his own counsel and put even greater pressure on himself, supplanting the label's efforts and doing his best to absorb their anxieties. The process of writing and recording *Loveless* had given him plenty of practice with these kinds of avoidance tactics, so he was used to it by now. Once Marot pulled the plug, however, things fell apart quickly. With his stipend cut off, Shields couldn't continue to hire engineers at the label's expense and hope to find his way forward. If he insisted on doing everything his way and according to his schedule, he would be forced to find other avenues to support himself.

•

Soon after Island cut off the funding, Bilinda Butcher moved out of the house in Streatham. Like Ó Cíosóig and Googe before her, she realized the situation wasn't going to improve, and she had exhausted her options. Though she would later say that she felt guilty about deserting Shields, she considered leaving to be an act of self-preservation. 'I just felt like I was the one who needed to sort myself out. It was hard, 'cause I felt like there wasn't any connection at all, you know, and I felt really sad. Really, really sad.'[18]

Butcher's departure brought an end to her intimate relationship with Shields, an end to the songs they were working on, and, at least for the time being, an end to MBV. 'It wouldn't be us if she wasn't in the band,' Shields had said in 1997.[19] And now she was gone. They had had many fights and difficulties over the previous ten years, both as lovers and as musical partners, but this time it seemed to both of them that they had truly fallen out. They were unsure if they would ever speak or work together again.

Over the coming years, Shields would take on work as a remixer, session guitar player, and producer. The money he made, along with the income he received from publishing and royalties for MBV's previous material, gave him more than enough to get by. Even if he wasn't doing exactly what he wanted to, his skills were nevertheless in sufficient demand that he was easily able to support himself.*

During that same period, Island underwent a series of changes that resulted in Shields being released from his contract. In 1999, the label merged with Universal, in the process becoming a much more corporate entity. Marot and Coxon left, and Nick Gatfield was installed as the label's managing director. By all accounts, Gatfield was a much more conventional kind of executive, and his promotion signaled the end of the old, artist-centered Island. By the time he took over, however, Shields had already moved on, and in that sense, Gatfield's leadership didn't change anything. Despite rumors of intrusive tactics and legal maneuvers, no one at Island would be able to get Shields to release any of the work he'd recorded using

---

* One of the first projects Shields was involved in outside of MBV was alongside choreographer Édouard Lock's Canadian dance troupe, La La La Human Steps. Exactly how he became involved with Lock is unclear, but he ended up contributing original music to two works by the troupe during the mid-to-late 90s. Their production *2* premiered in 1995, with approximately six minutes of Shields's music—instantly recognizable as his—appearing in the third segment, 'Old Young (Remembering).' He then contributed three original pieces to the 1998 work *Exauce / Salt*, amounting to seven minutes of music in total. Of all Shields's abstract works, these three pieces are among the hardest to place.

the label's money.* Further legal wrangling then led to Shields quitting the band and leaving Butcher as MBV's sole remaining member before Island finally released him from his contract in 2003.

In an extensive 2004 interview with the Irish music magazine *Hot Press*, Shields talked through the various options available to him, and Island, after he resigned from the band. His nonchalant tone when discussing his work from 1992 to 2003 made it seem like those years were a distant memory of little consequence. 'I basically had to leave the band, and they had the option to pick me up as a solo artist, but that would mean they'd have to give me a big advance,' he explained. 'And after giving me so much money and then me giving them nothing, it was too much for them to pay. It was just reality.'[20]

In retrospect, it's hard to know whether the difficulties Shields faced with installing the studio in Streatham and his inability to quickly get his ideas to tape were the cause of his creative stagnation and loss of momentum, or if they were a symptom of more fundamental problems, not least the intense pressure he felt to follow *Loveless* with something just as groundbreaking. But once the band finally had a working recording desk installed, the extensive, excited experimentation led only to dead ends—to recordings Shields would describe as 'stillborn' and unfit for release. Asked why he had decided not to put out any of this music, he explained, 'The answer is, it wasn't as good [as *Loveless*]. And I always promised myself I'd never do that, put out a worse record.'[21]

Only a handful of tracks that MBV recorded from 1994 to 1997 contained melodies that would haunt Shields sufficiently that he would

---

* The suggestion that Island sued Shields in order to induce him to release some of the tracks he'd recorded while signed to the label comes from a single source, an article by Jeremy Gordon published in the *New York Times* in March 2021. 'My Bloody Valentine has truly always done things its own way,' Gordon wrote. 'Other times, it has meant its label sue Shields rather than release music it didn't like. (That happened in 2001, after My Bloody Valentine had been signed with Island Records for nearly a decade without turning out a new album.)' There is no public record of any such case, however, suggesting that this may have been a misunderstanding, or perhaps that Island decided not to pursue a lawsuit after realizing that Shields would not be intimidated by the threat of legal action.

eventually return to them—his criteria for whether an idea was worth pursuing—but none of these songs were even close to being ready for release. Furthermore, because of the terms of the band's contract with Island, we've not heard the jungle-inspired 'skyscraper music' Shields made during this period, and it's unlikely we ever will.* We do have a few hints of what some of it might have sounded like, however. In 2003, Shields gave his most specific description of this material, explaining that he had been attempting 'to marry the kind of… do you know Neil Young's guitar sound when it's really distorted?' with the rhythms of drum & bass, so that the guitars and the fast, nimble programmed parts ripple together in time. 'But anyway, that's all concepts,' he concluded. 'It didn't actually pan out in the end because it's too difficult to do that intuitively. It's being a bit like Stravinsky, or something—pure fucking intellectual conceptuality.'[22]

Over the years, Shields would often imply that if only Island had given him more time, he might have been able to finish an album for the label. 'I was over-intellectualizing what I was doing,' he said in 2008. 'I lost the balance between the emotional side and the ideas side. I'd been thinking of doing this really mad drum & bass skyscraper-type music. That's where I was for a long time. But Island pulled the plug before I finished it.'[23] He is clearly rewriting history here, however. All the available evidence indicates that even if Island had continued to fund him for several more years, nothing was going to see the light of day. In retrospect, his assessment seems like a convenient justification for why the relationship went sideways—a necessary narrative built up to lessen the blow of things going so awry.

By 2021, Shields's viewpoint about his time with Island had shifted once again, and he began to indicate that the label had given him a fair shake. 'The record company quite fairly pulled the plug on me because I had reached the limit of the amount that they said they would ever give me to spend,' he told the Australian radio station Double J.[24] It had taken

---

* The closest we would get would be *m b v*'s 'Wonder 2,' though Shields has specifically stated that it doesn't represent the sound of the bulk of the music he was making during 1994 and 1995.

almost two decades for him to move past any bitterness or recriminations and publicly acknowledge that Island Records was not the villain.

It's hard, nonetheless, to resist the urge to speculate about what might have been, had things gone differently. Googe and Butcher have suggested several what-ifs. What if Butcher and Shields hadn't lived together? What if all four of them had simply taken six months off, away from each other, when they signed with Island in 1992? What if the band had gotten a recording console that worked from day one? How might things have played out differently if Shields had looked at Marot as a collaborator and taken his advice to make an album *before* undergoing the work of building their own studio?

Depending on how one looks at it, Shields's unwillingness to even consider any alternate working methods between 1992 and 1997 likely signaled a loss of productivity in the short term. For all we know, had Shields been more willing to confide in the top people at Island, they might have found ways to enable him to be more productive, which might in turn have led to one of the most creatively fruitful periods of his career.* Marc Marot was no slouch, having guided the careers of PJ Harvey and Tricky, among others. He had valuable skills and experience that would surely have been of use to Shields. But how useful, we'll never know.

Island's decision to cut Shields off actually helped him, in a way, by finally forcing him to acknowledge the dire straits he was in—something he'd previously seemed unwilling or unable to admit to himself, even with his band disintegrating around him. This might also be part of what allowed the band to eventually come back, as they never diluted their brand. Maybe Shields ended up doing the right thing in the long term, since his biggest fear was releasing something inferior to *Loveless* (in the process degrading the band's high standards and taking away from their mystique). Ultimately, the answers to all of these questions are unknowable. Or as the economist John Maynard Keynes put it, while weighing up short-term and long-term consequences, 'In the long run we are all dead.'

---

* Years later, Shields would be given a clear sense of what could be done with the right collaborator when he quickly made two recordings during a visit to Brian Eno's studio.

What is clear, however, is that by the end of his Island odyssey, Shields had done immense damage to his reputation and standing in the music industry. Everyone involved with Shields had wanted nothing more than for him to succeed, but he was struggling to figure out reality and his place in it. A great deal of time would pass before he could truly view this period of his life with a proper and honest perspective. But before he could look back and reflect on these years, he'd have to find a way to make it through them.

interlude five

hypnagogia

'I'm crazy but not mentally ill … there's a difference.'

KEVIN SHIELDS, 2004[1]

'I was on a journey from 1992 to the early 2000s.'

KEVIN SHIELDS, 2023[2]

Around 1996–97, Shields entered a period of semi-isolation that, according to interviews, lasted as long as a year. By the time Island had cut off funding for the band, he was barely leaving the house; speaking to *Sex* magazine in 2004, Butcher revealed that at times, he had refused even to get out of bed.

Whatever Shields was experiencing during this period, it isn't all that surprising, considering the intense pressure he was under to move things forward with his music. Most likely, he figured the safest option was simply to shelter in place. That decision can be viewed as a rational response to the unfulfilled obligations he may have felt toward his bandmates, his label, his fans, and himself. A few years later, asked point blank by the *Guardian* if he 'lost it' during this time, Shields replied, 'I think everyone does. Everyone has a certain thing and they lose it and they should move on.'[3]

He wasn't ready to move on, though. But having discarded the skyscraper project, he didn't know how to react when he no longer felt as inspired to create as he had in the past. Among the few people he confided in was Alan McGee, himself no stranger to emotional distress. In 2004, the former Creation boss recounted how Shields had locked himself away until no one—friends, the band—wanted to get in. 'It was definitely a meltdown,' said McGee.[4] Some years later, he would further describe the pressure Shields was under in an article for the *Guardian*. 'Shields was incredibly young when he was thrust into the spotlight (burdened with the tag of being the man who would "change the face of music"),' he wrote. 'He was ill-equipped to cope with the pressures of fame that followed. In five years Shields went from nowhere to being considered a world-class star and saviour of modern music.'[5]

Shields has since mentioned that some of the details that have been shared as evidence of his instability—including the fact that he had placed barbed wire and sandbags around the house—were actually related to crime prevention and soundproofing. He has also said that he played up the 'recluse' angle as a means to get Island off his back. But when we examine the evidence—and even after stripping away some of the more salacious details—it is clear that he was personally at sea during this time, and he has admitted as much. 'I was pretty crazy, for sure,' he told the *Guardian*, 'and it was a very manic, overdrive kind of state, but I never got out of control.'[6] He was nonetheless quick to point out that he remained able to look after himself; he had gotten away with living a particular lifestyle for so long that he could just continue to do so, and he did. The main drawbacks of his period of isolation, as he put it, were that he didn't get any work done and watched a lot of bad films.

•

Shields has credited a single book, *Hypnagogia* by Dr. Andreas Mavromatis, with saving his life, explaining that it offered some context to the altered states of reality that he was experiencing more and more as his isolation grew increasingly pronounced. Mavromatis's writings gave Shields insight into his 'insomniac habits and aesthetic preoccupations,' as he later put it, and 'made me feel sane.'[7]

Shields first came across the book at a time in the mid-90s, when he was having serious concerns about his sanity, due to the fact that, with little effort, he could simply close his eyes and have three-dimensional experiences so vivid as to be indistinguishable from the real outer world.

He seemed genuinely afraid that these sometimes-spontaneous states may have been an indication of mental illness or that he was bordering on mental illness.

He further summarized how important *Hypnagogia* was to him in a 2003 interview with *Arthur Magazine*. 'There are no books about that subject in English other than that one ... not only did he write a book about hypnagogia, he literally made *all* the connections to all other states of mind that are very similar.' Prior to joining Primal Scream in 1998, he noted, he would spend hours alone in his bedroom, tripping out. 'It was a four-year trip, basically.'[8]

Hypnagogia is broadly defined as 'hallucinatory and quasi-hallucinatory events taking place in the intermediate state between wakefulness and sleep.' It can include hallucinations, lucid dreaming, and lucid thoughts. Unlike a hypnopompic state, which is a period of transition from sleep back to consciousness, a hypnagogic state captures the body and mind's transition into unconsciousness. For convenience, Mavromatis uses the term 'hypnagogia' to encompass both states, though when it comes to thinking about how they might be harnessed for creative purposes, only hypnagogic states apply.

When one falls asleep in a conventional manner, this transitional state of consciousness usually lasts only for a relatively short period of time—one that's typically beyond our control, and likewise difficult to remember. One of the only ways people can tap into their thoughts from a hypnagogic state is by disturbing or extending this period, by arranging to be deliberately roused at the exact moment when they're losing consciousness on the journey to REM sleep.

For centuries, artists, inventors, and scientists have tried to harness and use these near-conscious moments productively. Edison, Brahms, Wagner, Puccini, Goethe, Dalí, Tesla, da Vinci, Keats, and Coleridge (who brought back some small part of his famous 'Kubla Khan' from a hypnagogic vision) have all used this technique for purposes of creativity and problem-solving. Mavromatis makes it plain that, like certain hallucinogens, the process aims to help a person 'lift one's logical "dampers" ... allowing the rising to consciousness of unconscious-nonrational and original combinations of associative elements.'[9] Another scientist describes hypnagogia similarly as 'the shortest path for communication from our subconscious. Your subconscious mind might send you solutions through imagery or other sensations.'[10]

Even in the early days, when MBV would all live in the studio together while recording, they would purposefully deprive themselves of sleep as part of their working method (often with the aid of marijuana). At some points, they were getting only an hour of sleep a night. Guy Fixsen has confirmed the role of sleep deprivation in the band's creative process, noting how they would 'stay up for twenty-four hours at a time, then sleep.'[11] While promoting *Tremolo* in early 1991, Shields explained how this helped drive the band's ideas in the studio. 'We just follow our instincts,' he said, 'There's a point on the verge of unconsciousness when you're more able to do something than you ever would otherwise.'[12]

Being stoned on marijuana and being in a hypnagogic state led the band to new ways to *hear* music—to really absorb it in an effortless yet deeply felt way that stays with you even after you are sober and awake. Of the two, Shields has said that he ultimately preferred hypnagogia, and many of his recordings from 1988 onward include moments that feel tailor-made for it, likely because they were written and recorded while he was methodically pursuing altered forms of consciousness himself. 'To Here Knows When' is a perfect illustration of this. To fully take it in, you have to pull back, in much the same way as you might dilate your pupil to take in a broader picture. If you aren't aware that the track was conceived in this way, the experience of listening to it can be highly disorienting.

Unusually, Shields was seemingly able to induce a hypnagogic state at will, to help explore the creative ideas that led to so many of his musical discoveries. On the flip side, the practice also seems to have led him to question his stability and sanity, though his drug use likely contributed to that too. He and his bandmates had been smoking pot regularly since the late 80s, and they have cited it as a key element in their early creativity, but by the mid-90s it may have been playing a more negative role. Google would later describe the Streatham house/studio as a kind of hallucinatory madhouse, such was the overindulgence with marijuana.* Shields has spoken of his ambivalence about his 'bad habit' with the drug while also admitting, 'It was necessary for me; it's my safety valve. I need to smoke to get to sleep every night.'[13]

Since the various states induced by hypnagogia, marijuana, and sleep deprivation are hard to distinguish between, and because they can have a cumulative effect, it's not surprising that Shields's comments about them can be confusing and contradictory at times. As Mavromatis writes, 'Sleep deprivation may be considered as a condition in which the need for sleep and the effort to stay awake place the subject in a vacillating intermediate state not unlike the naturally occurring hypnagogia.' He also noted how 'hallucinogenic-drug and hypnagogic experiences are found to summate.'[14]

In the period after the *Loveless* tour ended, Shields was pushing his experiments with sleep deprivation and fugue-like states even further. After reading a book by the prominent psychedelic writer Terence McKenna, he began hardcore experiments in his mind—visualizing a cow, for example, that felt solid and real; that he could not only see but could even move around. He began to look forward to the private time after everyone else was asleep when he could 'trip out' and enjoy infinite experiences in his own personal solar system—'my imagination.'[15]

Ultimately, Shields reached a point where it was hard to distinguish between what was real and what wasn't. 'The things I experienced were quite unreal,' he has since said. 'I've been totally out there, I can honestly say I've experienced everything Aldous Huxley wrote about in *The Doors Of Perception*.'[16] When he finally reached a breaking point, however, Mavromatis's insights helped put a name to what he was going through. But that process of understanding would take time, and in the meantime— in his 1997 AOL interview, for example—he would again attribute the delay in releasing new music through Island to 'mental illness.'[17]

---

* It was also the case that the marijuana itself was getting stronger and more potent. A study in *Neuropsychopharmacology* reported that the THC content in the drug doubled from 1990 to 2005.

By all accounts, Shields's struggles persisted until the Island funds were cut and he took some pressure off himself by turning his creative attention to remixes and playing with Primal Scream. But though the past few years had been difficult for him, he would look back on this period of exploration as a necessary journey he needed to get through to make peace with himself.

In later years, he would note that while he continued to have some of his best ideas while in a hypnagogic state, he would no longer try to stay in it. In 2003, while discussing tinnitus and silence, he noted, 'Silence doesn't exist anymore. I know states between being awake and sleep, a sort of narcotic state where I can experiment. Sometimes I keep mental images, even if my eyes are closed. Other times, everything is shut down. My brain, the sound, the visions. Only then do I have silence. But it's a place where you don't want to stay, so you try to come back quick.'[18]

In 2021, Shields spoke candidly about the metaphysical travels he'd been on during the late 90s and early 2000s, likening it to going to a Buddhist retreat to meditate for years to comprehend consciousness.

Silence doesn't exist for me. I know states between being awake and asleep, a kind of narcotic state where I can experience it. Sometimes images remain, even with my eyes closed. Other times, everything's off. My brain, the sounds, the visions. I have silence there but it's not a place you want to stay, so you try to come back quickly.[19]

chapter twelve

within: mbv arkestra • twenty-grand

rubbish • free reins • jazz-tinged

funk • *xtrmntr* • a loose collective •

broken punk • joy zipper

'MBV have effectively not released any new material since 1991, [yet] Shields continues to be a pervasive presence on the experimental side of modern rock music.'

PLAY GUITAR, 2002[1]

'Shields is not just a guitar fanatic and innovator. He's a musical modernizer, guitars, drums and all. And if you miss that, you only get half the story.'

BEN CARDEW, *PITCHFORK*, 2014[2]

'I hung out with Primal Scream from '98 to 2005, which was a strange block of time. I was taking drugs—just recreationally but ... a lot. I felt like I was on holiday.'

KEVIN SHIELDS, 2012[3]

The fallout with Island Records made Shields persona non grata as far as the record industry was concerned, but even if label executives saw him as dysfunctional, there was no shortage of artists who wanted to work with him simply because his approach to music was utterly unique.[*] And

---

[*] One of them was Charlotte Marionneau, who records as Le Volume Courbe. In 2015, she released 'The House,' written about the time she spent at Shields's home after Butcher moved out. Shields and other musicians in his orbit have contributed to various of her releases.

when he finally decided that there was not going to be a follow-up to *Loveless* anytime soon, he relied on his gifts as a remixer, guitarist, and producer to keep him busy and fed until he was ready to reengage with the group.

Since Shields was still officially under contract with Island, he was limited in the ways he could earn a living. Making original music for another label was out, but he could still remix other artists' material, do production work, and make guest appearances as a guitar player. Along with the royalties he continued to earn from MBV's previous albums, these outlets allowed him to stay afloat financially. At the time, due to the growing mainstream success of dance acts like Fatboy Slim, The Chemical Brothers, and The Prodigy, remixing was more popular than ever. Rock, pop, and dance acts would include remixes as B-sides on most of their singles—and the more exotic, the better. So, though the Island money had stopped, Shields was a long way from the days when he had to resort to squatting and scraping around for his next meal. Asked how he was getting by in 2003, he said simply, 'I get paid thousands every time somebody asks me to do a remix … every so often I get a nice royalty cheque. I've got enough money.'[4]

Between 1995 and 2005, Shields completed approximately twenty remixes. The vast majority were for bands he had some personal connection to, but one or two jobs may have just been for the cash, as it was hard to picture some of the bands he worked with as fellow travelers. (What was his connection to Placebo, for example?) Soon, however, some of his more accessible remixes could be heard on the hippest after-hours dance floors in New York, London, Berlin, Paris, and Ibiza.

Shields later expressed regret that he wasn't working on his own music during this time, describing remixing as 'a bad way to make a living … rubbish.'[5] But these sentiments seem offset by the fact that he was able to decide who to work with, and with managers calling him and offering him as much as £20,000 per remix, he could choose to remix the acts and songs that most interested him. He also challenged himself to only work with what the artist originally recorded, rather than composing new parts, but gave himself free rein to run his mixes through any sonic processing devices of his choosing.

Shields's remixes run the gamut from beautiful, delicate sculptures that clock in at under a minute to an epic, sixteen-minute track for Mogwai featuring unrelenting guitars and drums. There was something attractive to him about these jobs, possibly because there was little at stake but also a firm deadline each time. Over time, he created more than two hours of remixes, almost all of which are of interest for one reason or another; though they may not be as personal as the music Shields wrote with MBV, they compare favorably with it. And most of them could not have come from anyone else.

Among the most notable is Shields's remixes of Yo La Tengo's 'Autumn Sweater,' in which vocalist/guitarist Ira Kaplan describes wanting to slip away from a fall get-together with his wife (the band's drummer, Georgia Hubley). Bringing out the most melancholic elements of the original composition, the remix captures all the devotion and yearning in Kaplan's lyrics and delivery, though it's set to Shields's own take on the rhythm. Yo La Tengo were so impressed by it that they integrated certain elements of the remix when playing the song live, synthesizing the two versions into something new.

Shields also did several remixes for The Pastels. 'Cycle' is particularly affecting, beautifully emphasizing the mournful qualities in both the music and vocals, while 'Magic Nights' is noteworthy for its intriguing combination of hard and soft in a manner you might associate with an artist like Aphex Twin. He also remixed the band's 'Intro' as 'Outro,' resulting in a track that would have been a natural fit with the work he would later complete for the soundtrack to *Lost In Translation*.

Shields's version of Hurricane #1's 'Rising Sign' takes the original radio-friendly track and transforms it into an otherworldly soundscape designed, according to the accompanying press materials, 'to get you in the whirlwind … board up yer windows.' His remixes for GOD, The Frank & Walters, and Curve are also worth seeking out. He also contributed two short pieces—'Incidental One' with Mark Eitzel and 'Incidental Peace' with Skylab—to the Red Hot Organization's charity album *OFFBEAT: A Red Hot Sound Trip*. The first is a short track reminiscent of the segues on *Tremolo* or *Loveless*; the second is longer, with the first minute featuring just Shields alone, before Skylab takes over the remix, and you can't help but wonder where it would have gone had he developed it further.

Shields's last remix from this period was for The Go! Team, for whom he combined the tracks 'Lady Flash' and 'Huddle Formation' into 'Huddle Flash' in 2006. Asked about this track several years later, however, he left no doubt as to where he now stood with this kind of work. 'I don't do that anymore. I wouldn't say I wouldn't do it ever again, but, uh, I've got no plans to or anything like that.'[6]

•

As noted earlier, Primal Scream's *Screamadelica* was one of three seminal albums—alongside *Loveless* and Teenage Fanclub's *Bandwagonesque*—released by Creation Records in 1991. Combining the talents of the band's core members—Bobby Gillespie, Andrew Innes, Richard 'Throb' Young, and Martin Duffy—with the work of DJ Andrew Weatherall and other talented producers, it helped connect the group with the sounds of the ecstasy-fueled dance scene. The album proved hugely successful and influential, but like MBV, Primal Scream had issues creating the follow-up, which was eventually released in 1994 as *Give Out But Don't Give Up*. The singles 'Rocks' and 'Jailbird' were greeted with some enthusiasm, but overall the album and its retro Rolling Stones vibe were not the success the band or Creation had hoped for, especially considering the rumored costs (before marketing) of £400,0000 plus.

The band regained their stride on their next album, 1997's *Vanishing Point*, and consolidated their return to form on the two that followed, *XTRMNTR* (1999) and *Evil Heat* (2002), which were much truer to the band's disaffected, nonconformist origins. Innes and Gillespie led the way, fusing together a potent update of dub, industrial, punk, and more. Gillespie came from a working-class Scottish family with connections to organized labor, and it's clear that he and Innes were galvanized while making these records by US hegemony and what they saw as unhinged globalization. The scuzzy, malevolent recordings on *Vanishing Point* helped steer the overall direction of the band's next two records, both of which involved significant contributions from Kevin Shields.

It was Innes who first initiated Primal Scream's collaboration with Shields when he went over to the guitarist's home studio around May 1997—coincidentally, right around the time Island Records cut the band's stipend—and asked him to do a remix of the *Vanishing Point* track 'If They Move, Kill 'Em.' From there, Shields gradually fell in with the band, enjoying both his secondary role within the group and their casual way of working together.

Reportedly created during one twenty-four-hour session, the remix was released in early 1998 as a promotional single with the title 'If They Move, Kill 'Em (Kevin Shields Mix).' Shields's radical take on the track got the music world's attention, electrifying all who heard it. As well as leading to many other remix offers for Shields, it became a key signpost toward the kinds of dark, futuristic, jazz-tinged funk the band would develop on *XTRMNTR*. *Vanishing Point* contains some outstanding original moments, but for *XTRMNTR*, Primal Scream were in pursuit of something that hit even harder, and Shields pointed them where they needed to go.

Even in light of the high expectations attached to Shields name, his remix of 'If They Move, Kill 'Em' is truly exceptional. As Kris Needs, an archivist and confidante of the Primal Scream, wrote, 'It's the epic track that manages to work in a Moroccan percussion groove, incorporate a fatter-than-fat hip hop beat, plus dissonant free-jazz assaults and a mean rock guitar swagger.'[7]

Though Shields limited himself, as always, to working only with the original recordings, the new track seemed to feature elements that weren't there previously—a mystery Gillespie would clear up in a subsequent interview:

We record way more than we use. Like when we did 'If They Move, Kill 'Em' and Kevin Shields remixed that, he didn't add any music to it. He just used what was there. If you shoot a movie, I'm sure directors shoot a lot of scenes that they don't use because they're trying stuff [out]. They shoot a lot more than they use and eventually they'll edit that down to a narrative that makes sense to them, and they tell the story they want to tell. That's what we do with music; we do the exact same thing.[8]

Shortly before Primal Scream finished *Vanishing Point*, there was another good omen when bassist Gary 'Mani' Mounfield, formerly of The Stone Roses, joined the group, along with Darrin Mooney, a jazz drummer with the John Bonham–like power they'd always needed. They also brought in Jim Hunt and Duncan MacKay on horns, and with these four added to the core lineup of Innes, Young, Gillespie, and Duffy, Primal Scream became a kind of supergroup, firing on all cylinders in the studio and on tour. They'd never sounded better.

For *XTRMNTR*, Primal Scream worked in a similar way to musical collectives like Parliament/Funkadelic, recording whatever or whenever someone had something that inspired them. Shields found himself circulating among the rotating constellation of musicians, engineers, and producers who contributed to the sessions, among them Hugo Nicholson, Adrian Sherwood, David Holmes, Brenden Lynch, and Jagz Kooner. He had already begun recording music for *XTRMNTR* by August 1997, and he quickly found the relative anonymity (and regular paycheck) refreshing. As he became more involved with the group, he realized he could blend naturally into the background; no one in the band or in the audience at gigs would ask him about MBV or the status of his new album. Working with Primal Scream provided him with a much-needed change of scenery after the years of struggling to make a follow-up to *Loveless*.

With *XTRMNTR*, Primal Scream assembled the album that best reflected who they really were if you got down to the marrow. In the twenty years since punk had first reared its head, a whole new set of social and economic evils had emerged, and the band wanted to make a modern-day punk record in response. *XTRMNTR*, Gillespie explained, was meant to reflect all the tensions of modern society, from the Gulf War to the exponential pace of social and technological change. It's no surprise that it also drew inspiration from the darkest elements of Sly Stone, Fela Kuti, and Miles Davis and, as the press kit put it, 'took improvised funk to extremes of abstraction and evil'—a description that certainly applies to tracks like 'Swastika Eyes,' 'Exterminator,' 'Blood Money,' and 'Insect Royalty.'

Shields's 'If They Move, Kill 'Em' remix, now retitled 'MBV Arkestra,' is included on the album alongside two new tracks featuring his guitar and mixing prowess, 'Accelerator' and 'Shoot Speed/Kill Light.' The former qualifies as one of his all-time great efforts and one of the best songs Primal Scream ever committed to tape. Gillespie later recalled telling Shields, 'You don't know how happy you made me—I made a punk rock record at last.'[9] Innes agreed, calling the song 'the best racket we've ever made.'[10] If you wanted to know what a modern take on The Stooges or MC5 should sound like, 'Accelerator' was the answer.

The track originated at a session that had been booked for the band and jazz legend Pharoah Sanders, until the planned collaboration fell through when Sanders's manager doubled the fees previously agreed to at the last minute. Undeterred, the band used the time to quickly bash out 'Accelerator' instead. The first mix was reportedly atrocious, with Shields recalling that with the speakers turned up to full blast, it sounded broken. He then realized he could use this to his advantage and 'decided to make the mix like that.'[11]

In October 2000, 'Accelerator' was released as *XTRMNTR*'s third and final single. It was also the last single ever released by Creation Records; the album, likewise, had been the label's final full-length release. In November 1999, Sony had bought out the remainder of the label for $24 million; McGee, having lost interest in running the label, had for all intents and purposes jumped ship long before the sale went through. Despite the upheaval, *XTRMNTR* went to number three on the UK album charts and sold well across Europe and in Japan. It made numerous 'best of' lists at the end of the year and has since been cited as one of the greatest albums of the twenty-first century by the *NME* and the *Guardian*, among others.

Even after *XTRMNTR*, however, the radical sound of 'If They Move,

Kill 'Em' remained a key inspiration to other artists and a calling card for Shields. Bobby Gillespie left a copy for Robert Plant after a Page & Plant show at the Shepherd's Bush Empire, and while a proposed slot opening on the duo's upcoming European tour fell through, the former Led Zeppelin frontman was sufficiently impressed that he found the time to play a wicked harmonica part on Primal Scream's next album.

That album, *Evil Heat*, was the band's first release for Sony, but despite deft contributions from the likes of Plant and Jim Reid of The Jesus & Mary Chain, it seemed to get lost in the shuffle. It deserves a close listen from Shields fans, though—as well as anyone interested in cutting-edge music in general—as he produced six of the ten tracks and contributed guitar to 'City.' By now, Shields was also a regular part of the live Scream experience, with McGee noting, 'Kevin's virtually a member of Primal Scream now.'[12] Gossip made the rounds about his considerable pot smoking while on tour with the band, while bass player Mani noted, 'We're probably a pressure-free zone for Kevin.'[13] Innes, meanwhile, gave him the nickname Bagpuss, after the 'saggy old cloth cat' of the UK children's TV show—a playful jibe at his dormancy and somewhat soft physical shape.

Overall, the fruits of Shields's collaboration with Primal Scream make a good case for the importance of his role in the larger musical collective. He helped them expand their sound in the studio and offered added heft to their live sound, initially only venturing onstage to play the songs that featured his work but by August 2001 contributing to the entire show. Innes would call this configuration the best lineup Primal Scream ever had. In 2003, the group released *PRML SCRM Live In Japan*, featuring highlights from *Evil Heat* and *XTRMNTR* along with their best-known singles. Shields appears throughout and also mixed the album with Mads Bjerke.* The live version of 'Accelerator' is particularly noteworthy, managing to sound even more extreme than the studio take.

---

* Shields was also namechecked on the cover of the twentieth-anniversary reissue of *Screamadelica*, which had a sticker on the front stating that it had been 'remastered by Primal Scream and Kevin Shields,' though the credits inside reveal that the album was actually remastered by John Davis and merely 'approved' by Shields.

•

Another band that Shields worked with around this time was the married US duo of Vincent Cafiso and Tabitha Tindale, who record together as Joy Zipper. The group had already made a splash in the UK with their debut but struggled to capitalize on that with their second album, 2002's *American Whip*, as their record company went under. Nonetheless, the time Shields ended up investing in the record—alongside many other very talented musicians, including David Holmes, Guy Fixsen, Hugo Nicholson, and Tony Doogan—is indicative of the unique music Joy Zipper made and the esteem he held it in.

Initially, Shields had agreed to a fee of around £3,000 for mixing one song, but he ended up coming to every mixing and mastering session without asking for any further remuneration. There's not really any other example of Shields volunteering so much time to another band or artist, with the possible exception of his close friend J Mascis. This presumably was because he realized how special Joy Zipper's music was, while perhaps also sensing a parallel with how he and Butcher documented their relationship on MBV's two Creation albums. Either way, *American Whip* stands out as one of the better albums Shields has contributed to, even if we don't know the full extent of his input. (Cafiso and Tindale are credited with producing and mixing the album, while Shields is listed as pitching in on five songs.) Cafiso has described his time working with Shields as 'like going to school.'[14]

Meanwhile, after MBV's unraveling in the mid-90s, the other members of the group had become involved in a number of new projects. Colm Ó Ciosóig remained in London initially and worked on some demos with Simon Johns (soon to become the bass player for Stereolab), two of which would gain release as a seven-inch under the name Clear Spot in 1998. This short-lived collaboration hinted at some very interesting music that Ó Ciosóig would never pursue further, however, as he abandoned it when he left for the San Francisco area that same year to work with Hope Sandoval of Mazzy Star. He ended up moving in with Sandoval, creating three albums with her under the moniker Hope Sandoval & The Warm

Inventions, released in 2001, 2009, and 2016, respectively. The overall sound is similar to Mazzy Star's, and Ó Cíosóig's experience as a musician and engineer is put to good use, although they lack the kind of aggressive drumming that is usually his forte.

After Debbie Googe left MBV, she began collaborating with her girlfriend, Katharine Gifford, best known for her work with Moonshake and Stereolab. As Snowpony, they released *The Slow-Motion World Of Snowpony* in 1998. Although it was produced by John McEntire of Tortoise, it didn't quite take the indie music world by storm. They released a second LP together, *Sea Shanties For Spaceships*, in 2001. Since MBV's reunion in 2008, Googe has continued to squeeze in other work, touring with Primal Scream during the summer of 2012 and playing on an ongoing basis with The Thurston Moore Group since 2014 (as part of a rhythm section with ex–Sonic Youth drummer Steve Shelley). She has also taken the opportunity to support other female artists and musicians, including Ann Waldman and Brix Smith.

Bilinda Butcher, meanwhile, stayed largely out of the musical limelight. She had a second child, Davy, before meeting and marrying Eugene Coyne (the son of the musician Kevin Coyne) and having a third child, Billy, with him. She also found her way back to one of her first loves, dance, and began teaching flamenco classes. The only non-MBV music of hers ever to see the light of day were 'Ballad Night' and 'Casino Kisschase,' a pair of tracks from the 1996 album *C**ler* by Collapsed Young, to which she contributed lyrics and vocals. Her melodies and voice 'add ethereal depth to the late-night soulful grooves,' as one *NME* reviewer put it, making it abundantly clear that no one else could ever take her role in MBV.

·

In later years, Shields would say that he wished he'd spent more time on his own music during this period and less time on his 'semi-job' working with Primal Scream and completing the occasional remix. But despite his reservations, it's clear from the outside that Shields's non-MBV work from 1995 to 2005 led to some fascinating collaborations and remixes that don't sound like anything else of his. Perhaps more importantly, they helped prepare him to go back into the studio and follow his own muse again.

Shields ended his working relationship with Primal Scream around April 2006. By that time, it was extremely clear that there was a pent-up demand for MBV's return. Other prominent artists had also sought him out for collaborations, giving him the confidence he needed to dive back into his own work again. Most crucially, two noteworthy musicians who had been profoundly affected by *Loveless* contacted him in the hope of working together, and both of them would play a key role in helping him overcome the psychological barriers he was facing in terms of making and playing his own music.

chapter thirteen

within: brian reitzell • eight hours

of equalization • grossly overpaid

and lost in translation • patti smith

and benedictory qualities • avant-

garde sheet metal distortion

'They said I was crazy, that it wasn't going to happen.'

BRIAN REITZELL, 2004[1]

'I'm quite proud of 'City Girl' because that song, even though it's used in the end credits [of *Lost in Translation*], is somehow really is that movie to me.'

BRIAN REITZELL, 2022[2]

After working on side projects throughout the mid-90s and 2000s, Shields only became ready to return to My Bloody Valentine after interacting with two other musicians who each played an important role in helping him regain the confidence to strike out on his own again.

The first was Brian Reitzell, who worked primarily as the music supervisor for the independent filmmaker Sofia Coppola. He had previously played drums in Redd Kross alongside bassist Steve MacDonald, who dated Coppola for a brief period. Through MacDonald, he eventually became one of Coppola's trusted friends, and in 1999, she asked him to be the music supervisor for her first film, *The Virgin Suicides*. Despite having no prior experience in the role, Reitzell showed he had a natural ability to work with people, enabling him to secure the songs he needed for Coppola's films while staying within their relatively small budgets.

Reitzell first met Shields at the 2001 Summer Sonic Festival. At the time, Shields was touring with Primal Scream and Reitzell was playing drums in the French band Air. Like so many other musicians, Reitzell thought *Loveless* was a masterpiece—'It was what was keeping me alive when I was still touring with Redd Kross,' he later said—so he decided to throw caution to the wind and approach its creator.[3]

The two men hit it off right away, and as they walked drunkenly through the deserted streets of Osaka at 4:30 in the morning, Reitzell decided to ask Shields if he might be interested in contributing to a film score, if ever he found a suitable project. 'Sure,' Shields replied. His only prior experience with film music had been a $5,000 payday he'd shared with J Mascis to demo a version of the *Mission Impossible 2* theme song. (In another win for mainstream American culture, Limp Bizkit got the gig instead.)

Reitzell knew of Shields's recent difficulties with Island and his inability to finish new solo work in the studio, but he seemed undeterred. His desire to help Shields get back on track creatively ultimately stemmed from both the high esteem in which he held him and his wish to put Shields back in a position to make his own music. And if he could harness Shields's amazing gifts to help Coppola and her films, so much the better. Crucially, having already accomplished a great deal at a young age through hard work, talent, charm, and luck, Reitzell wasn't intimidated by the naysayers who warned him that Shields wasn't ready to make new music.

For Coppola's first three films (*The Virgin Suicides*, *Lost in Translation*, *Marie Antoinette*), Reitzell would make mixtapes for the director that would play a role in her ultimate vision, his choice of songs helping shape the aesthetics of the movies. By the time they began working together on *Lost In Translation*, Coppola had already chosen to use MBV's 'Sometimes' in the film, so they decided to involve Shields from the earliest stages of production. This is not typical of how things are usually done; soundtracks are traditionally one of the last things in the production cycle, and their makeup is often dependent on the look of the film and on how much of the budget is left. 'This was a pretty unusual experience,' Shields remarked in 2004. 'They gave me the script before they shot the film [and] they were kind of as inclusive as possible, which is great.' Music became one of the main drivers of the film, via the mix CDs Reitzell made for Coppola and her own understanding that Shields could bring the kind of romantic melancholy that was so key to the movie's atmosphere. 'She was making a movie based on what she was listening to even when she was writing it.'[4]

Reitzell's plan was to get Shields to write again by offering him unwavering support within very specific parameters. He wanted first-rate music for Coppola's film, but he also wanted to ease the guitarist back into the saddle of making his own music. A soundtrack seemed like the perfect opportunity as it gave Shields the chance to write original material with relatively low stakes. Shields would deal solely with Reitzell and Coppola, and because he was one of many artists lined up to write music for the movie, there wouldn't be too much pressure, even if things did not work out.

As it transpired, Reitzell managed to get seven new compositions out of Shields, four of which ended up on the soundtrack. From the outside, it seemed that his attitude of 'do whatever, and we'll see what works' was the ideal strategy in terms of how Shields generally worked and how he was feeling around this time. And the timing was providential, with Shields finding his way after years in the wilderness to join Coppola in what would become both her most personal and successful film.

That didn't mean the process was quick or easy. 'City Girl,' Shields's most conspicuous contribution, is less than four minutes long, but the journey to complete it required unprecedented drudgery and dedication from Reitzell. Across three separate, weeklong sessions spanning November 2002 to March 2003, he met up with Shields in a studio in Camden. Each time, Reitzell encountered a new engineer, Shields having worn out the previous one.

Shields would only work at night, and he smoked pot constantly. He insisted that Reitzell partake too, to make sure he was in the same head space. On one occasion, it took him eight hours to get his guitar equalized properly. Hours of useless, random bits of music were recorded, but Reitzell maintained the low-pressure approach. 'I never forced Kevin into anything,' he later said.[5] Finally, after weeks of dead ends, it all came together in an instant. Reitzell was exhausted, past the point of being stoned, on the verge of falling asleep, only to hear Shields announce, 'Okay, Brian, I'm ready.'

> The guitar was so loud. Kevin's whole trip is volume, that relationship of extreme volume with microphones. There were no effects pedals. He uses fewer effects than anyone I ever worked with. It's pure science, it's that physical air moving: that's how he gets those sounds. He started playing these chords, and a few minutes later, that song was done. It took weeks to get to that point, and we played it once.[6]

Reitzell further expanded on how they got to that point in another interview, echoing earlier sentiments Shields had made about *Loveless* and how it was basically about recording moments of spontaneity as they arose naturally. It was about eight in the morning, around the time their workday typically ended, when Shields ordered Reitzell to get behind the drum kit. He then started playing the chords to 'City Girl,' teaching the track to Reitzell during that one take. After overdubbing the bass, vocals, and a second guitar, they were done.

> Literally it's a guitar; there's no distortion pedals, either. It's just a guitar, a certain Vox head, a little speaker, and a microphone … you cannot be in the room, it will kill you. Your bones will break, it's that loud. What happens with the translation of the volume, the microphone, the desk, the EQ, the dude is a master of EQ. He's got really sensitive ears. I love it. Those chords in that song I think are absolutely beautiful. It's two guitars, a drum set, and a bass, that's all it is.[7]

The 'City Girl' session offers a great illustration of Shields's creative process. It may take forever for things to line up, but when they do, the music flows like water. Shields would call the session 'liberating.'[8] Three more songs resulted, including two with vocals, which Shields was happy enough with that he noted that they might eventually see the light of day later.

Shields would record three further subdued and fragile tracks that ended up on the soundtrack ('Goodbye,' 'Ikebana,' and 'Are You Awake?') soon after. He went on to say of the challenge:

> It was a giant learning curve for me because I hadn't done anything like this before. I was barely aware of the language of music that's not essentially just for your ears. I was just learning as I went along. I suppose we [himself and Reitzell] were under the influence of the film. Looking at it and trying different things. In the end, just the physical movement of the film, that was a delicacy. And I supposed that's why I ended up doing stuff that was delicate.[9]

Lost In Translation received glowing reviews and great word of mouth. It earned $118 million on a $4 million budget and secured four Oscar nominations, with Coppola winning one for best original screenplay, as well as a BAFTA nomination for best soundtrack (which it lost out to *Cold Mountain* by T-Bone Burnett and Gabriel Yared). Without realizing it, the film also introduced millions of people to Kevin Shields's talents as a songwriter. The *Guardian* speculated that his work on the soundtrack, which developed a cult following along with the movie, might have earned him his first million-dollar payday.

Reitzell next worked with Coppola on *Marie Antoinette*, for which, in a feat of amazing interpersonal diplomacy, he managed to work his way into Malcolm McLaren's confidence and get hold of the original tapes for 'Fools Rush In' and 'I Want Candy' by Bow Wow Wow.[*] Thanks to the success of *Lost In Translation*, Reitzell had a great deal of latitude with Coppola's new film, and by all accounts he 'grossly overpaid' Shields to assemble relatively straightforward quadraphonic mixes of the two tracks.[10] *Marie Antoinette: Original Soundtrack* was released in 2006, just

---

[*] McLaren had previously driven EMI crazy by holding onto the original master recordings of many of his acts, including the Sex Pistols.

as Shields left Primal Scream and began to work on the CD remasters of the MBV albums.* His Bow Wow Wow mixes do bring a tiny bit of unrealized potential out of the original recordings, but the work he did was presumably not commensurate with the large sum he received for it.

Shields repaid the favor some years later, when he contributed to Reitzell's 2014 solo album *Auto Music*, playing organ on the opening track, 'Last Summer.' Like Shields, Reitzell had a fundamental interest in the mechanics of sound and would go to whatever necessary lengths to realize his ideas. Explaining the concept behind the album, he recalled, 'The first piece that I did was an experiment based on something Kevin Shields told me that he did for the song "Sometimes." It was about how he EQed and layered guitars. So I took that concept and did my own experimenting, and then I actually had Kevin play on it.'[11] Influenced by Krautrock rhythms, cult soundtracks of every sort, and composers like Toru Takemitsu (best known for his film soundtrack work of the 60s and 70s), the resulting music works on several levels: you can absorb it fully while relaxing, but it's also great to listen to while your conscious mind is occupied with something else.

•

After Reitzell, it was Patti Smith who would next play a critical role in helping Shields get back on track creatively. Another huge fan of *Loveless*, the punk poet invited him to collaborate before ever getting to know him or even discussing the project when she curated the 2005 edition of the annual Meltdown Festival in London. She approached him specifically to back a narrative poem she'd written about her intimate friendship with photographer Robert Mapplethorpe, who died of AIDS in 1989. Smith heard something in *Loveless* that led her to believe Shields would intuitively understand the project.

---

* The timing may not have been coincidental. Speaking to *Uncut* in 2018, Reitzell speculated that Shields felt financially trapped in Primal Scream—not the worst place to be, but a trap nonetheless. If true, the rumored payout for *Marie Antoinette* would have given him the financial cushion he needed to get back to working on his own music.

Shields may also have seemed like the logical choice for this project because he shared many attributes with Jimi Hendrix, a key inspiration behind Smith's groundbreaking 1975 album *Horses* and its goal to 'merge poetry with soundscapes.'[12] After Shields agreed to participate, he and Smith spent a few hours together one afternoon while she explained how she envisioned the project. There was no other preparation.

The collaboration consisted of Smith reading her extended poem 'The Coral Sea' while Shields provided an improvised accompaniment to the drama of the story in real time, laying on a sofa with his guitar and utilizing various pedals and processors, all in front of a live audience. Having considered himself 'on holiday' between 1998 and 2005, he had not played his Jazzmaster using his glide-guitar style for years—not even when Reitzell specifically asked him to utilize those methods for *Lost In Translation*. (Shields declined.) After meeting Smith, however, he decided it was time to reconnect with his signature technique.

Reviewing the performance for the *Guardian*, Alexis Petridis wrote, 'The effect is magical, in that what he does with his hands frequently bears no relation to what comes out of his amplifier. At times, his guitar drones woozily, matching the onstage films of sea images. At others, it sounds like a church organ. At the piece's climax, he prods an effect pedal and something approximating a protracted thunderstorm consumes the venue.'[13]

Looking back on the project in a 2021 interview with Keith Cameron, Shields said, 'Patti was the catalyst for me to go back and re-explore everything, the way I used to do it. ... When Patti asked me to do that, I got inspired. I spent an evening familiarizing myself with all these guitars and tunings I hadn't touched since '96 or '97. We didn't rehearse. It was a wonderful opportunity to work with somebody who was truly a kind of genius at being improvisational.'[14] It was like he had been hypnotized by Smith into being able to go back to playing that way. Cameron also surmised that this was the turning point for Shields in terms of writing his own material again. 'There was,' he wrote, 'a benedictory quality to Smith's approach that allowed him to safely reconcile with the past.'[15]

After Meltdown, two further performances by the duo were recorded and eventually prepared for release, which involved Shields removing some 3,200 aural imperfections. The album was eventually issued in 2008, with Smith writing in the liner notes, 'It was a privilege working with Kevin, a gifted, humble, and extremely confident musician.'

Not everyone was impressed with the results. For Alex Gillis of the Australian magazine *Time Off*, Shields 'doesn't do anything remarkable here, but what he does do is soften Smith's coarse voice.' Ultimately, he concluded, 'Two legends do not a legendary release make!'[16] Barry Walters of *Spin* got more out of the collaboration, noting how Shields's playing 'matches the ebb and flow of her morphing prose with thunderstorms of guitar sustain that weep and roar empathetically.'[17]

•

Although *The Coral Sea* was one of Shields's last well-publicized collaborations before he returned to MBV full-time, he was also working in relative obscurity at the same time on another project: the sound mix for Douglas Gordon and Philippe Parreno's 2006 documentary *Zidane: A 21st Century Portrait*. This novel documentary follows the French star footballer Zinedine Zidane throughout a whole ninety-minute match, regardless of where on the field the action is taking place, and is set to a soundtrack by Mogwai. One review focused on how Shields, credited as 'noise consultant,' elevated the overall production:

> That label of his contribution might seem slightly absurd, but in fact, Shields's contribution to *Zidane* is anything but inconsequential. Any My Bloody Valentine acolyte that sees the movie in the theater will hear the unmistakable sound of Shields as he wields layers of crowd noise with the same hallucinatory impact he's brought to the electric guitar. His contribution proves to be as important as Mogwai's score, and perhaps a perfect corollary to Darius Khondji's seventeen-camera cinematography. Shields makes a symphony from stadium noise, and the result lures one deeper into a viewer facsimile of Zinedine Zidane's consciousness.[18]

Unfortunately, I was not able to see this film in a theatre with a suitably significant sound system, but if anyone could make crowd noise sing, I would imagine Kevin Shields is up to the task.

•

After being released by Island Records in late 2001, Shields had sold his house in Streatham, leaving its bad memories behind, and bought a place in Camden. There, he began a relationship with a young band initially known as The Beatings, who helped him build his new studio. In exchange, he gave them studio time and produced and mixed their first (and only) album.

The group's first single, 'Bad Feeling,' was released in 2002 and was the only record they made before they were forced to change their name—which it turned out was already in use—to The Beat Up. The catchy single has some rather extreme guitar tones, though they weren't the kind you would expect to find on an MBV record. Still, Shields enjoyed the challenge the band presented, explaining, 'It's kinda got a really serrated and raw and in-your-face sort of sound. It's something you just can't EQ, you can't get a plug-in to make this happen … [they're] guitar sounds that feel like if you were to rub them across your face, it would really hurt.'[19]

With ten tracks produced and mixed by Shields (along with six worthy B-sides), The Beat Up's *Black Rays Defence* was released in 2005 to mixed reviews. Some of the negative assessments give the impression that the album suffered as a result of the unusually high expectations attached to it due to Shields's involvement. Pat Gilbert, who reviewed it for *Mojo*, was one critic who was able to successfully put the record in context:

> The consummate auteur, [Shields] treats The Beat Up's fast, gutter-snipe rock'n'roll guitars exactly as you'd imagine, creating layers of thick, nasty fuzz noise riddled with shrieking lead. … However, bluesier tracks like 'When I See My Mind To Forget' and 'The Flame' expose the group's genuine originality and unexpected lyrical depth—dark psycho poetry about girls, drug-befuddlement,

and self-doubt, unquestionably meritorious of the avant-garde sheet metal distortion … first class punk rock.[20]

With the band coming to Shields with solid songs set to a wide variety of dynamics, listeners are treated to the appealing album from a hungry young band with an uncommon authenticity to whom the closest point of comparison might be The Icarus Line. But they had a not-so-secret weapon in Kevin Shields. The single that proceeded his involvement, 'Jailhouse,' sounds run of the mill when compared to the album.

When examining these many side projects, a few things come to mind. So long as Kevin Shields's name (or MBV's) is not at the top of the marquee, he is able to get things done on time without feeling the weight of the world on him; we have a solid ten years of great music that is worth going back over outside of MBV. Additionally, one can't help but notice his genuine curiosity about *all* sound in any context. Whether it's to accompany spoken word, dance, still images, or film, he intuitively understands their relationship to sound.

Side projects like these would take a backseat now as Shields again assumed the mantle as MBV's leader, but they nevertheless offer a wide-ranging insight into his work that only reinforces his spirit of exploration and his unique musical abilities.* Now, however, after collaborating with an unprecedented number of artists across the past decade, he was refocusing on MBV. Though there hadn't been any new music from the band for a long time, the genius of *Loveless* had continued to reverberate with listeners, and the interest levels were about to reach a tipping point.

---

* For a complete list of Shields's side projects, visit turnmyheadintosound.com

interlude six

who are mbv really?

Almost all of MBV's records include the following credits, or a variation thereof:

KEVIN SHIELDS guitar, vocals, samplers

BILINDA BUTCHER guitar, vocals

DEB GOOGE bass

COLM Ó CÍOSÓIG drums, samplers

In interviews, however, they have said that their roles in the band go beyond what these credits suggest, while Shields has always made it clear that he is responsible for writing all of MBV's music and for a great deal of what goes on in the studio. In fact, because he spent so many months working alone on *Loveless*, the record has come to be seen in some ways as a solo effort. So how exactly did the group work *as* a group? What did each of the members do? Were there actually two MBVs—one that put together work in the studio and the other that played the songs live?

It's well documented that all four members were present for MBV's recording sessions in 1987 and 1988, making for a true band atmosphere, where everyone contributed and gave their input. By 1989, however, Butcher and Googe were showing up less and less, and after Ó Cíosóig's breakdown, Shields worked largely by himself (alongside an engineer) to complete *Glider* and much of *Tremolo* and *Loveless*.

So much goes on within any band to make recordings and tours happen, however, and it goes far beyond the primary instrument each band member plays. I suspect one reason why the album credits list all four band members is because Shields wanted to make sure there was no misunderstanding of MBV's existence as a four-person venture, even if—with the exception of Butcher's role as muse, lyricist, and vocalist—it was Shields who was the primary creative force. Everyone was essential, and onstage if not in the studio, they all fulfilled their roles as they were listed on the records. And what they explored and achieved live likely carried over in some spiritual, esoteric way into the studio.

In 2004, Butcher broke a ten-year silence when she gave an interview to Swedish journalist/editor Ika Johannesson for *Sex* magazine.* It was her first in-depth interview of any kind, conducted at a time when she was unsure if the band would ever reform, and in it she offered some particularly candid views:

> Kevin always wanted to uphold the myth about us being a band. In interviews, he never said that he was the one making all the music. He would probably be pissed off if he knew that I'm saying this now! But time has flown since then. I think it was obvious that Kevin did everything. Colm had good ideas, but since we were always in a hurry when we made records, Kevin asked us not to play anything.[1]

Butcher's comment somewhat downplays Ó Cíosóig's input, particularly early on the band's career. During their relatively anonymous formative years, when Shields was struggling to say anything truly original with his guitar, many of the earliest reviews of their live performances singled out the positive impact of Ó Cíosóig's ferocious drumming. He would often be compared to the Who's Keith Moon, and deservedly so. After seeing MBV open for the Soup Dragons in 1987, *Melody Maker*'s Glasgow correspondent, Tom Morton, called Colm 'the most astonishing drummer I've ever seen or heard' before lamenting, 'unfortunately, he's the only good thing about this band. Great haircuts, though.'[2]

---

* The interview later reappeared online (undated) at TotallyDublin.ie, just as MBV's reunion was being promoted, which caused some confusion.

Besides Moon, the other drummer Ó Cíosóig was regularly compared with was Animal, the frenzied, deranged, and misunderstood percussionist for Dr. Teeth & The Electric Mayhem in *The Muppet Show*. The official video for 'Only Shallow' features him playing both in real time and slowed down, and it's probably the best source of what his manic playing looks like. A little before the three-minute mark, he is intensely lost in the moment; watching it, it's not hard to imagine how his demeanor would invite flippant comparisons like those mentioned above.

'My technique is totally wrong,' Ó Cíosóig himself would note in 1988. 'The timing, everything, I can't play quietly. I have to play hard and fast otherwise it goes wrong. Sometimes I just go mental because it's fun.'[3] A year later, he admitted in a TV interview that he sometimes drifted off while playing. 'Using so much energy I get such a…high [from] adrenaline.'[4] (These comments might be more indicative of a young Ó Cíosóig's inability to accept a compliment, however, than a self-conscious admission of any inadequacies on his part.)

Ó Cíosóig is often portrayed as the unsung hero on *Isn't Anything*, given the prominence of his drumming. Later, even as the band's rhythms slowed down and became less busy, he remained a jack-of-all-trades, switching his focus to sampling and drum programming. In 2012, Shields noted how important he was as a collaborator, revealing that Ó Cíosóig would take on the responsibility of getting familiar with the relevant technologies, freeing up Shields to focus on other areas. And it was an unqualified disaster, as far as Shields was concerned, that Ó Cíosóig wasn't available to play when they started *Loveless*.

While he is a skilled musician, Ó Cíosóig also has a special chemistry with Shields in the studio. The most obvious point of comparison is Ringo Starr. Starr may not have been the most technically perfect drummer, but there was no one on earth who could have worked so well with the other Beatles. When one hears Shields and Ó Cíosóig's ferocious playing together on 'Feed Me With Your Kiss,' or the push and pull of 'You Never Should,' it's difficult to imagine two musicians being more in sync with each other. As a drummer, engineer, and friend, Ó Cíosóig was an indispensable collaborator from day one; without him, Shields's journey might not have been anywhere near as successful as it was.

The same could be said of Googe, even if her own feelings about the band were complicated at times. She wasn't under any illusion that her live bass playing would have the same feel as Shields's, and she knew it was much more efficient for him to write and play the parts. And, with Ó Cíosóig and Shields having known each other for so long, and with Butcher and Shields being in a relationship, she felt superfluous and estranged at times, but she was nevertheless a valued member of the band.

It was the ferocious attack of all four members playing as a unit that caught the attention of Alan McGee and Dick Green in early 1988. This, in turn, got them their first recording deal with Creation, which led to their revolutionary records of the late 80s and early 90s. Googe's muscular approach to bass playing was well-suited to Ó Cíosóig's unbridled live percussion. The two of them worked in lockstep, show after show, providing a powerful rhythm section in support of Shields's and Butcher's guitars and vocals.

'The band becomes a proper band mainly outside of the studio, when we tour and stuff,' Shields noted in 1991. 'That's when it's a real band, and that identity and that kind of atmosphere gets carried into the studio. It's the atmosphere that really tends to dictate.'[5] He would continue to make similar points years later. 'Live, it's kinda its own thing,' he said in 2018, making clear his appreciation for his bandmates. 'Debbie very much puts her personality into the way she plays, and so does Colm. That's the cool thing about not playing with just a bunch of session people—they're people with their own way of doing things.'[6] Asked by the French magazine *Les Inrockuptibles* if he felt possessive about the band, Shields replied, 'You have to be realistic. I'm the leader of the band. I'm doing the driving more than the others. But they're more down to earth than me. They allow me to function … I need them to realize my ideas. Besides, I'm the handicap when we need to be dynamic, like onstage. I'm the weak link there. My place is in the studio, which is really where the spirit of the band comes out.'[7]

It's difficult to see MBV's career panning out the way it did—

particularly between 1988 and 1991—if the four members didn't care so much about each other as individuals or about the success of the band as a whole. Shields's comment that they allow him to 'function' is particularly telling in light of how things played out at Island. Besides one or two snide comments he made in 1997, they never turned on each other, acted out, or imploded.

Butcher made another revealing insight about the dynamics of the band in her interview with *Sex* magazine when she noted, 'We never got the chance to go through the same process as with the earlier albums. Everyone was fighting, and we went our separate ways. That's why Kevin couldn't be creative. It sounds exaggerated—that he was the goose that was gonna lay the golden egg and that he should've been wrapped in cotton wool to be able to create the next masterpiece—but the feeling of us being a band didn't exist anymore.'

Even though Shields wrote the majority of the music, everyone's input was needed to make it work. 'He knew that too,' Butcher emphasized, 'and that's why he was so frustrated. He understood that it wouldn't be good enough if we didn't all fight together.'[8]

Butcher and Shields have both spoken of each member of the band holding the power to veto any part of a song, and how none of them ever wanted to let the others down. Right back in the afterglow of the *You Made Me Realise* EP, Shields had noted, 'I write most of the songs, but it's not like someone solo with a backing band. Each song reflects the character of everyone's playing.'[9]

Interpersonal dynamics are a strange thing, and they can't always be articulated clearly. On his own, Shields probably would have become some sort of noteworthy cult figure no matter what, but the prominence and financial security he and the band enjoy today is a result of a chemistry that goes beyond his own work. Even with all of his talent, it's hard to see him having the same success without the other members of the band alongside him. And they in turn were not merely his backing band but instead members of a family of outsiders that they had all chosen to be part of. This became most evident during their public reunion in 2008, in particular during the interviews they did after receiving their *Mojo* 'Classic Album' award. You can't fake that kind of camaraderie and affection.

Asked in 2021 how MBV had been able to stay together for so long, Shields chalked it up to a mingling of complementary personalities. He then offered a rundown of the roles each member played, saying, 'It's a mix of personalities. Each takes the lead, depending on the context. Colm is in charge on the bus, Debbie runs the party after a show, dressing up and goofing around. Bilinda dictates the atmosphere of the band, and I take care of the music. ... The band is balanced. When we broke up, we didn't fall apart. We stayed in touch. That's why we were able to get back together quite easily. It's thanks to that balance of energy that we're still going.'[10]

When you put it like that, it all sounds so simple.

chapter fourteen

within: newfound recognition • red,

green, yellow, purple, and blue •

a proper live show • barry hogan •

remastering for cd

'Maybe that was the last great rock record that was going somewhere new. Instead of staying where everyone else was, going backward.'

BOBBY GILLESPIE, 2010[1]

Although it had been over a decade since the release of *Loveless*, it was clear from the coverage Shields received for his work on *Lost In Translation* that demand was building for MBV to return. In the intervening years, the press continued to publicize his various collaborations, while a wide range of artists and critics regularly cited the importance of his work. Gavin Friday of The Virgin Prunes, whose advice the band had sought when they were just starting out, brought things full circle when interviewed for the Creation Records documentary, *Upside Down*, describing *Loveless* as what might happen if Lou Reed's *Metal Machine Music* 'became a pop album.'[2]

As new generations of musicians—professional and otherwise—discovered MBV, a stream of tribute albums devoted to the group and their catalog began to appear in all manner of genres and languages: *Red Loveless* (Spanish), *Pas De Printemps Pour Marnie* (French), *Yellow Loveless* (Japanese), *Indonesian Loveless* (Indonesian), and *Blue Loveless* (Korean), among others. Other versions include Kenny Feinstein's heartfelt *Loveless: Hurts To Love*, Athens, Georgia's Japancakes' eccentric instrumental take, and a classically orchestrated version of 'To Here Knows When' featuring vocals by the Canadian opera singer Rachel Zeffira.

Deep down, Shields was always confident that *Loveless* was a great record, but he also suspected that it would take time for people to catch up with it. That process really seemed to pick up speed as the new millennium neared and various magazines began running lists of the best music of the decade. 'It became apparent that it really connected with a lot of people,' he noted. 'Well, after having seven years of people not really getting it and ignoring it, it's sort of a nice balance!'[3]

At the same time, MBV's connection to bands like Ride and Chapterhouse fell away with each passing year, their status now cemented instead as indie-rock trailblazers and among the canon of the all-time greats. To cite one random example, in 2002, the filmmaking magazine *RES* published a special issue primarily devoted to movies and technology that had 'restarted' the medium. It also included a column about music that had proven similarly seminal and forward-thinking. The list of records the magazine's editors considered 'progressive in spirit and futuristic in feel' included *The Velvet Underground & Nico*, *Bitches Brew*, *The Dark Side Of The Moon*, *Head Hunters*, *Another Green World*, *Trans-Europe Express*, *Low*, *Planet Rock*, *Selected Ambient Works 85–92*, and *Loveless*.

•

In the years after the band's dissolution, Shields would see Googe around town on occasion, at gigs and family events, and he would catch up with his old friend Ó Cíosóig when the latter came back to the UK from San Francisco. But he had little contact with Butcher. She was on the opposite side of the Thames, so they didn't cross paths that often, while their romantic history meant they needed time before they could reach out to each other. All four of them were in the same room for the first time since their breakup when they went to see Ó Cíosóig play with Hope Sandoval & The Warm Inventions in London in 2002. Their first public reunion, however, would have to wait until 2008, when they appeared together at the Mojo Music Awards to receive the 'Classic Album' award for *Loveless*.

Even with all of the new accolades, the possibility of a reunion was still up in the air in terms of when it would happen or if it would happen at all. Fans and critics knew not to get their hopes up too quickly. In 2006, Paul Tollet, a promoter at Goldenvoice, had offered MBV $300,000 to headline the following year's Coachella Festival—an offer that would eventually increase to $1,000,000 for the 2008 event. The rumor mill quickly started up again, with *Billboard* running an article entitled 'My Bloody Valentine Mulling Coachella Reunion.' While the group ultimately passed on Tollet's initial offer, deciding that they did not yet have everything in place to make it happen, he had planted a seed.[4]

Meanwhile, Barry Hogan, the founder of All Tomorrow's Parties (ATP), had been pursuing Shields to curate and/or play at one of his festivals. A decade of correspondence passed between them, during which time Shields attended various ATP events and watched it grow into arguably the best-curated music festival around. With its humble origins and independence, ATP seemed like the ideal partner for MBV if they ever decided to play together again. As the writer Sharon Nichols put it, 'What makes Hogan's events special is that he chooses a band as curator to select the lineup: kinda like a mix tape for the stage, he explains.'[5]

Hogan, like many others, didn't understand the hype around MBV when he first saw them live in 1991, but as the years passed, he eventually got it, and he had let Shields know that he was interested in backing the group financially when the time came. So, when Shields told Hogan that he was thinking of getting the band back together, the promoter immediately went into action.

The reunion wasn't about cashing in. MBV could have easily opted for a much smaller effort with a smaller outlay and quickly come away with a huge windfall. Instead, the undertaking with Hogan was about properly presenting their music in a live setting for the first time. Shields was committed to investing the money and taking the time to 'do it right,' as he put it, and having only really toured for six months following the release of *Loveless*, they were all still excited to play the songs from the album when the opportunity arose.

Shields always felt that the band never had a proper PA system on their earlier tours, and though he did everything he could to make each show sound as true to his vision as possible, it always felt compromised. Because they were dropped by Creation soon after the release of *Loveless*, the only financial support they received for the ensuing tour was some publishing money from EMI that the label had negotiated earlier. As such, in direct contrast to Shields's perfectionism in the studio, the band's live shows had always been a case of making do. Now, however, he was truly galvanized; the deficiencies in their live sound that had been on his mind since 1992 could finally be fixed, and he could approach playing live much as he had the recording of *Loveless*—free from any compromises.

ATP loaned Shields around $600,000 to buy equipment—analog mixing desks and amplifiers, various pedals and rack-mounted processors, including duplicate pieces so they didn't have to take things apart and rearrange them between songs—and pay for other sundry expenses involved in a proper setup, such as engineers and a suitable rehearsal space. 'We could actually buy equipment and rehearse properly and do it really well,' Shields said. 'Last time we toured, it didn't sound right. We didn't have control of the environment. So we were kind of excited to play the songs properly.'[6]

In an interview with *Guitar Player*, Michael Brennan, the front-of-house engineer for the 2008 tour, said that the PA MBV used was partly inspired by the 'Wall Of Sound' the Grateful Dead had in 1974; it used exactly twelve guitar cabinets, with Shields's guitar able to go as loud as 116 decibels. Photographs of the setup show dozens of processors, pedals, and rack-mounted equipment, as well as a variety of amplifier heads and cabinets.

Properly reproducing MBV's music live required a specific blend of sounds with enough volume as well as a certain kind of energy and passion from the other band members. They spent a total of seven weeks buying and testing the equipment and integrating it into their setup to figure out what worked best. They then committed to their first reunion shows at London's Roundhouse Theatre, first playing a pair of rehearsal gigs for family and friends at the Institute Of Contemporary Arts (ICA) to ensure they could get through all the songs.

The first three shows at the Roundhouse sold out in six minutes, prompting the band to add two more. MBV played their first full concert in sixteen years on June 20, 2008, with the run of shows quickly becoming the kinds of events that fans just *had to* attend, regardless of price, many in the audience no doubt wondering if this might be their last or only chance to see the band play live.

The group often opened these shows with 'I Only Said.' Now that they could obtain any piece of gear that had been used to record the song—or, alternately, purchase the best substitute to be used in a live setting—they could finally offer a closer approximation to the studio version, and it seemed fitting to open their new shows with something so massive yet relatively straightforward as 'I Only Said.' They had played it on previous tours, but it had never sounded anything like this, with its massive main guitar riff grinding away. Shields must have felt a certain delight each night as he kicked off the shows, having had to wait sixteen years to finally present the *Loveless* songs as they were meant to be heard.

Although the band used a much wider array of equipment than on earlier tours, the set lists in 2008 didn't include any songs they hadn't previously played live, with tracks like 'Loomer' and 'Swallow' remaining impossible to play as a four-piece outside of a studio. Not that it mattered. The band's extended hiatus had only increased their fans' (and the media's) affection for the band, which Shields saw as both weird and unintentionally brilliant. Noting that *Loveless* had come out at the same time as Nirvana's *Nevermind,* he felt the album hadn't received as much publicity at the time of its release as it might have, but also that the fact that they were cited more regularly by other bands and fans than by the press gave them more credibility and probably also a longer lifespan.

Hogan's support of the band was rewarded with MBV's first American show in fifteen years, for which they headlined and curated one day of the three-day ATP festival in Monticello, New York, in September 2008. For the rest of the bill, MBV chose a number of friends and peers who also put artistry before commerce, including Mogwai, Yo La Tengo, Dinosaur Jr., Lilys, Mercury Rev, Bob Mould, Gemma Hayes, Spectrum, The Wounded Knees (Jimi Shields's band), The Brian Jonestown Massacre, Robin Guthrie of Cocteau Twins, EPMD, and … And You Will Know Us By The Trail Of Dead.

Speaking to the *Village Voice* on the eve of the event, Hogan described MBV's performances as 'the most sonic force of sound I've ever heard in my entire life. People are going to lose their minds when they see it. It sounds 1,000 times better than anything you have seen in a long time. You're in for a treat.'[7] (It wasn't all fun and games, however. While he enjoyed the high of seeing MBV play together again, Hogan was seemingly unprepared for their very onerous technical requirements. 'Kevin Shields is not exactly a laugh a minute,' he noted in another interview. 'It should be fun, but he had all these demands.'[8])

The ATP event would be followed by seven more sold-out performances across the USA, grossing almost a million dollars. The tour then moved on to Spain, France, Canada, Denmark, Ireland, Japan, Norway, Belgium, the Netherlands, Portugal, and Sweden, before the band returned to the UK to headline and curate another ATP festival. This edition, billed as 'The Nightmare Before Christmas,' ran from December 4 to December 6, 2009, in Somerset, England, and included an even wider array of performers: Sonic Youth, De La Soul, EPMD, Sun Ra Arkestra, the Horrors, Buzzcocks, Spectrum, Fucked Up, Le Volume Courbe, Wounded Knees, The Pastels, Witch, Lilys, A Place To Bury Strangers, J Mascis + The Fog, Bob Mould, Swervedriver, Dirty Three, Primal Scream, Television Personalities, Serena Maneesh, Yo La Tengo, Brightblack Morning Light, The Membranes, Josh T. Pearson, Ariel Pink, Lightning Bolt, That Petrol Emotion, múm, Harmony Rockets, Th' Faith Healers, School of Seven Bells, No Age, Robin Guthrie, The Robert Coyne Outfit, and The Pains Of Being Pure At Heart.

•

Shields was also taking new steps to release more MBV material, though none of it was technically new. Sony had bought out Creation completely in 1999, and in 2001, Shields approached the label to see about digitally remastering the band's four Creation EPs for CD and putting them out as a single package, along with some rarities and unreleased tracks from sessions in 1988 and 1989. For distribution purposes, MBV had been signed to various labels around the globe via Creation, yet most of those contracts, with the exception of the one with Sire Records in America, had expired by 1994. After that, the rights reverted first to Creation and then to Sony. Eventually, it was decided that Shields might as well remaster *everything* from the Creation years for compact disc, so *Loveless* and *Isn't Anything* were added to the project as well.

Remastering might have seemed like a straightforward enough idea, but there were several obstacles for Shields to get past in order to make it happen. His first problem arose when Metropolis Studio, where the original tapes were stored, said they couldn't be found. Shields was convinced that someone was deliberately putting barriers in his way. 'They wanted me to use a digital source and save loads of money,' he explained.[9] In his mind, this meant turning the remastering process into an exercise in making the songs louder without any concern for improving their fidelity, whereas proper remastering required going back to the original multitrack analog tapes. As long as those tapes stayed missing, the rights to them would not revert back to the band. Shields told Sony that he was going to bring in the police to help look for them. He believed his threat made the tapes 'magically, suddenly reappear,' but it's impossible to know this for sure, with the different regime changes at Sony Music. (It's also difficult to know if the police could have really done anything to help.)[10]

After finally getting his hands on the original multitrack tapes, Shields then had to deal with other issues of breach of contract and bad faith. He would finally overcome everything and complete all of the digital remastering for compact disc around 2011, with the label duly announcing plans for their release for the following year. 'We have really enjoyed working on these hugely iconic re-issues with Kevin,' a Sony representative said, 'and can't wait for the release.'[11] The label did not address any of Shields's issues or explain why the process had taken so long, although, with his track record, it's hard to know which party was most responsible for the delays.

Everything the band recorded for Creation was released in remastered form across three titles on Sony, containing five CDs: *Isn't Anything*, a two-CD set entitled *EP's 1988–1991*, and a package containing two separate remasters of *Loveless* taken from two different sources.

EP's 1988–1991 features the band's four Creation EPs plus three previously unreleased tracks and four rarities: the two instrumental tracks originally given away on a seven-inch single included with the first five thousand copies of *Isn't Anything*; 'Sugar,' which was first released on a flexi-disc with *The Catalogue* magazine in 1989; and 'Glider (Full Length Version),' which until now had only been available as the B-side to the twelve-inch release of Andrew Weatherall's 'Soon' remix. All four had already been released in digital formats on one obscure compilation or another over the years, but now they were available in one place at last, alongside three previously unreleased tracks from 1988–89: 'How Do You Do It' and 'Good for You' were leftovers from the *Feed Me With Your Kiss* / *Isn't Anything* sessions, while 'Angel' stemmed from one of the aborted 1989 EP sessions.*

A new version of *EP's 1988–1991* would appear in 2021 after MBV signed a distribution deal with Domino Records. From the outside, the only difference was a change of logo on the sleeve, but in fact, Shields had also appended two unlisted bonus tracks to the second disc. The first is a not particularly interesting alternate mix of 'Don't Ask Why,' but the second has a providence worth noting. Though it has come to be known as 'What Can You See,' the previously unknown and officially untitled track was recorded sometime in 1989 and was, according to Shields, a precursor to 'Soon.'[12]

The remastering of *Isn't Anything* was fairly straightforward. The new release, consisting of one disc with no bonus tracks, improved the analog-

---

* When *EP's 1988–1991* was first planned for release in 2004, initial promotional copies included another unreleased track from 1989, 'Kevin Song' (aka 'Just Like Us'), but it was pulled from the 2012 release, reportedly because Shields was unhappy with the mix and was unable to locate the original multitrack recordings so that he could rework it.

to-digital conversion and raised the volume. The remastering of *Loveless*, by contrast, was much more involved. As Shields later explained to *Pitchfork*, because the album has such a wide dynamic range, it is actually a very quiet record. 'Most of it is about four or five decibels below zero, while most modern records are about six or seven above zero. That's a huge difference in volume, because every three decibels is perceived as being twice as loud.'[13] The remastering process wasn't about just turning up the volume; instead, it involved the creation a new set of tracks that would work with the updated technology of compact discs. That was no easy task—especially if you wanted it to sound perfect.

Shields ended up presenting two digital remasters of *Loveless* on CD. The first is from the same PCM-1630 digital videocassette the band had originally used, while the second was taken from the half-inch analog tape that Shields had been unable to use previously (with the interstitial tracks recorded from a digital source). Remastering those tapes was only made possible through recent technological improvements, allowing him to correct the stereo image so that the guitars are positioned correctly in the mix. 'The analog one is clearer and more in your face so you have much more of a sense of human beings playing it,' he said after its release.[14]

As far as Shields was concerned, for those who listen to music closely and care about such things, the difference between the two CDs is plain to hear. 'They're both good for different reasons,' he explained. 'The digital one is slightly more like an inner head trip and the analog one is more physical, like you're conscious that some people did this.'[15]

MBV had come a long way through a decade of being out of the public eye. But though they were back to playing live, Shields was talking more readily to the press, and the remasters were giving fans brand-new ways to experience the band's earlier work, there was still one glaring elephant in the room. Would there be a new record?

chapter fifteen

within: accepting no substitutes •

m b v • the end of the world •

financial independence • fully

analog vinyl • andy savours •

the correct version

'When seventeenth-century Irish philosopher Edmund Burke said: All that is necessary for the triumph of evil is that good men do nothing, he was thinking about Kevin Shields.'

JOHN DORAN, *THE QUIETUS* CO-FOUNDER, 2013[1]

Economics 101 teaches the basic concept of substitution. When one particular product isn't available, people inevitably substitute in another one—or, at least, that's the theory. If apples aren't available, then people buy oranges, and they are usually able to make do. But what if there is no real substitute for what you need? For more than a few devotees, Kevin Shields's music has become a genuine necessity. So, perhaps unsurprisingly, as the deadlines passed and the follow-up to *Loveless* failed to appear, the invective began to appear. The remasters were something, but what MBV fans really wanted was new material, and they were growing impatient.

Things seemed to come to a head for fans toward the end of 2012, as the gap between releases entered its third decade. Brian Anderson made his opinion clear in an essay entitled 'Watch My Bloody Valentine's Kevin Shields Reaffirm His Brilliant-Asshole Status':

Kevin Shields is a liar. Straight up. Creating music at a glacial pace is one thing. Creating music at a glacial pace (and that doesn't even do it justice . . .) while saying repeatedly in the decades between releases that the next opus is just around the bend—always just around the bend—is an entirely other thing. . . . Just shut up and release the damn thing when it's done, Kevin. The world will be waiting—and willing, if I can hazard the guess, to actually buy the thing. But until then, just shut up, already.[2]

Paula Mejia, a writer at *Vice*, voiced similar sentiments in her online diatribe 'An Open Letter To Kevin Shields Of My Bloody Valentine,' in which she wrote, 'The year ended but the world didn't, and *Loveless*'s follow-up remains the stuff of vague statements from you and lucid dreams from your fans. Yes, the purity of artistry and beauty of what you do, yes all good things come with time, but c'mon dude, it's been twenty years. At some point, you gotta shit or get off the pot.' Later in the article, she accused Shields of 'trolling us all.'[3]

The best contribution of all came from John Doran, the journalist/provocateur and co-founder of *The Quietus*, who pretty much laid all of the world's problems at Shields's feet. From the new age that was supposed to be ushered in according to the Mayan calendar, to the evil that men do, it all rested upon Shields's shoulders, he concluded:

So please join me in saying, 'Thanks, Kevin. Thanks a fucking bunch for taking twenty-two years to make a record that could have saved the world.' All you had to do was make a bunch of songs that sound like being hit on the head with a shovel after doing poppers while listening to a melancholy whale sighing. But you couldn't be bothered and now we're all going to die in planet-wide nuclear annihilation.[4]

Doran's piece was a parody of what had by then become well-worn territory, although it's unclear if he was taking aim at the fans' sense of entitlement, critics' over-the-top writing, or the whole circus surrounding and including Shields—or all of the above. By now, we were two decades into a sequence of think-pieces filled with grand pronouncements about how, to quote Jim Butler of *Jockey Slut*, Shields had simultaneously supplied 'the blueprint for anyone who's interested in manipulating the traditional notions of sound' while also being a 'one-off genius' incapable of regaining the heights of his former glories.[5]

In 2004, *Uncut's* David Stubbs had offered a similarly provocative analysis of how, in his view, Shields was unable to make music equal to his overreaching ambitions:

> And maybe he never will. But maybe that's the point. Perhaps 'To Here Knows When' (which actually went Top 30 as part of the *Tremolo* EP) wasn't a new beginning for rock but an end—less a show of strength than a final, spectacular hemorrhage, the last supernova, an unconscious act of self-immolation. To attempt to exceed it has meant drifting off into the more amorphous and ironically less effective realms of keyboards, sampling, electronica, and sound engineering.[6]

If *Loveless* was, indeed, the last reinvention of what it was possible to do with the guitar, would there ever be a follow-up?

•

The long odyssey toward *m b v* began sometime in 1996 when Shields decided to start afresh on his follow-up to *Loveless* after Ó Cíosóig and Googe had left the group. He has indicated that, by then, he was done with his foray into drum & bass, but he was still challenging himself by trying out new modes of composing. 'I was purposefully *not* trying to write songs with a beginning, middle, and end,' he said of the album's earliest days. 'I was trying to pull myself away from the part of my brain that makes things linear and toward something more impressionistic.'[7]

Shields has often mentioned the influence of Brian Wilson's *Smile* on his way of working around this time, and Wilson's approach gave him new inspiration.* Rather than work in the way he had before—writing songs and only recording them when they were complete—he was now attempting something more abstract, recording various melodic and/or percussive riffs that at some point he would look back on and decide how to fit together. But that opportunity would have to wait. When Butcher left MBV in 1997, the new project was abandoned, and Shields didn't give any more thought to this material until 2004, when he began going through tapes for the digital remastering of all the Creation material. He was surprised by what he found. By 2006, he had come to realize that these last recordings represented something unique. 'It wasn't just a collection of songs,' he later noted. 'The mood and the attitude and what I was doing was really worth finishing.'[8]

In 2008, Shields reassured fans that those same recordings would serve as the basis for a new album. But, as ever, that would take time. And, as ever, the accounts he has given about the process vary considerably.

In one, he described narrowing down about seventeen recordings to eight proper songs he felt good about. But other interviews from around the time of the album's release muddied the waters as to when and how the album came to be. Early on, Shields said that around thirty percent of *m b v* was completed during his time at Island, though he offered no details beyond that. In fact, most of the album originates from 1996–97, though a demo for one song, 'New You,' inspired by the death of Kurt Cobain in April of 1994, was recorded around that time. Based on more recent interviews, however, it would be more accurate to say that around a third of the tracks (primarily 'Is This And Yes,' 'Nothing Is,' and 'Wonder 2') were recorded in 1996 and 1997, with overdubs added later; some fragments from other tracks may have also been used for other songs, but the majority of them were rerecorded later.

---

* At this particular time, before Wilson returned to *Smile* in 2004—first onstage and then with a rerecorded album—it existed mainly as a series of bootlegs and tracks on other Beach Boys LPs from which anyone could construct their own versions of the songs and the album. The song 'Heroes And Villains,' for example, has dozens of parts that could be assembled into a large number of variations, as well as melodies and rhythms that recur in various other *Smile* songs.

Shields had previously noted that if he isn't able to recall a melody over a significant period of time, it's a sign that it wasn't of much value to begin with. He first mentioned this when discussing why most of the drum & bass tracks he recorded throughout 1994 and 1995 were discarded. But even though 'She Found Now,' 'Only Tomorrow,' and 'In Another Way' weren't recorded until a decade later, Shields has specifically mentioned that their melodies stem from 1996 and 1997. The most significant overdubbing and additional writing for the record occurred between 2011 and 2012, with at least two songs being completely recorded or rerecorded from scratch around this time.

When *m b v* finally appeared, there was so much excitement about its mere existence that many reviews failed to mention what a truly diverse collection of songs it is. More than a few critics viewed the album as a collection in three parts, each consisting of three songs. But what stands out twelve years later is the record's seemingly boundless creativity. Because it was created in small fragments, some of the individual songs contain three or four completely novel, completely different elements.

The new recordings were also very different from Shields's earlier work with Creation, which had primarily used his glide guitar parts as a starting point. During that period, this one setup—made up fundamentally of the same guitar processor and two pedals—seemed limitless. But in an exhaustive 2021 interview with the Japanese *Guitar Magazine*, Shields was able to further articulate all the ways *m b v* originated from a totally different place. In it, he discussed his use of a series of new devices, no longer limited to rack-mounted processors and pedals, and his novel integration of flanging—a particular kind of modulation that had been used by the first generation of shoegazers, but which he had stayed away from until now.

As the breadth of material on *m b v* makes clear, there was no single jumping-off point for the various tracks, though Shields was still able to stitch together a cohesive set of songs. 'She Found Now,' the last song recorded for the album, contains more guitars than any of the others, with additional, double-tracked rhythm and acoustic guitars building during the second half of the song. 'Only Tomorrow,' which runs the main guitar through a Univox Uni-Tron 5 (an envelope filter pedal) connected to a 1954 Fender Tweed Deluxe, also has a wholly new sound—one that, in Shields's estimation, is more distorted than anything on *Loveless.*[*]

'Is This And Yes' was in part recorded in 1996, and Shields has described it as using an old-school Brian Wilson-style chord progression, though he has noted a debt to Sean O'Hagan of The High Llamas, who also did arrangements and other work as a part-time member of Stereolab, notably on the mid-90s albums *Emperor Tomato Ketchup* and *Dots And Loops.* The brass part intermingled with Butcher's vocals toward the end of the song is also reminiscent of the Anglo-French group.

'Who Sees You,' 'If I Am,' 'In Another Way,' and 'Nothing Is' all contain drum parts that Shields originally programmed using samples. Some were done by his brother, Jimi Shields, due to his close proximity, though Ó Cíosóig returned to play live drums over the existing loops on some tracks to give them a more human feel—some 'push and pull,' as Shields put it.[9]

'In Another Way' and 'Nothing Is' are among the most aggressive tracks on the album. While 'In Another Way' began in 1996, a great deal was done later, including adding an EBow (a device placed directly on a guitar string to make it vibrate), which Shields first tried using with Brian Reitzell but was able to experiment with more extensively while touring with Primal Scream. Also of note is the way his glide guitar is altered during each section of the song. Again, in contrast with the more straightforward structures of *Loveless,* within this one track there are so many different changing and shifting variables. 'Nothing Is' is one of the more difficult tracks to take in, as it is made up of loops and guitar parts without any overt melody. With no steady beat to latch on to either, it was designed to be more of a sensory experience; at least one writer felt its irregular rhythm putting them into a trance.

---

[*] In this context, the term 'envelope' refers to the overall shape of a sound's loudness contour, including its attack, decay, sustain, and release. An envelope filter affects how the loudness of a sound changes over time. These pedals can dynamically control other parameters like filter cutoff frequencies, creating unique and expressive sounds.

The album's closing track, 'Wonder 2,' seems to be a one-off piece made during Shields's 'skyscraper' experiments of the mid-90s. He first discussed it back in 1999, during his 'Invisible Jukebox' interview with *The Wire*, when he detailed a track running at around 160bpm that was in a drum & bass style 'except that it's mostly snare-based, like a constant rollercoaster effect, or like a mixture of a train and a rollercoaster. It's really heavily phased and distorted, so instead of sounding like a drum track, it sounds like a kind of strange rhythm track.' After clarifying that the piece wasn't purely percussive, he sounded pleased that he had managed to pair the rhythms with 'kind of optimistic Beach Boy chord changes. Well, Bacharach meets Beach Boys.'[10]

A decade and a half later, six months after the album's release, Shields told the Italian magazine *Rumore* ('noise') that his drum & bass experiments had been an attempt to create 'a slower and jazzier version of our sound but, in the course of the long process that makes a song yours, things change. We lost interest in an exploration of that type of sound.' He went on to cite 'Wonder 2' as 'the only fragment that we have kept and that reflects in any way those attempts,' revealing that it originally had the working title 'Airplane Song.'[11]

Speaking to *The Quietus* around the same time, Shields gave further context to this phase of the band's recording—and, perhaps, the reason it became so protracted:

> We were actually inventing a new sound—and this song doesn't really represent it, but—we were doing slowed-down drum & bass music around 1993, 1994. But it just came to nothing, mainly because we didn't know how to do it. We didn't realize that you use just a few good samples, then it's about how you stretch them on the computer. We were trying to program it, work out every beat.[12]

In multiple interviews, Shields has stressed how, to him, little of value is recorded without the elements of chance and spontaneity, using live instruments, which allow you to record relatively quickly, and that making music on computers was not something he wanted to try again. If that is the case, it makes 'Wonder 2' all the more intriguing.

In 2014, journalist Ben Cardew wrote a piece for *The Quietus* entitled 'In Another Way: My Bloody Rhythmic Invention.' In it, he argued that because so much emphasis has been placed on Shields's guitar playing over the years, many fans and critics have overlooked the fact that MBV 'innovated a great deal in the world of drums, rhythm and percussion over their thirty-year career.'[13] In Cardew's view, it was only after 'Wonder 2' appeared that listeners really began to notice Shields's rhythmic innovations, though in my estimation the track still hasn't received the attention it warrants. This is likely in part because of its placement at the end of the album, following the similarly challenging 'Nothing Is'; many listeners might have stopped after the first seven, relatively more (MBV) conventional tracks on the album.

'Wonder 2' is certainly one of the most disorienting tracks in the MBV catalog. The ascending chord sequence that forms its melodic backbone only gradually reveals itself (you can make out the complete cycle most clearly from 1:26 to 1:50); the underlying drum loop implies 4/4 time, but the chord sequence—which has a striving, ascending pattern that gives the sense of a bird trying to gain flight—changes in a way that suggests a different meter.

The song's other elements are even harder to distinguish, as Shields offers his own oblique angle on the untamed drum & bass he and Ó Cíosóig first heard on pirate radio. Drums roll like waves, the other percussive elements are more akin to tornado winds, and the guitars create updrafts and low-pressure surges. It's easy to hear why Shields initially dubbed it 'Airplane Song.' He finally revealed some of the track's mystery in a recent interview, explaining that the drums are processed with reverse reverb, distortion, compression, and flanging (inspired by J Mascis). It's probably the band's wildest, most convulsive, turbulent track, uncovering yet another new world of sound.

•

As early as 2008, Shields and his bandmates had been talking about releasing *m b v* on their own label, which is ultimately what they did. With the income they had received from touring since 2008, they had finally attained the financial independence needed to operate outside of the music industry's typical constraints and timetables. And so, without advertising, the band released *m b v* digitally through their own website on February 2, 2013. Demand for the album promptly crashed the site's server. But what's another day or two when you've been waiting twenty-one years?

The band offered a vinyl edition through the site some weeks later and sold around eight thousand copies in the UK immediately after release; by comparison, Daft Punk sold ten thousand vinyl copies of *Random Access Memories* the same year after a huge media blitz. Although Shields was reluctant, later, to reveal the total number of physical sales, he did note that MBV would have had to have sold 1.5 million copies through a major label to make a comparable profit by the end of the year.

The band's first proper release since *Loveless* inevitably brought another wave of publicity. Unsurprisingly, given the growth of their status in the intervening years—plus the fact that they had recently toured and remastered their old catalog—it seemed as though every print and radio outlet in North America, the UK, Europe, and Japan took the opportunity to recount the band's convoluted story to some degree when reviewing the new record. There were prominent reviews for *m b v* in almost every noteworthy periodical and website. Most of them were positive, though as had been the case with *Loveless*, there were some listeners who didn't quite know what to make of the album at first.

Shields had always believed that it would take time for *Loveless* to be fully appreciated by the public, and he was right.* It may be that *m b v* requires a similar span of time before it too is put in its proper context.

---

* To take one further example, in a 2008 review of the *Loveless* remasters for *Uncut*, Stephen Troussé demonstrated that the album was now considered among the most seminal popular music of the past half-century when he observed that it was 'the last real sonic innovation in indie rock, a deconstruction of rock's riffing presence into an intimately immense, roiling colourfield.'

For his part, Shields had always been adamant that he would never release anything that he felt was inferior to *Loveless*, and while *m b v* may not be the equal of its predecessor in terms of articulating one specific vision—Shields has always said that he sees it as a much more 'impressionistic' record—it contains so many new and undefinable moments that it is an undeniably essential part of the group's catalog.

Musical duo Beach House offered a succinct yet insightful review of the album, describing *m b v* as 'completely worth the long wait after *Loveless*. There are some moments that connect back aesthetically to their earlier records, but there are also new, deeper forms and vibes that materialize throughout. To us, it's a great example of how a band can progress naturally. It feels like a perfect blend of lovely melodic songs and wild harsh moments. It also feels timeless.'[14]

Despite the long gap between releases, Shields has said that he sees *m b v* as the final phase of the period that began with 'You Made Me Realise' in 1988, noting that it was about death, change, nostalgia, and his perception of the world in the 90s. Considering the fact that most of the album was conceived in 1996 and 1997, it makes sense to see it as the conclusion of a ten-year creative period. The band's next recordings—if and when they arrive—will mark the start of a new phase of their career.

•

The band decided to tour again after *m b v*'s release, with about sixty dates taking them to twenty-seven countries around the globe, adding relatively exotic places to their list of venues and including several songs from the new record to their set lists. In addition to the UK, USA, France, and all the places they'd played in 2008 and 2009, they added shows in Hungary, Italy, South Korea, Austria, the Czech Republic, Finland, Croatia, Poland, Slovenia, Slovakia, and Taiwan. And with the band having paid off all of their equipment costs by 2009, one can reasonably assume that these tours were very profitable. Things would only get better after that, as MBV found themselves in the position of being able to choose to play lucrative festival dates rather than stage a full-blown tour.

More shows would follow across Europe and North America in 2013 and 2018, with Seattle-based journalist Dave Segal noting the uniqueness of MBV's situation:

> Very few rock bands in 2018 can take a five-year hiatus from releasing music and touring and then fill all 2,800 seats in the Paramount Theatre. But the English/Irish quartet My Bloody Valentine pulled off that feat, proving against the odds that an innovative group with no stage presence, no label, and no hits since 1992 can still draw large crowds despite going dormant for half a decade.[15]

The last of these shows was an appearance closing out the main stage on the final night of the Desert Daze Festival in Moreno Beach, California, on Sunday, October 14, 2018. Nice work if you can get it.

The 2018 shows coincided with the release of remastered vinyl editions of *Isn't Anything* and *Loveless*, which the band referred to as 'Fully Analog' cuts of the albums. Since they were still under contract to Sony at the time, these were done as a limited self-release only available through the band's website. In 2021, once Sony's ownership of the masters expired, MBV signed a distribution deal with Domino Records, which made the analog remasters more widely available, in the process ensuring that no one had to pay outrageous prices for earlier pressings from 1991 or 2018.

Pitchfork's Mark Richardson explained how Shields had gone the extra mile to make the vinyl remasters in the first place, spending his own savings (and a great deal of time) reconstituting the band's classic records to 'honor the spirit of the original while inevitably imparting its own subtly different character.'[16] Prior to 2018, all that was available were the original vinyl pressings, various awful bootlegs, and some atrocious re-pressings that Sire (part of the Warner Music Group) had licensed to Plain Records in 2003 and 2009. According to Shields, the latter outfit had simply ripped the audio from a CD and cut it to vinyl; the sound was '100 percent wrong.' He sought an injunction to prevent these copies from being imported to the UK, claiming it was technically a bootleg there. 'Warners operate under their own law,' he added, 'so it might have been slightly legal in the United States.'[17]

Shields had also discovered that most earlier pressings of MBV's records—and most records generally since the late 70s, for that matter—were often not truly analog. There is a three-letter designation printed on materials with records, tapes, and CDs that is supposed to tell you the providence of the recording using the Society Of Professional Audio Recording Services (SPARS) code. DDD, for example, would denote it was recorded to a digital format (typically a hard drive or digital tape), mixed using digital equipment, and then mastered digitally, while AAA would denote all these steps were done with analog equipment. But these binary A/D labels, created in the 80s, fail to represent the many different types of equipment and other complexities that don't fit neatly into an analog or digital realm.

For example, the use of digital videocassettes such as the Sony PCM-1630 had become a standard for production masters around the mid-80s, even for many 'analog' albums. When Shields went back and played the original analog tapes, he was surprised by what came over him:

Hearing the true analog, it was like when you smell something you haven't smelled since a child—it brought back memories and feelings together. Memories I hadn't thought about since I made the record. It was a time machine effect. My brain had stored these memories somewhere that could only be accessed by these analog recordings. So I realized there really is a profound difference between analog and digital. So I've become determined to let other people experience that too.[18]

This, of course, was coming from a man who had said in 1992 that he only wanted *Loveless* to be released on CD because vinyl and cassettes sounded antiquated; the quote above, from 2013, speaks to why Shields released two CD editions of the album before there was ever any talk of an analog vinyl cut. Five years on, however, his view on digital music had changed:

> Back in the 80s and 90s, I didn't see digital as a bad thing because
> I could hear all the good things that the digital world had to offer,
> basically, which is a very accurate representation of the waveform
> and the frequency response of the record. Eventually, people started
> to go, 'I don't really like the sound.' And then, when they go back
> to analog, they go, 'Oh my god, it sounds so much nicer,' and that's
> [how] the whole analog concept sort of becomes an issue.[19]

Speaking to NPR, Shields revealed that when he originally mastered *Loveless*, he had a certain sound in mind. 'The sound of *Loveless* that was mastered digitally back in '91 had a certain lack of transient information, as I preferred the sound of the DAT—that sound, whatever it made—to anything else. That, to me, was close to what I was trying to achieve and what I was mixing in the studio.'[20] Another incitement that reinforced his new mission was hearing the mono remasters of the Beatles catalog, which were pressed in 2014 using the original analog tapes.

While reviewing the original masters of *Isn't Anything* from 1988, Shields learned that more liberties had been taken when mastering it than he was aware of at the time. In 2004, he gave an in-depth interview to Aaron North from The Icarus Line, discussing how—to his increasing dismay—certain steps in the mastering process had been handled by the companies used by Creation Records, despite his best efforts at the time. He explained that *Isn't Anything* was mastered very quickly, possibly in a few hours—a low standard of care even by Creation's standards. Due to spikes in the vocal signal, the whole album was run through a De-Esser (a processor typically used to remove sibilance in vocals, although it can be applied in many ways to many elements to smooth things over), before the engineers added treble and compression, further changing the sound in the process. Now, he was eager to find out what the album would sound like without those elements.[21]

Shields went on to detail the active role he took in remastering the two Creation albums for these new vinyl editions, which even involved visiting the record-pressing plants to observe the process and ensure quality control. A project he initially thought would take no more than six months ended up occupying the next two years of his life, eating up hundreds of thousands of dollars of his own money in the process. But he felt compelled to complete it now because he wasn't sure how good his hearing might be five years down the line.

The fully analog pressing of *Loveless* would prove particularly challenging. Shields had used cutting-edge computer technology to mix and master the album back in 1991; now, he and engineer Andy Savours, whom he had first met during the *m b v* sessions, would have to work painstakingly to take measurements of the original album using digital equipment, transfer that information to analog tape, create new edit blocks, and hand-splice them together, often cutting the tape into unorthodox shapes, so that the final album would flow identically to the 1991 version.

Creating a truly analog master was just the first step in the process. The next challenge was finding a record-pressing plant able to faithfully transfer the new analog master to vinyl without using any equipment that violated Shields's objective in any way. When he started to ask around, he didn't like what he found:

> It turned out that a very small percentage of albums is mixed and mastered analog these days. They generally work with digital files they get sent. If you want to go all analog, they really have to dust off the gear. A lot of knowledge has disappeared. Making a vinyl record the way people used to do hardly exists anymore. There are now more obstacles than in the past. I think we succeeded in making really good-sounding albums, which are very close to the intentions we had when we created them.[22]

Ultimately, Shields found only three pressing plants across the UK and Europe that would agree to forgo any digital steps in the process. Upon hearing all three outfits' efforts, he chose Optimal Media in Germany, though he ended up giving away some of the other companies' 'audition discs' of *Isn't Anything* to whoever ordered the album first. The discs were unlabeled, so it was impossible to know whether they came from France, Great Britain, or Germany. Receiving what Shields called an 'alternate cut and pressing' would be a pleasant surprise for those lucky fans.

In 2021, in a relatively obscure interview with the *Manila Times*, Shields announced a further surprise: there was to be yet another pressing of *Loveless* and *Isn't Anything*, this time from a high-resolution digital file:

> It's a 24-bit 96kHz high-res thing with no compression. Just because with the analog thing I realized there is a certain limit to a certain frequency response phenomena. ... I know a lot of people, especially young people, they've only ever heard us on CD or digitally. Besides the fact that I really need the analog versions out there, I also have a need for versions that sound as good as possible and that they're not just different from the CD, but as good as the CD, even a bit better.[23]

Years earlier, speaking to *Pitchfork* in 2013 after the release of the previous digital remasters, Shields went into great detail about digital versus analog, starting out with an important underlying concept of what happens when you record anything: 'The very nature of limiting something from an infinite to moments in time creates distortion.'[24] His point was that unless you are there to hear a performance, the very nature of recording something places limits on the sound and distorts it. So, the question becomes: how do you want to limit or distort something to tape? Digital may be more accurate, but Shields had noticed a profound three-dimensionality when playing back the analog tapes of *Loveless*, which he felt more engaged with.

Many listeners may not have had the opportunity to hear the many benefits of each format. But for those who are unaware of just how varied any one album can sound depending on the many steps that go into preparing the material, the differences can be astonishing. And an album like *Loveless* is a perfect test case as to what is possible. On a decent-quality stereo with a proper setup, there are distinct differences to be heard. The new analog vinyl pressing of *Isn't Anything* is much less ear-fatiguing and is improved immeasurably as a result, while *Loveless* takes on a three-dimensional quality you simply can't get from the original. Only now can we hear how Shields intended for them to sound on vinyl.

If nothing else, these different versions make clear that there is no one 'right' version of any recording, although some can be horribly inferior if they're done poorly or without care.* The general consensus is that digital music, whether it's on a CD or pressed to vinyl, will have a truer and wider frequency response, although it can also often bring about a kind of listener fatigue (as well as a lack of warmth). Analog presents a three-dimensional depth that is unique, particularly on *Loveless*, and warmer, but perfectly accurate highs and lows can be lost due to the inferior frequency response. And more upkeep is involved to keep vinyl records sounding like new, although you may be surprised at how well they can stand up over time if maintained properly.

Either way, by virtue of taking a live sound or performance and committing it to any media, there will always be a compromise. But Shields's main priority—made clear when he finally allowed his music to be put on streaming services in 2021, despite their compromised sound—has always been about creating music that can reach and speak to listeners, regardless of what format it takes. In other words, the process isn't about correcting, it's about *connecting*.

---

* Even records from the same run at the same record plant can vary substantially, depending on how new the stamper is. The website ontherecord.co is a useful free resource offering accurate, impartial information on vinyl releases.

interlude seven

the science of sound

To fully appreciate the significance Shields attached to MBV's live shows as far back as 1987, it's vital to know the very specific ideas and experiences that have shaped his artistic sensibility and why he makes music in the first place. Knowing this also helps give some insight into one of the most talked-about elements of the band's live shows, commonly known as the 'holocaust'—an extended stretch of noise and volume that usually comes toward the end of their shows—and why Shields wants to take the audience on that kind of sonic journey.

The first thing that's critical to understand this is that hearing, like vision, is a subjective phenomenon. It takes input from every part of our being, which is then interwoven with our very essence and lived experiences. As such, there is no objective way to hear sound; it is all uniquely processed by your brain and all the individual baggage you possess.

In 2017, Elizabeth Hellmuth Margulis, director of the music cognition lab at the University Of Arkansas, explained some recent discoveries about how music affects the brain:

When people listen to music, no single 'music center' lights up. Instead, a widely distributed network activates, including areas devoted to vision, motor control, emotion, speech, memory, and planning. Far from revealing an isolated, music-specific area, the most sophisticated technology we have available to peer inside the brain suggests that listening to music calls on a broad range of faculties, testifying to how deeply its perception is interwoven with other aspects of human experience. Beyond just what we hear, what we see, what we expect, how we move, and the sum of our life experiences all contribute to how we experience music.[1]

Shields, who has devoted a great deal of his life to working with and thinking about sound, certainly understands that hearing is a unique experience. One anecdote about the 'holocaust' section of the band's performance of 'You Made Me Realise' makes this abundantly clear. On multiple occasions, journalists have asked Shields about things they have heard, thinking they'd caught some specific melody or countermelody buried beneath the noise, only to be told by Shields that there are no melodies to speak of; those elements were purely things these listeners had created in their minds. 'Hearing,' he told NPR, 'is very much a mental process as much as a physical process.'[2]

When *Pitchfork* contributor Mark Richardson spoke to Shields in 2017, he came away with a definite impression of the guitarist's overall approach to sound:

> It's clear that sound itself is a holy thing for Shields. He speaks of it in almost mystical terms, the way a certain kind of circuitry can alter the texture in tiny ways that, he feels, can have an overwhelming impact. In his world, every piece of equipment has a role to play in the final product of a piece of recorded music, and each changes the final product in a way that can be expressed emotionally.[3]

The earliest origins of the 'holocaust' grew out of live versions of 'Claire,' with which MBV would close their concerts until as late as 1988. It was not unheard of for them to try to provoke a reaction by experimenting with different unpleasant frequencies, depending on how they felt about the audience or venue. A bootleg from a show at Dingwalls in 1988 has them playing the song for seventeen minutes.

The idea of combining extreme frequencies with volume to bring about transcendence was further solidified after an incident in the summer of 1989, which Shields has recounted in multiple interviews over the years.

The band had just taken up residence in a studio in South Kensington, one of London's more affluent neighborhoods. The studio had an adjoining art gallery, and in the middle of the day, when the gallery was empty, he and Ó Cíosóig set up their amps in the larger art gallery. They then made a huge racket purely for the sake of doing it, for the gratification the volume and tone gave them, with Shields playing guitar and Ó Cíosóig on a bass with the strings loose and detuned.

The intense sound helped them achieve an altered state, as Shields later recalled:

> We just started giggling, and then we kept on doing it, and it was over an hour later before we stopped. We just found that something happened in that long process of sounds that took us somewhere else. We were like children, and we couldn't stop laughing and smiling. … We felt like we were on the strongest drug in the world. That's when we realized, 'There's something in this. What would happen if other people got to feel this, too?'[4]

As they continued and the volume increased, the light fixtures and the pictures were shaking. Eventually, the huge, rumbling noise shook the building and made the lights flicker, disturbing the typically exclusive and quiet neighborhood. Just as they were taking a break, they heard a loud knocking at the entrance. It was the owner of the studio, who had been frantically pounding on the door for forty minutes. He had heard their playing from several streets away.

•

The 'holocaust' segment of MBV's shows started properly with the first leg of the tour supporting *Loveless*, which was also noteworthy for the addition of a fifth member to their touring lineup. Anna Quimby, a classically trained flutist, was brought aboard to replicate some of the high frequencies Shields had created in the studio. While the flute is not usually associated with sonic terror, as journalist Sean O'Hagan recalled in the

Guardian, 'the instrument added an almost unbearable shrillness to what was already a blizzard of sustained sonic overload.'[5]

After the band's break with Creation forced them to tighten their belts in 1992, they dropped Quimby from the lineup and continued as a four-piece, but the 'holocaust' remained a key part of their live performances. They would use this extended period of more abstract music and noise, in which the second wordless chorus of 'You Made Me Realise' breaks off into another discrete section of the song, as an opportunity to experiment with (and on) the audience, with the stated goal of taking listeners on a transcendent musical journey. Shields was fascinated by watching the crowd and messing with their reality, using volume to get to a point where people could imagine hearing most anything.

The middle-eight noise section of the studio version of 'You Made Me Realise' is forty seconds long. Onstage, however, it could expand to ten, twenty, even forty minutes. As it has grown to ever greater lengths, the experience has become a hot topic of conversation among fans and journalists. The band have registered each country's reaction, in effect making it a kind of Rorschach test for an audience's view on sound, noise, control, and tolerance. Reviewers can be counted on to mention that MBV's show is one of the loudest they've ever attended, often without even hinting at—much less explaining—the larger context and purpose behind the incredible volume.

Shields has expounded on what he sees as the band's main aim, and it seems directly related to the ideas and the altered sense of reality at the heart of what he and Ó Cíosóig felt in their session at the art gallery. 'What I do is about consciousness,' he said while touring America in 1992, 'being conscious of a feeling in my whole body. The trouble with the attitude toward psychedelic music is that it's about your head only. And to me, all non-Western people when they get into altered states of mind, it's the whole body that's involved.'[6]

The aggressive and confrontational nature of the 'holocaust' was partly a way to ensure that MBV's music wasn't perceived as too dreamy or lightweight, but it wasn't just about volume. Rather, for Shields, it's about creating an environment where listeners are utterly surrounded by sound. Keenly aware of how sound can affect the brain and a person's sense of balance, he explained, 'We play with low frequencies that are nothing like anyone has ever heard before—it's a chaos that sets off a kind of inbuilt alarm system. We use psychoacoustic effects so it sounds louder than it actually is in sound pressure levels.'[7]

Michael Brennan, who worked on the 2008 tour, subsequently described the overall vision for the 'holocaust' section of the show, which only expanded in scope when the band added hundreds of thousands of pounds in new equipment following their reunion:

> Shields has a total plan; it is totally orchestrated. If you really listen, he is playing little parts and little bits and looping them during 'You Made Me Realise' and still keeping that outrageous noise going. He has a master plan of the journey that he wants to take people on sonically. He knows exactly where he wants it to go, and I put in some sub stuff to add to the dynamics of what is going on.[8]

The band's sonic assault on the audience—which would also include the sound of a jumbo jet taking off—was one of the central themes of reviews of their reunion tour. Example headlines include 'And Then Transcendence: My Bloody Valentine's Sensory Assault,' 'The My Bloody Valentine Endurance Challenge,' and 'My Bloody Valentine In Santa Monica: How Could Something So Loud Be So Subtle?' One fan wrote, 'The show as a whole—and especially the holocaust section—felt transformative and far exceeded any expectations I had going in. Unless MBV tour again in the future, I doubt that I'll ever experience something so majestic ever again. But I will always cherish what transpired last night.'[9]

Barry Hogan summed up what he saw as the element that distinguished MBV from other live acts: 'My Bloody Valentine define the word sonic. Their live sound is like nothing else. It's harsh but beautiful. For years, we have seen or worked with various noise acts, but after seeing the band live, everyone will re-evaluate what they are doing. Everything else is like Diet

Coke to My Bloody Valentine's real thing. To say it has raised the bar is an understatement.'[10]

Despite this, Shields has regularly pushed back against the accusation that MBV's concerts are too loud, or that he mindlessly turns up the volume as far as he can. 'It does bother me,' he has said. 'That's why I made sure earplugs were available and that we play within tried-and-tested sound pressure levels with a limit of 119dB(A). We also never overdrive the PA, which can provide spikes of distortion up to 130dB. We'd like to say that it is cool to wear earplugs; it's not cool to get your hearing damaged. And anyway, feeling the music is a great experience.'[11]

There are many misconceptions—some bordering on the hysterical—about how attending too many loud concerts can cause tinnitus and other hearing problems. In fact, these issues often have more to do with prolonged exposure to loud sounds without letting your ears rest. The damage Shields has done to his own ears, for example, has resulted from listening to mixes very loudly in headphones and not giving his ears time to recover.* Having had his concerts' volume measured by environmental inspectors, Shields has noted that they are no louder than your average underground train.

Shields further discussed volume's importance in an interview with Gary Canino of the *Creative Independent* in 2018:

In itself, volume creates a more personal interpretation of what's happening … doctors are discovering that's biologically true. It's also true from the perspective of perception because when something is that loud, you're hearing different harmonic relationships and you're also hearing your own ears start to distort the sound. Your hearing is your own personal version of what your relationship to sound is. What I find good about loud volume is that I actually perceive it more as an expression of freedom and individuality … if something is loud, it forces you to just experience and accept it.[12]

---

* Butcher had an unrelated hearing issue when she suffered a perforated eardrum due to a one-time event involving a speaker that accidentally emitted a massive blast of feedback for a moment. She temporarily lost hearing in one ear before getting treatment.

Almost three decades earlier, Shields had told *Hype* magazine, 'Just about every sound we can experience implies a thing or motion ... Everything is actually a big giant connection of ... language.' The 'holocaust'—and MBV's explorations in sound more generally—can be just as transformative for him as they are for audiences. Asked in the same interview whether he enjoyed the creative release that came with these extreme sonic experiments, and whether it was about 'self-assertion, or self-obliteration,' he responded, 'It's both. It's everything.'[13]

chapter sixteen

'Ultimately, where we're all heading in music is a sort of integration of the reality of what it's all about in the end, and that's extremely psychedelic in the purest sense. Music can remind you of what else is out there. It's a guidepost or a stepping-stone.'

KEVIN SHIELDS, 1995[1]

'If I've learned one thing about myself, it's that I'm one hundred percent incapable of knowing when things will happen.'

KEVIN SHIELDS, 2012[2]

A lot has changed for Kevin Shields over the last fifteen years, and yet people still seem to be asking the same question: 'Where is the next album?' Let's take a quick look at where things stand now to help answer that question or to help us understand if that's even the question we should be asking in the first place.

In 2025, Shields is an established musical icon whose every significant move is reported by the press. One indication of just how prominent he has become in recent years was a 2021 *New York Times* profile—a big deal by any metric—that was essentially nothing more than a status report. The article, by Jeremy Gordon, was noteworthy because it contained the first public mention of Shields's marriage to Anna Davolio, a Danish model. The other big news was My Bloody Valentine's decision to allow their full catalog (from 1988 to the present, anyway) to be streamed by Apple Music, Spotify, and other music services. The article also detailed MBV's licensing of their analog vinyl remasters and CDs to Domino Records, an independent UK label.

Finally, everything the band had issued on CD or vinyl since 1988 was back in print, with a few very notable exceptions.* The timing of the deal stemmed in part from the fact that the rights to the Creation material had now fully reverted to the band from Sony, but among other motivations it's likely that MBV had probably had enough of running their own record sales and distribution business, having done so since *m b v* was released in 2013. Now, Shields and his bandmates had the best of both worlds: full control of the rights to everything they had ever released, and the discretion to rerelease only what they wanted as part of their official discography, distributed on a much wider scale by Domino.†

The *New York Times* profile showed the status MBV had attained among the cognoscenti, but it didn't answer the question of when fans could expect them to release new music. Elsewhere, as has always been the case, every rumor or prediction about a possible new album gets reported. Shields has promised 'one hundred percent' at least one more tour to promote new music. But he has always made promises, offering confident, concrete indications to fans to expect new material at various points over the past thirty-five years, sometimes even detailing distinct projects that have then failed to appear. This type of teasing—the perpetual possibility that a new MBV record, or two, could be just around the corner—has frustrated many fans.

---

* The band's four Creation EPs were reissued on CD in 2012 but have not been rereleased on vinyl. They are easily the most important recordings yet to be remastered or reissued on vinyl, as they track the band's development in a very specific way that the albums fail to capture.

† At the time of writing, nothing of the band's output from before Butcher joined in 1988 has been reissued in any format without the band's oversight, though for streaming purposes, the songs contained on *Ecstasy & Wine* (recorded in 1987) fall into a grey area: at the time of writing, they are available to stream on Pandora but not for download.

The fact remains that there's been only one MBV album since 1991, and the overarching feel or theme of the material included on it was originally conceived two decades earlier. So, why haven't we gotten more new music? One can't help but think back to a comment Shields made in 2004: 'I've never been normal and never will be. The world will change before I will.' Asked if there was an industry mogul who could rein him in, he replied, 'No … but that's only because I can't control myself.'[3]

•

In 2017, Shields described some of the new music he was working on to *Rolling Stone*, noting that he wanted to keep the band's next album to around five to seven tracks and forty minutes total. He framed the material as a departure from the band's earlier work, grouping their previous records into a kind of trilogy. '*Isn't Anything* is a kind of metaphysical record, very sexual, dealing with things like madness. It was like a diary of when we were living in squats. And *Loveless* was more intimate. And the *m b v* record was a bit like the end of something.'[4] What came next, he said, would be about freedom of the soul. He also seemed confident enough to reveal that he was readying two separate album-length works: one would be 'warm and melodic,' the other 'more experimental.' Elsewhere, he claimed that one of the planned new albums 'is like if somebody took [*m b v*] and dropped some acid on it or created a dimensional clash or something.'[5] Maybe, in hindsight, those descriptions will mean something.

Though the aforementioned *New York Times* profile did not offer any truly earth-shattering news, it did provide some new insights into how time had taken on a new relevance for Shields, and how he felt he needed to finish his new music sooner rather than later. At the time of the interview, he was two years away from turning sixty, and he may have come to realize that he had let his creative pendulum swing too far in one direction, as Gordon would note in the conclusion to his article:

When he was young, Shields said, he thought he needed to peak before he turned twenty-five; after My Bloody Valentine achieved some success, he stopped thinking about time altogether, hence the long layover. Those days have passed.[6]

It seems clear that once Shields became financially independent, everything fell into place for him. By then, the world had ample time to catch up with *Loveless*'s true greatness. On tour, he had the sound system he'd always wanted, and after paying off the cost of that equipment, playing live began to provide a more than decent income for the band—without the constraints of a record company. Once Shields achieved that kind of independence, that's when things truly changed for him. At that point, I believe, he felt he could take as much time as he needed on the projects he wanted to pursue.

But even with this newfound freedom—a type of autonomy that very few artists ever achieve—even Shields began to feel that he'd been a bit lax in his ambitions. 'Time is a bit more precious,' he said in 2021. 'I don't want to be seventy-something wanting to make the next record after *m b v*. I think it'd be cooler to make one now.'[7] The COVID-19 pandemic likely complicated those plans, of course, and at the time of writing, it remains unclear whether Shields is any closer to putting out the band's next album, or albums, though the band are due to tour again in late 2025.

There have been some efforts by Shields to break out of his usual way of doing things. In 2017, for example, he played a live piece alongside Godspeed You! Black Emperor drummer Tim Herzog at Norður og Niður, Sigur Rós's festival in Reykjavík, Iceland. A year later, he completed an encouragingly quick two-song collaboration with Brian Eno ('Only Once Away My Son' / 'The Weight Of History') that showed him how complex technology could be set up in such a way as to allow him to arrange and record his music quickly and still allow for spontaneity and accidents. 'It's directionless and purposeful at the same time,' he noted.[8]

Since then, however, there's been nothing to indicate that he fundamentally was able to change his way of working. Shields has shown again and again the incredible artistic heights he's capable of when he's given enough time and space. But as he's made clear on countless occasions, he's also only capable of doing so when his mind and body are in sync and in a good place. And, of course, he only has to answer to one person, which suits him just fine. In a world of contemporary music that is increasingly built on saturation, consumption, and easy access, it's refreshing to be reminded that truly great art takes time, thought, and effort. He's always shown that the wait is worth it.

•

In 2003, Alan McGee said something that seems just as discerning now as it did back then: 'Kevin Shields is the most fascinating musician I have ever met or worked with … [he is] probably the most talented musician in the world and [MBV are] this generation's Velvet Underground in waiting. People will be playing *Loveless* in twenty-five years. I said that in 1991 when I released it, and I stand by that comment.'[9]

When all is said and done—when all the top ten lists have been written, when all the reunion shows have been played, and when all the rumors have been bandied about—what exactly does Shields himself want? The answer is pretty simple: he just wants to make his music on his terms.

Early in his life, Shields came to understand that pop music—The Beatles being the most obvious example—could be as important and as life-altering as any other art form. He believes that his music—when it's done right, when it matches the way he hears things in his head—can have the same type of impact as a great novel, movie, symphony, painting, or sculpture. And, in thinking along those lines, his mind has moved toward permanence, toward building something that truly lasts:

> Music might be a throwaway culture, but we don't make records to be thrown away. We don't share that philosophy of some bands that it's only for the moment. Compare it to books—if you want to be a writer it takes years to get even your first little thing published. And getting a film together takes years. People in their forties are considered young in those fields, but in rock music people laugh at them 'cos they're considered old.[10]

Shields said that in 1990, when MBV were still putting out new music with some regularity. Since then, of course, the gaps between releases have grown greater and greater, but in the future, no one will care about how much time he took to make his music. The only thing that will matter is that it exists at all.

Today, Shields works at two studios, one in London and one outside of Dublin, where he's resided since 2015, and where, during the COVID pandemic, he and his wife learned to handle all the engineering and other technical aspects themselves. He practices Wing Chun martial arts and is on good terms with his bandmates, with whom he remains in regular contact about MBV business and life generally. By all indications, his mental health is good, and his hearing is still in a good place, if an interview from 2017 is any indication. 'After years of practice, you just learn to work hard,' he said. 'Like muscles.'[11]

On the possibility of new records, Shields said back in 2007, 'I do feel like I will make another great record.' It seems that *m b v* was not that album, being more of a closing out of MBV 1988–1997, so I remain optimistic of good things to come.

Speaking just prior to the pandemic, Shields said something he'd never said before about his ultimate ambitions and how he sees himself while acknowledging his past mistakes and wariness about burning himself out.

'You see, I don't feel like I'm finished. I will be exploring things until I'm dead. I feel like if I don't do this myself, no one else is going to do it.'[12]

Amen to that.

appendix one

mbv timeline

1963 Kevin Patrick Shields is born in Queens, New York, on May 21.

1973 The Shields family moves back to Ireland.

1978 Shields meets Colm Ó Cíosóig.

1983 Shields meets Dave Conway.

1984 Conway, Tina Durkin, Ó Cíosóig, and Shields leave for Europe, spending time in the Netherlands and Germany.

1985 The mini-LP *This Is Your Bloody Valentine* is released on Tycoon. *The Man You Love To Hate*, a cassette tape collection of live songs, is released on Schuldige Scheitel Tapes. The band move to London, where Debbie Googe begins rehearsing with them. The *Geek!* EP is released on Fever in December.

1986 Another EP, *The New Record By My Bloody Valentine*, is released on Kaleidoscope Sound.

1987 The *Sunny Sundae Smile* EP is released on Lazy Records. Dave Conway decides to bow out of the band in March. Bilinda Butcher joins the band around April. 'Strawberry Wine,' a non-album single, is released in early November. The mini-album *Ecstasy* follows a few weeks later.

1988 After being thoroughly astonished by MBV's live sound at a venue in Kent in January, Creation Records offers the band the chance to record a one-off EP. Their first Creation EP is recorded in the spring at Bark Studios. *Untitled (You Made Me Realise)* is released in August; The band's second EP and *Isn't Anything* are jointly recorded and mixed in August and September, taking about five to six weeks in all. On September 25, MBV record a Peel Session, which airs on BBC Radio One on October 5. The *Feed Me With Your Kiss* EP is released on October 31. *Isn't Anything* follows on November 21. The album goes to no. 1 on the UK indie chart in December.

1989 'Sugar' is recorded quickly and released as a free flexi single with *The Catalogue* magazine. MBV spend approximately ten days recording at Blackwing Studios in Southwark in February but are unsatisfied with the results, which all go unreleased at the time. Unbeknownst to the band, their last two Lazy releases are collected as *Ecstasy And Wine* and released in February. MBV tour from February through June in support of *Isn't Anything*. They are then booked into Elephant Studios in Wapping in September, the same month Creation drops Rough Trade as its distributor. During these sessions, Ó Cíosóig is incapacitated for a handful of months.

1990 The *Glider* EP is released in April, followed by a brief tour; it reaches no. 41 on the national charts, and the lead-off track, 'Soon,' raises the band's profile.

1991 The *Tremolo* EP is released on February 20; it eventually goes to no. 1 on the UK indie chart and no. 29 on the national charts. *Loveless* is released on November 4.

1992 In January, MBV are dropped by Creation Records. They sign to Island Records UK in October.

1993 MBV issue 'We Have All The Time In The World,' their first release for Island, on July 19.

1995 Ó Cíosóig leaves the band's Streatham home in June. He continues to help with engineering for a few additional months before permanently leaving the band. Googe leaves the band in November.

1996 MBV's cover of Wire's 'Map Ref 41° N93° W' is released on March 11; it will be only their second proper song released on Island.

1997 Wary of throwing good money after bad, Island cuts off all financing to the band, which now consists only of Shields and Butcher. Butcher leaves the Streatham home she shared with Shields; with her departure, all recording comes to a halt.

1998 Shields's radical reworking of Primal Scream's 'If They Move, Kill 'Em' generates a great amount of demand for him as a remixer. He begins working with Primal Scream while also doing remixes to make ends meet, resulting in some twenty or so remixes between 1995 and 2005.

2001 Shields 'quits' MBV to get around his contract with Island Records UK in order to work on the soundtrack to *Lost In Translation* under his own name, leaving Butcher as the sole remaining member of the band. He will only get completely free of his obligations and regain possession of the My Bloody Valentine name in 2003.

2003 *Lost In Translation* and its soundtrack are released; Brian Reitzell's dogged efforts to help Shields make original music is rewarded with four new songs and a BAFTA nomination for Best Soundtrack.

2005 Shields next collaborates with Patti Smith, using his glide-guitar setup for the first time in eight years; two of their performances together are released in 2008.

2006 Shields stops playing and recording with Primal Scream in order to focus full-time on MBV.

2008 The MBV reunion shows begin.

2012 CD remasters of *EP's 1988–1991*, *Isn't Anything*, and *Loveless* are finally released by Sony, which bought out Creation in 1999.

2013 *m b v* is released by the band through their website.

2018 'Fully Analog' vinyl remasters of *Isn't Anything* and *Loveless* are released in January via the band's website.

2021 Free from Sony, MBV sign a distribution deal with Domino Records, which makes available the analog remasters of *Isn't Anything* and *Loveless*. With the exception of vinyl editions of their four seminal Creation EPs (which have never been remastered and repressed for vinyl), Domino distributes everything from 1988 onward on vinyl and CD, and for download and streaming. Shields states that approximately two albums and several EPs will be released in the near future through various outlets.

2025 MBV return to the stage with concerts in Europe and Asia.

appendix two

shields's sense of

harmony & melody

by joe kennedy

Kevin Shields is often thought of primarily as a sonic innovator—a master at creating gorgeous, mind-bending soundscapes. But there is another element of his music that doesn't get quite as much attention, and that is his highly developed sense of harmony and melody. He is just as adept at using the twelve notes of the scale as he is at using varied production techniques; just as skilled at writing a melody as he is at creating previously unheard tones on the guitar. If you were to simply sit at a piano and play a stripped-down version of an MBV song using only its basic chords, it would still sound great because so much of the mystery and beauty of it is right there in the harmonic content.

Shields is comfortable using chord structures that are often associated with sophisticated songwriters like Brian Wilson, Burt Bacharach, and Antônio Carlos Jobim. MBV's music is full of what we usually think of as jazz chords: major sevenths, major ninths, suspended chords, chords with fourths and fifths in the bass, and so on. That isn't to suggest the band's music can be filed under the 'easy listening' genre, like that of the songwriters mentioned above, nor is Shields's use of harmony as traditional and conventional as theirs is. Though they may be using the same building blocks, Shields's lush chord structures have a very different end result—something vastly dreamier and more hallucinogenic. It's a well-known fact that Shields intentionally tries to capture the phenomenon of hypnagogia in his work, and, in fact, he often writes in that state himself. And with a lot of MBV's songs, they seem to be floating in a liminal space somewhere between consciousness and dreams.

Before diving into how Shields does this exactly, first, a brief and very basic primer on how chords work. The standard, most common chord in pop music is the triad, which is made up of a scale's first, third, and fifth notes. The triad is extremely stable, it has a consonant sound, and it's free of any tension. But when you take that stable triad and start adding other notes to it, each change alters the chord's overall feeling, allowing you to create tension and a higher degree of harmonic sophistication. And Shields is drawn to these chords with extra notes, particularly combinations that might evoke a melancholic 'happy/sad' feeling.

The verses of 'Soon' are a good example of how he deploys these kinds of chords in fascinating ways. The song's introduction establishes that it's in the key of F sharp. When the song moves to the verse, Shields moves to a B major chord, but he doesn't play it as a straight B major triad. Instead, the first two chords in the verse sequence are suspended chords (specifically, sus2 chords). This means that, in these instances, he is playing the scale's first and second notes, which, due to the short interval between them, creates a more dissonant tension. That tension only gets released with the sequence's third chord, which goes back to a solid F sharp. It's a particularly stable iteration of the chord, too, as it is an F#5, which only consists of two notes. The fourth chord in the sequence is a lovely, lush D major ninth. That chord has both major and minor triads embedded in it, which is how you achieve that 'happy/sad' kind of feeling. Shields's sequences are often like this. He rarely uses chords that are simple triads, unless they are there for the purpose of releasing a sense of tension he has created.

It's important to point out that Shields doesn't really think about all this in terms of conventional music theory. He doesn't sit down with the guitar and say to himself, *I'm going to go to this major ninth chord right now*. His use of advanced harmony is instinctual; he just does whatever sounds most pleasing to his ear. Many of his songs were created using open tunings, which is another way he puts his unique harmonic fingerprint on his music, as they allow him to find unexpected patterns and intervals in his chords. As he said in a 1992 interview with *Guitar World*, 'My use of alternate tunings just comes from the song side of it. If I wasn't writing songs with them, I wouldn't do it.'[1]

Ultimately, it's Shields's merging of harmonic sophistication with his otherworldly production techniques that creates the magical whole that is more than the sum of its parts. 'Only Shallow' wouldn't have its introspective feeling without the suspended chords Shields uses in the verses. 'To Here Knows When' wouldn't create its swirling, disoriented effect without its breezy major seventh chords and sweet melodies. And the sublime chorus of 'Lose My Breath' wouldn't have anywhere near the effect it does without the dissonant chords that set it up in the verse.

You can buy all the gear that Kevin Shields has, and you can imitate his production techniques, but his real secret is that he's a great songwriter too. Strip away all the production and the songs would still be great. The fact that the production elevates the material the way it does is just another testament to his mastery.

JOE KENNEDY is a Los Angeles–based songwriter, producer, and multi-instrumentalist who has collaborated with artists such as Lil Yachty, Yves Tumor, Kurt Vile, Kim Gordon, Sia, Blondshell, Pete Yorn, Ariel Pink, and many others.

appendix three

notes & sources

ACKNOWLEDGMENTS

Love to my parents, Harriet and Howard Perer, and my best friend, Neva Grout. • Next, I want to thank freelance editor Michael Jauchen, who is most responsible, after me, for making this book happen. With his guidance, his pitch-perfect proposal, and general support, Mike made this such a great experience. • Thanks to Tom Seabrook at Jawbone Press, who read my proposal and saw the possibilities. He is so considerate, and he was so invaluable in too many ways to enumerate. Tom and owner Nigel Osborne run this press, putting out truly high-quality books, and I can't think of a better place to have it published. • Thanks to Joe Kennedy for helping from day one to the very end. And thanks to my dear friend Damian Divney and his wife, Michel. • Thanks to my cousin Josh Shifrin for his guidance. • Thank you also to Jay Stewart, Hershal Shevade, Karina Argudo, and Eugene Iwasa for their friendship and help. • Love and thanks to Britt Sorensen, as this book wouldn't exist without her. • Thanks to photographer Richard Bellia for his time, friendship, and guidance. • Thanks to Matt Anker for use of his truly creative Lime Lizard photo and his support. • Thanks and love to Judy Secher, David and Sylvia Shifrin, Betsy and Ramana Mallysetty, Matthew, Priyanka, and Sapna Mallysetty. • I am indebted to Swedish journalist Ika Johannesson for her in-depth interview with Bilinda Butcher. • Thanks to my UK friends Ben Allan, Mayuko Kai, Fergus Lawrie, and Nick Soulsby. Ben and Mayuko did an amazing translation of the Japanese *Guitar Magazine*, and Fergus was my guitar guru. They all provided valuable info and insights. • Thanks to former Island UK director Marc Marot for his time, insight, and trust in me. His concern for telling a balanced story and even challenging his own memories and perceptions was refreshing. Thanks also to Nigel Coxon for taking the time to speak with me. • Thanks to Takanori Kuroda, Brandt Larson, Bob Divney, and Barry Rothberg for taking the time to help me. • Thanks to Dave Anderson, Angus Cameron, David Conway, Guy Fixsen, Simon Johns, and Nick Hallam for answering questions by email or letting me interview them by Skype. • Thanks to Naomi Eagleson at artfuleditor.com for her support on multiple fronts and for finding Michael Jauchen for me. • Thanks to translators Eugene Iwasa, Josephine Baldwin, and Simonetta Carr. • Thanks to Amy Wuelfing at DiWulf Publishing for reaching out with some business advice and making things a little more fun. • Thanks to Jane Friedman personally and janefriedman.com. If you need to figure out anything about the world of publishing, start with her. • Thanks to Will Myers for his excellent early editorial work on this book. • Thanks to Ned Raggett for his review and input. • Thanks to Glaiza Ganaba at Grid Creative Solutions for my website. • Thanks to Barney Hoskyns and the people at rocksbackpages.com for providing an excellent yet inexpensive research resource that would be hard to replace. • Thanks to the librarians at the Edendale Library. • Thanks to Dr. Frank Young and Dr. Abigail Stanton. • Thanks to Dr. William King and his staff for all their care. • Thanks to Alan McGee and Dick Green for starting Creation Records and for all the amazing music they gave us, including but not limited to My Bloody Valentine, Felt, Primal Scream, Teenage Fanclub, The Boo Radleys, Swervedriver, Super Furry Animals, and The Telescopes. • Thanks to the people behind *Honey Hunt* and *Woosh!* and the many other wonderful fanzines put out by fans through the years. • Thanks to My Bloody Valentine (1987–present). Colm, Debbie, Bilinda, and Kevin did not participate in the making of this book, but I appreciate what they have accomplished, and I hope I accurately represented their story. I've never worked on anything harder in my life. • Lastly, thanks to Kevin for his music and efforts to make us all feel more connected to each other and part of something bigger.

AUTHOR'S INTERVIEWS

Dave Anderson, owner/engineer at Foel Studio. Skype, 2023.

Angus Cameron, video director. Skype, 2018.

David Conway, original MBV vocalist. Email, 2023.

Nigel Coxon, A&R, Island Records UK. Skype, 2018.

Nick Hallam, member of Stereo MC's. Email, 2023.

Simon Johns, Colm Ó Cíosóig collaborator. Email, 2022.

Marc Marot, managing director of Island Records UK. Skype, 2023; Facebook, 2024.

Brian O'Shaughnessy, owner/engineer at Bark Studio. Email, 2023.

BOOKS

Cavanagh, David. *The Creation Records Story: My Magpie Eyes Are Hungry For The Prize*. Virgin Pub, 2001.

DeRogatis, Jim. *Turn On Your Mind: Four Decades Of Great Psychedelic Rock*. Hal Leonard Corporation, 2003.

Hewitt, Paolo. *Alan McGee And The Story Of Creation Records*. Mainstream, 2001.

King, Richard. *How Soon Is Now? The Madmen And Mavericks Who Made Independent Music 1975–2005*. Faber, 2017.

Leech, Jeanette. *Fearless: The Making Of Post-Rock*. Jawbone Press, 2017.

Macari, Steve, and Anthony Macari. *Level & Attack: The Untold Story Of The Tone Bender Fuzz*. 11 Publishing, 2018.

Mavromatis, Andreas. *Hypnagogia: The Unique State Of Consciousness Between Wakefulness And Sleep*. Routledge, 1991.

McGee, Alan. *Creation Stories: Riots, Raves And Running A Label*. Macmillan, 2001.

McGonigal, Mike. *My Bloody Valentine's Loveless*. Continuum, 2007.

Needs, Kris. *The Scream: The Music, Myths, & Misbehavior Of Primal Scream*. Plexus Publishing Limited, 2003.

Reynolds, Simon. *Blissed Out: The Raptures Of Rock*. Serpent's Tail, 1990.

Reynolds, Simon. Blissed Out: The Raptures Of Rock. Backpages Classics Kindle edition, 2011.

Reynolds, Simon. *Retromania: Pop Culture's Addiction To Its Own Past*. Farrar, Straus And Giroux, 2011.

Strong, Hannah. *Sofia Coppola: Forever Young*. Abrams Books, 2022.

Vasudevan, Alexander. *The Autonomous City: A History Of Urban Squatting*. Verso, 2017.

NEWSPAPER AND MAGAZINES

Anderson, Donald. 'Interview Simon Reynolds—Co-Author Of The Sex Revolts.' *The Space Age Bachelor* no. 7, 1996.

Aston, Martin. 'My Bloody Valentine Catalogue Interview.' *The Catalogue* no. 67, February 1989.

Azerrad, Michael. 'The Sound Of The Future.' *Rolling Stone*, February 6, 1992, 20.

Barnes, Mike. 'Come On, Feel The Noise.' *The Guardian*, January 9, 2009.

Barron, Jack. 'Dream Demons.' *NME*, December 10, 1988.

Bates, and JD Beauvallet. 'La Fleur Du Dragon.' *Les Inrockuptibles* no. 32, January 1992.

Beaumont, Mark. 'Creation Was Like An Asylum.' *NME*, May 21, 2011.

Beaumont, Mark. 'The Making Of *Loveless*… "It Was A Fucking Nightmare!"' *NME*, June 2, 2012.

Beaumont-Thomas, Ben. 'Stereolab: There Was Craziness In Getting Lost And Dizzy." Music. *The Guardian*, September 4, 2019.

Bonner, Michael. 'An Audience With … Kevin Shields.' *Uncut*, January 2014.

Bonner, Michael. 'Going Blank Again.' *Uncut*, July 2017.

Bonner, Michael. 'Perfect Sound Forever.' *Uncut*, March 2018.

Boyd, Brian. 'Prune Power.' *The Irish Times*, October 3, 2009.

Brown, Nick. 'My Bloody Valentine.' *Spiral Scratch*, February 1991.

Butler, Jim. 'The Art Of Noise.' *Jockey Slut* no. 4, May 2003.

Cairns, Dan. 'Lost And Found.' *Sunday Times*, September 28, 2003.

Cameron, Keith. '(No) Sign Of The Valentines.' *NME*, April 15, 1995.

Cameron, Keith. 'Of Sound Mind.' *Mojo* no. 331, June 2021.

Cameron, Keith. 'Reading The Label: Keith Cameron On David Cavanagh's Creation Records Story.' *The Guardian*, November 25, 2000.

Cameron, Keith. 'Songs In The McGee Of Life.' *NME*, February 12, 1994.

Cavanagh, David. '3am Eternal: My Bloody Valentine.' *Select*, February 1992.

Collins, Andrew. 'World War Skreeeee!' *NME*, November 9, 1991.

Dalton, Stephen. 'The Sound Of Violence.' *Vox*, February 1991.

Diederichsen, Diedrich. 'My Bloody Valentine: Occasional Lapses Into Laziness.' *Spex* no. 3/100, March 1989.

Doyle, Tom. 'Classic Tracks: My Bloody Valentine "Only Shallow."' *Sound On Sound*, May 2018.

Dubrowa, Corey. 'Going Blank Again.' *Magnet Magazine* no. 53, April 2002.

Finlay, Leo. 'To Here From God Knows Where.' *Sounds*, February 9, 1991.

Fulton, Ben. 'Immediate Feedback: My Bloody Valentine Shakes Some Reaction.' *Option* no. 35, December 1990.

Gabriel, Clive. 'My Bloody Valentine.' *Lime Lizard* no. 15, December 1991.

Gilbert, Pat. 'The Beat Up: Black Rays Defence.' *Mojo*, January 2005.

Gillies, Andrew. 'Patti Smith & Kevin Shields: The Coral Sea Review.' *Time Off*, August 6, 2008.

Gittins, Ian. 'Single Of The Week: My Bloody Valentine—Glider EP.' *Melody Maker*, April 28, 1990.

Gittins, Ian. 'The Excellence Of Ecstasy.' *Melody Maker*, January 30, 1988.

Gordon, Jeremy. 'Kevin Shields On My Bloody Valentine's Return: Time Is "More Precious."' *New York Times*, March 31, 2021.

Gore, Joe. 'The Savage Beauty Of My Bloody Valentine.' *Guitar Player*, May 1992.

Hodgkinson, Will. 'Hey, Big Fender: The Iconic Instrument Of Hendrix, Clapton And Richards.' *The Times* (UK), May 22, 2010.

Hodgkinson, Will. 'My Bloody Valentine.' *Make It Ongar Fanzine*, November 1987.

Holland, Roger. 'My Bloody Valentine, *This Is Your Bloody Valentine*.' *Sounds*, October 5, 1985.

Hoskyns, Barney. 'The Angry Brigade.' *Select*, April 2000.

Houseman, Danny. 'Hype: My Bloody Valentine.' *Hype*, August 1992.

Hsu, Hua, and Jay Babcock. 'Perfect Sound Forever: Kevin Shields Of My Bloody Valentine Interviewed.' *Arthur* no. 7, November 2003.

Huston, Johnny. 'The Future Of … Rock: #8—My Bloody Valentine's Next Album.' *Spin*, November 10, 1995.

Jones, Cliff. 'Valentine's Day.' Guitar The Magazine 2 no. 3, 1992.

Joyce, Stephen. 'Woosh! 1.' *Woosh Fanzine* no. 1, Winter 1988.

Joyce, Stephen. 'Woosh! 3.' *Woosh Fanzine* no. 3, Winter 1989.

Keenan, David. 'Invisible Jukebox: Kevin Shields / My Bloody Valentine.' *The Wire*, March 1999.

Lagambia, Gregg. 'The *Loveless* Waiting Room.' *Filter* no. 8, November 2003.

Lawrence, Sara. 'What The World Is Waiting For…My Bloody Valentine.' *Number One* no. 359, May 1990.

Lester, Paul. 'I Lost It.' *The Guardian*, March 12, 2004.

Maconie, Stuart. 'The Artery Of Noise.' *NME*, April 21, 1990.

McCobb, Rosie. 'No Love Lost: My Bloody Valentine.' *Boston Rock* no. 121, March 1992.

McGee, Alan. 'McGee On Music: The Twin Talents Of Charlotte Church And Kevin Shields.' *The Guardian*, April 21, 2010.

McGonigal, Mike. 'Into The Abyss.' *Maggot Brain* no. 17, Summer 2024.

Morton, Tom. 'Live Review: My Bloody Valentine And Soup Dragons.' *Melody Maker*, 1987.

Mulkerns, Helena. 'Valentine Days.' *Hot Press* no. 16, 1989.

Murphy, Peter. 'Lost In Transmutation.' *Hot Press*, April 7, 2004.

Nation, Lucy. 'My Bloody Valentine.' *Ablaze* no. 9, Winter 1992.

Needs, Kris. 'How Was It For You? My Bloody Valentine.' *Mojo* no. 177, August 2008.

O'Hagan, Sean. 'Daydream Believers.' *The Guardian*, May 18, 2008.

Oldfield, Paul. 'Immolation Time.' *Melody Maker*, September 24, 1988.

Pareles, Jon. 'Pop/Jazz; Slightly Skewed Valentine.' *New York Times*, February 28, 1992.

Pareles, Jon. 'Reunited, Loud And Finding The Love.' *New York Times*, September 22, 2008.

Paytress, Mark. 'Record Collector Profile: My Bloody Valentine.' Record Collector no. 128, April 1990.

Perna, Alan Di. 'Bloody Guy.' *Guitar World*, March 1992.

Perna, Alan Di. 'Quiet Riot: Dinosaur Jr.'S J Mascis And My Bloody Valentine's Kevin Shields Speak Softly—Very Softly—But Carry Big Axes.' *Guitar World*, April 1993.

Perna, Alan Di, and Joe Gore. 'My Bloody Valentine's Disposable Tunings.' Guitar Player, December 1992.

Perry, Andrew. 'My Bloody Valentine: Barbed Wire And Aliens In The Garden.' *Daily Telegraph*, June 19, 2008.

Petridis, Alexis. 'My Bloody Valentine's Kevin Shields: "We Wanted To Sound Like A Band Killing Their Songs."' *The Guardian*, May 27, 2021.

Petridis, Alexis. 'The Coral Sea.' *The Guardian*, June 24, 2005.

Powell, Austin. 'An Interview With Kevin Shields.' *Austin Chronicle*, April 16, 2009.

Relyea, Lane. 'Sugar Rush.' Artforum, November 1992.

Reynolds, Simon. 'Day Of Creation, Doing It For The Kids.' *Melody Maker*, August 13, 1988.

Reynolds, Simon. 'Electric Warriors.' *Spin*, July 2000.

Reynolds, Simon. 'More Music.' Arts. *The Observer*, November 27, 1988.

Reynolds, Simon. 'My Bloody Valentine: The Opposite Of Rock'n'roll.' *Spin*, August 5, 2008.

Reynolds, Simon. 'Pop View; 'Dream-Pop' Bands Define The Times In Britain.' *New York Times*, December 1, 1991.

Reynolds, Simon. 'Suicide Kisses.' *Melody Maker*, October 15, 1988.

Reynolds, Simon. 'Valentine Daze.' *Melody Maker*, November 2, 1991.

Reynolds, Simon. 'When You Wake You're Still In A Nightmare.' *Alternative Press*, October 1995.

Robb, John. 'Blood On The Tracks.' *The National*, May 1, 2008.

Robb, John. 'Blown A Wish.' *Louder Than War* no. 6, October 2018.

Roberts, Chris. 'My Bloody Valentine: Glide On Time.' *Melody Maker*, April 28, 1990.

Roberts, Chris. 'Sky Scrapers.' *Melody Maker*, November 5, 1988.

Robson, Michael. 'Michael Robson Tracks The Indie Band Who Arrived With A "Crash."' *Record Collector*, October 1990.

Rogers, Jude. 'Diamond Gazers.' *The Guardian*, July 27, 2007.

Savage, Jon. 'Feedback To The Future: My Bloody Valentine.' *20/20*, Spring 1991.

Segal, Dave. 'Feed Me With Your Bliss.' *Alternative Press* no. 45, March 1992.

Selzer, Jon. 'My Bloody Valentine: *Loveless* Review.' *Lime Lizard*, December 1991.

Sprague, David. 'Pop Shredded Through The Looking Glass.' *Request Magazine*, February 1992.

Stanley, Bob. 'My Bloody Valentine—Ecstasy.' *NME*, January 1988.

Stubbs, David. 'Feedback To The Future.' *Uncut*, February 2004.

Stubbs, David. 'My Bloodier Valentine.' *Mojo*, June 2012.

Stubbs, David. 'My Bloody Valentine: All Hail The Future!' *Melody Maker*, January 26, 1991.

The Stud Brothers. 'My Bloody Valentine: The Class Of '91.' *Melody Maker*, November 2, 1991.

Thompson, Ben. 'Alive And Kicking At The Country Club.' *NME*, August 1, 1988.

Thompson, Jody. 'Please Release Me!' *NME*, April 5, 1997.

Tischler, Eric. 'Kevin Shields: From My Bloody Valentine To … ?' *Tape Op: The Creative Music Recording Magazine* no. 26, December 2001.

Troussé, Stephen. 'My Bloody Valentine—*Isn't Anything | Loveless | The Coral* Sea.' *Uncut*, August 2008.

Wilkinson, Roy. 'Sonic Youth: A Load Of Tony Baloney.' *Sounds*, September 1, 1990.

Wilson, Mackenzie. 'Kevin Shields Sets The *Loveless* Record Straight.' *Magnet Magazine*, March 2007.

Yamamoto, Rye. 'Kevin Shields Interview Series.' Translated By Tomohiro Moriyo. *Guitar Magazine* Japan no. 6, June 2021.

— 'About Bloody Time Too!' *NME*, July 26, 1997.

— 'Big Bangs: 100 Records That Shook Up The World.' *Mojo*, June 2007.

— 'Fact! All The President's Men.' *Select*, April 1994.

— 'Guitar Greats: Kevin Shields.' Play Guitar no. 35, 2002.

— 'Majors Court Indie Giants.' *NME*, August 1, 1992.

— 'My Bloody Valentine: Whore.' *NME*, February 24, 1996.

— 'Now Let's Talk About Kevin …' (translated by Simonetta Carr). *Rumore*, August 2013.

— 'Review Of 1990: Symphonic Chaos.' *Melody Maker*, December 22, 1990.

ONLINE ARTICLES

Anders, Tiffany. 'My Bloody Valentine: It's Quite Simple, Really.' larecord.com, October 11, 2018.

Anderson, Brian. 'Watch My Bloody Valentine's Kevin Shields Reaffirm His Brilliant-Asshole Status.' vice.com, December 7, 2012.

Antonuccio, Josh. 'Twenty Years Ago: My Bloody Valentine's *Loveless*.' popmatters.com, March 1, 2011.

Berkowitz, Joe. 'How A Classic Is Created: My Bloody Valentine And The Making Of *Loveless*.' fastcompany.com, October 28, 2014.

Beta, Andy. 'How Composer Brian Reitzell Became Hollywood's Recluse Whisperer.' spin.com, July 24, 2014.

Boinet, Carole. 'Kevin Shields, "I Have A Zero Compromise Policy."' lesinrockuptibles.com, April 22, 2021.

Bonifacio, Mark. 'Full My Bloody Valentine Digital Catalogue Now Available For The First Time.' manilatimes.net, June 3, 2021.

Brewster, Will. 'The 10 Most Iconic Fender Jaguar Players Of All Time.' mixdownmag.com, February 21, 2023.

Bromhead, Erin. 'Fender 60th Anniversary Classic Jazzmaster—Kevin Shields.' fender.com, 2018.

Brown, Nick. 'Archive: My Bloody Valentine Interview From February 1989.' louderthanwar.com January 28, 2013.

Burns, Todd L. 'Brian Reitzell At Red Bull Music Academy.' redbullmusicacademy.com. October 8, 2018.

Canino, Gary. 'On Finding The Soul Of A Song.' thecreativeindendent.com, October 8, 2018.

Cardew, Ben. 'In Another Way: My Bloody Valentine's Rhythmic Invention.' thequietus.com, January 13, 2014.

Chester, Tim. 'Great Lost Albums.' nme.com, February 7, 2012.

Clay, Joe. 'Baker's Dozen | A Sucker For Melody: Martin Carr's Favourite Songs.' thequietus.com, October 28, 2014.

Dansby, Andrew. 'Kevin Shields On *Lost In Translation* Soundtrack.' rollingstone.com, September 24, 2003.

Dawson, Nick. 'The Music Of Sofia Coppola.' focusfeatures.com, November 8, 2010.

DeRogatis, Jim. 'A Love Letter To Guitar.' jimdero.com, December 2, 2001.

DeRogatis, Jim. 'Valentine's Day Again.' jimdero.com, September 26, 2008.

Dombal, Ryan. 'Interview Kevin Shields: Speaks On The Long And Laborious Process Of Recording The Follow-Up To *Loveless*.' pitchfork.com, August 9, 2013

Dombal, Ryan. 'Kevin Shields Interview Outtakes.' pitchfork.com, August 12, 2013.

Dombal, Ryan. 'Interview Kevin Shields: The Shoegaze Titan On The Strange Saga Behind My Bloody Valentine's Remasters (2012).' pitchfork.com, April 30, 2012.

Doran, John. 'Why My Bloody Valentine's *m b v* Has Come Too Late To Stop The End Of The World.' vice.com, February 4, 2013

Fisher, Joseph. 'My Bloody Valentine's *Loveless* And The Un-Invention Of Cock Rock.' popmatters.com, June 17, 2020.

Flint, Tom. 'Alan Moulder: Recording My Bloody Valentine's *Loveless*.' polymathperspective.com, April 4, 2013

Gourlay, Dom. '"We Became Seminal For Doing Nothing": DIS Meets Debbie Googe Of My Bloody Valentine.' drownedinsound.com, December 6, 2012.

Gregpore, Carolyn. 'Hypnagogia, The State Between Sleep And Wakefulness, Is Key To Creativity.' huffpost.com, February 22, 2016.

Grow, Kory. 'My Bloody Valentine's Kevin Shields On The Agony And Ecstasy Of *Loveless*.' rollingstone.com, November 15, 2017.

Haagsma, Robert. 'Book Excerpt: Kevin Shields On Vinyl And Analogue Audio.' thevinylfactory.com, January 18, 2024.

Headly, Janice. 'From The Kexp Archives: An Interview With Kevin Shields Of My Bloody Valentine.' kepx.org, December 5, 2021.

Huston, Johnny Ray. 'MBV Top—Kevin Shields And Zidane: A 21st Century Portrait.' sfbgarchive.48hills.org, February 1, 2008.

Hvum. 'Interview: Deb Googe—With Musical Attitude And Edge, She's Shaping Modern Music.' horizonmusic.com, November 24, 2017.

Jazairi, Adam. 'The Magnificent '90s: Kevin Shields Of My Bloody Valentine.' guitar-muse.com, October 6, 2011.

Johannesson, Ika. 'Life's A Picnic: Interview With My Bloody Valentine.' totallydublin.ie, February 1, 2008.

Kennedy, John. 'Alan McGee: My Bloody Valentine Made You Made Me Realise As A Joke.' radiox.co.uk, November 15, 2013.

Kuroda, Takanori (translated by Eugene Iwasa). 'Kevin Shields Japan Exclusive Interview Part 1, The Truth Of The "New Acoustic Experience."' rollingstonejapan.com, February 2, 2018.

Leonard, Michael. 'How Kevin Shields And My Bloody Valentine Changed The Course Of Guitar Playing Forever.' guitar.com, April 7, 2021.

Margulis, Elizabeth Hellmuth. 'Music Is In Your Brain And Your Body And Your Life.' aeon.co, November 2, 2017.

Marszalek, Julian. 'Vitamin Gee: Primal Scream's Bobby Gillespie Sees The Light.' thequietus.com, April 30, 2013.

McPherson, Jerry, and Jack Steel. 'Unlimited Decisions: Record Label Battles.' vice.com, November 30, 2003.

McVicar, Georgie. 'Mechanics Of Perception: Caterina Barbieri Interview.' straylandings.co.uk, June 30, 2018.

Mejia, Paula. 'An Open Letter To Kevin Shields Of My Bloody Valentine.' vice.com, January 4, 2013.

Morrison, John. 'The Engineer Who Helped Save MBV's *Loveless* & Oasis' Debut.' reverb.com, November 15, 2022.

Murphy, Tom. 'My Bloody Valentine's Kevin Shields On The Early Days Of The Band, Using Synths And Tape-Loops.' westword.com, August 14, 2013.

Murphy, Tom. 'My Bloody Valentine's Kevin Shields Talks *Loveless* And The Influence Of Bands Like Sonic Youth And Dinosaur Jr.' westword.com, April 23, 2009.

Pitchfork Staff. '33 Musicians On Their Favorite Albums Of The Last 25 Years.' pitchfork.com, October 13, 2021.

Nichols, Sharon. 'There's No Place Like Drone.' chronogram.com, August 26, 2008.

North, Aaron. 'Kevin Shields: The Buddyhead Interview.' buddyhead.com, January 19, 2005.

Parkes, Taylor. '"Not Doing Things Is Soul Destroying": Kevin Shields Of MBV Interviewed.' thequietus.com, May 10, 2012.

Pearis, Bill. 'An Interview With Kevin Shields Of My Bloody Valentine.' brooklynvegan.com, October 29, 2013.

Price, Huw. 'My Bloody Valentine, Kevin Shields And Me: Recording Guitar With A Shoegaze Icon.' guitar.com, April 6, 2021.

Raggett, Ned. 'My Bloody Valentine Interview At KUCI.' kuci.org, April 1996.

Reynolds, Simon. 'My Bloody Valentine: The Resurrection Director's Cut, *Spin*, August 2008.' reynoldsretro.blogspot.com, February 8, 2011.

Reynolds, Simon. 'When You Wake You're Still In A Nightmare AKA Where The Fuck Are My Bloody Valentine.' reynoldsretro.blogspot.com, February 2013.

Richardson, Mark. 'My Bloody Valentine's Kevin Shields Dissects His New *Loveless* Vinyl Remaster, Talks New Album.' pitchfork.com, November 1, 2017.

Robinson, Julius. 'Music Supervisor Report #2.' wegetartists.com, December 2019.

Rosenborg, Rutger. 'Blue Angel Of Noise: Lilys' *Loveless* Affair With Drama And Time.'nbbcsandiego.com, January 30, 2017.

Segal, Dave. 'Why You Should Still Give A Fuck About My Bloody Valentine.' thestranger.com, July 4, 2018.

Shamoon, Evan. 'Hank Shocklee's Temple Of Boom.' native-instruments.com, May 3, 2018.

Sodomsky, Sam. 'Kevin Shields Talks New My Bloody Valentine Album And Tour.' pitchfork.com, November 15, 2017.

Sweeney, Eamon. 'Not Your Bloody Valentine— My Bloody Valentine.' independent.ie, August 22, 2008.

Taj. 'And Then Transcendence: My Bloody Valentine's Sensory Assault.' javacrossknitmusic.com, September 28, 2008.

Tatlock, John. 'The Noise And How To Bring It: Hank Shocklee Interviewed.' thequietus.com, February 4, 2015.

Venutti, Isabella. 'Gear Talks: An Interview With Kevin Shields Of My Bloody Valentine.' mixdownmag.com, June 19, 2023.

Walters, Barry. 'Patti Smith And Kevin Shields, *The Coral Sea*.' spin.com, July 8, 2008.

Wray, Daniel Dylan. '"It Wouldn't Have Been Done By Anyone In Their Right Mind"— The Oral History Of ATNP.' vice.com, July 1, 2021.

— 'Interview: Barry Hogan, Creator Of All Tomorrow's Parties.' villagevoice.com, September 17, 2008.

— 'MBV Rumor: Andy Wilkinson.' expectdelay.com, February 24, 1997.

— 'My Bloody Valentine Are Back! Here's The Gear Guide.' guitarplayer.wordpress.com, November 24, 2007.

— 'No Valentines This Year From Mr. Shields.' nme.com, January 4, 1999.

BROADCASTS / MISCELLANEOUS

Boilen, Bob. 'My Bloody Valentine's Kevin Shields Gets Deep Into *Loveless*.' *All Things Considered*, NPR, March 14, 2023.

Burgess, Tim. '*Loveless* Twitter Listening Party Replay: My Bloody Valentine.' timstwitterlisteningparty.com, March 16, 2023.

Burgess, Tim. '*Isn't Anything* Twitter Listening Party Replay: My Bloody Valentine.' timstwitterlisteningparty.com, May 15, 2021.

Cameron, Angus, Matthew Amos, and Douglas Hart (directors). *The Story Of Creation*. Band Song Videos / Creation Films VHS, 1992: 1h.

Connor, Danny (director). *Upside Down: The Creation Records Story*. Document Productions Ltd., 2010: 1h41m.

Green, Eric (director). *Beautiful Noise*. Hypfilms DVD, 2014: 1h30m.

Leng, Karen. 'Kevin Shields Interview With Double J, 2021 (Unedited).' Double J, April 8, 2021: 3hr32m; via YouTube.

Lester, Paul. 'Kevin Shields Video Interview In 1991.' March 1991: 5:54; via YouTube.

Pearson, Jesse (director). *Soft Focus Invades The British Isles* with Ian Svenonius. Vice Studios, 2007; 29:09.

Peel, John. *John Peel*. BBC Radio One, June 11, 1993.

Snub TV. 'My Bloody Valentine Interview (Unedited).' 1991: 21:46.

Stereo.Typen. '#051podcast My Bloody Valentine.' stereotypenpodcast.de, October 31, 2021: 92:32.

— 'Celebrity Photocalls And Interviews; Kevin Shields And Colm Ó Cíosóig.' Getty Images, 2008: 8:46.

— 'My Bloody Valentine Backstage Interview *Mojo* Awards 2008.' *Mojo* magazine, 2008: 1:48; via YouTube.

— 'Radio France Interview With My Bloody Valentine.' Radio France, February 2, 1991.

— *Rockin' In The UK* with Rachel Davis. Channel 4, January 24, 1989: 5:33; via YouTube.

endnotes

INTRODUCTION

1 'Soft Focus Invades The British Isles'
2 Needs, 'How Was It For You?'
3 Needs, 'How Was It For You?"
4 Bromhead, 'Fender 60th Anniversary Classic Jazzmaster—Kevin Shields'
5 McVicar, 'Mechanics Of Perception'
6 Jazairi, 'The Magnificent 90s'
7 O'Hagan, 'Daydream Believers'
8 Wilson, 'Kevin Shields Sets The *Loveless* Record Straight'
9 Fulton, 'Immediate Feedback'

CHAPTER ONE

1 Lester, 'Kevin Shields Video Interview 1991'
2 Hsu and Babcock, 'Perfect Sound Forever'
3 Dombal, 'Kevin Shields Interview Outtakes'
4 Bonner, 'Perfect Sound Forever'
5 Bonner, 'Perfect Sound Forever'
6 Boyd, 'Prune Power'
7 Mulkerns, 'Valentine Days'
8 Mulkerns, 'Valentine Days'
9 Stubbs, 'My Bloody Valentine: All Hail The Future!'
10 Jones, 'Valentine's Day'
11 Sweeney, 'Not Your Bloody Valentine—My Bloody Valentine'
12 Interview with David Conway
13 Venutti, 'Gear Talks'
14 Holland, 'This Is Your Bloody Valentine'
15 Beaumont-Thomas, 'Stereolab: There Was Craziness In Getting Lost And Dizzy'
16 HVUM, 'Interview: Deb Googe'
17 'Big Bangs: 100 Records That Shook Up The World'
18 Leng, 'Kevin Shields Interview With Double J, 2021'

19 Paytress, 'Record Collector Profile: My Bloody Valentine'
20 Hsu and Babcock, 'Perfect Sound Forever'
21 Brown, 'My Bloody Valentine'
22 Joyce, 'Woosh! 1'
23 Brown, 'Archive: My Bloody Valentine Interview From February 1989'

CHAPTER TWO

1 Barron, 'Dream Demons'
2 Leonard, 'How Kevin Shields And My Bloody Valentine Changed The Course Of Guitar Playing Forever'
3 Robson, 'Indie Band Who Arrived With A Crash'
4 Reynolds, 'Suicide Kisses'
5 Brown, 'Archive: My Bloody Valentine Interview From February 1989'
6 Stanley, 'Ecstasy'
7 Chester, 'Great Lost Albums—Recommend A Neglected Classic'
8 Pareles, 'Pop/Jazz; Slightly Skewed Valentine'
9 Gittins, 'The Excellence Of Ecstasy'
10 Paisley, 'The Designer Pudding Basin Of Pop'
11 Gittins, 'The Excellence Of Ecstasy'
12 North, 'Kevin Shields: The Buddyhead Interview'

CHAPTER THREE

1 *The Story Of Creation*
2 Gourlay, 'We Became Seminal For Doing Nothing'
3 McCobb, 'No Love Lost'
4 *The Story Of Creation*
5 McGee, *Creation Stories*
6 McGee, *Creation Stories*
7 Cavanagh, *The Creation Records Story*

8   McCobb, 'No Love Lost'

9   Brown, 'Archive: My Bloody Valentine Interview From February 1989'

10 Di Perna, 'Quiet Riot'

11 Grow, 'The Agony And Ecstasy Of *Loveless*'

12 Bromhead, 'Fender 60th Anniversary Classic Jazzmaster—Kevin Shields'

13 Reynolds, 'When You Wake You're Still In A Nightmare'

14 Reynolds, 'Doing It For The Kids'

15 Oldfield, 'Immolation Time'

16 Kennedy, 'Alan McGee: My Bloody Valentine Made You Made Me Realise As A Joke'

17 Finlay, 'To Here From God Knows Where'

18 Clay, 'A Sucker For Melody: Martin Carr'

19 Stud Brothers, 'My Bloody Valentine: The Class Of '91'

INTERLUDE ONE

1   King, *How Soon Is Now?*

2   Hodgkinson, 'My Bloody Valentine'

3   Aston, 'My Bloody Valentine Catalogue Interview'

4   Wilkinson, 'Sonic Youth: A Load of Tony Baloney'

5   Rosenborg, 'Blue Angel Of Noise'

6   Finlay, 'To Here From God Knows Where'

7   DeRogatis, *Turn On Your Mind*

8   Barron, 'Dream Demons'

9   Leech, *Fearless*

10 Parkes, 'Not Doing Things Is Soul Destroying'

11 Shamoon, 'Hank Shocklee's Temple Of Boom'

12 Leng, 'Kevin Shields Interview With Double J, 2021'

13 Parkes, 'Not Doing Things Is Soul Destroying'

14 Tatlock, 'The Noise And How To Bring It: Hank Shocklee Interviewed'

CHAPTER FOUR

1   Troussé, '*Isn't Anything* / *Loveless* / *Coral Sea*'

2   King, *How Soon Is Now?*

3   Interview with Dave Anderson

4   Burgess, '*Isn't Anything* Twitter Listening Party Replay'

5   Interview with Dave Anderson

6   Everett, 'The First Time With Kevin Shields'

7   Cavanagh, *The Creation Records Story*

8   Burgess, '*Isn't Anything* Twitter Listening Party Replay'

9   Reynolds, 'Doing It For The Kids'

10 Reynolds, 'Suicide Kisses'

11 Reynolds, *Blissed Out*

12 Roberts, 'Sky Scrapers'

13 Bonner, 'Going Blank Again'

14 Maconie, 'The Artery Of Noise'

15 Snub TV, *MBV Unedited Interview*

16 Reynolds, 'More Music'

CHAPTER FIVE

1   Robb, 'Open Heart Purgery'

2   Joyce, 'Woosh! 3'

3   Joyce, 'Woosh! 3'

4   North, 'Kevin Shields: The Buddyhead Interview'

5   Stud Brothers, 'My Bloody Valentine: The Class Of '91'

6   King, *How Soon Is Now?*

7   Dubrowa, 'Going Blank Again'

8   Cavanagh, *The Creation Records Story*

9   Wilson, 'Kevin Shields Sets The *Loveless* Record Straight'

10 Cavanagh, *The Creation Records Story*

11 McGee, *Creation Stories*

12 Flint, 'Alan Moulder: Recording My Blood Valentine's *Loveless*'

13 McGonigal, *My Bloody Valentine's Loveless*

14 McGonigal, *My Bloody Valentine's Loveless*

15 Flint, 'Alan Moulder: Recording My Blood Valentine's *Loveless*'

INTERLUDE TWO

1   Hodgkinson, 'Hey, Big Fender'

2   Brewster, 'The 10 Most Iconic Fender Jaguar Players Of All Time'

3   Mulkerns, 'Valentine Days'

4   Doyle, 'Classic Tracks: Only Shallow'

5   Gore, 'The Savage Beauty Of My Bloody Valentine'

6   Stereo.Typen podcast #51

7   Tischler, 'Kevin Shields: From My Bloody Valentine To … ?'

8   Murphy, 'Kevin Shields Talks Influences'

9   Yamamoto, 'Kevin Shields Interview Series'

10 Crawford, 'First Australian Interview With My Bloody Valentine'

11 Yamamoto, 'Kevin Shields Interview Series'

12 Savage, 'Feedback To The Future: My Bloody Valentine'

CHAPTER SIX

1   Gittins, 'Single Of The Week'

2   'Review Of 1990: Symphonic Chaos'

3   Price, 'My Bloody Valentine, Kevin Shields And Me'

4   Price, 'My Bloody Valentine, Kevin Shields And Me'

5   Murphy, 'Kevin Shields Talks Influences'

6   Di Perna and Gore, 'My Bloody Valentine's Disposable Tunings'

7   Price, 'My Bloody Valentine, Kevin Shields And Me'

8   Bonner, 'Perfect Sound Forever'

9   Diederichsen, 'My Bloody Valentine: Occasional Lapses Into Laziness'

10 Segal, 'Feed Me With Your Bliss'

11 Di Perna, 'Bloody Guy'

12 Lawrence, 'What The World Is Waiting For'

13 Raggett, 'My Bloody Valentine Interview At KUCI'

14 Raggett, 'My Bloody Valentine Interview At KUCI'

15 Powell, 'An Interview With Kevin Shields'

16 Interview with Angus Cameron

CHAPTER SEVEN

1   Morrison, 'The Engineer Who Helped Save MBV's *Loveless* And Oasis's Debut'

2   Reynolds, 'It's The Opposite Of Rock'n'roll (Director's Cut)'

3   Bonner, 'Perfect Sound Forever'

4   McGonigal, *My Bloody Valentine's Loveless*

5   Cavanagh, '3am Eternal'

6   McGonigal, *My Bloody Valentine's Loveless*

7   Sprague, 'Pop Shredded Through The Looking Glass'

8   *The Story Of Creation*

9   Cavanagh, *The Creation Records Story*

10 Stubbs, 'My Bloody Valentine: All Hail The Future!'

11 Sprague, 'Pop Shredded Through The Looking Glass'

12 Savage, 'Feedback To The Future'

13 Berkowitz, 'How A Classic Is Created'

14 Cavanagh, *The Creation Records Story*

15 Cavanagh, *The Creation Records Story*

16 Doyle, 'Classic Tracks: Only Shallow'

17 Interview with Angus Cameron

18 Stubbs, 'My Bloody Valentine: All Hail The Future!'

INTERLUDE THREE

1   Fulton, 'Immediate Feedback: My Bloody Valentine Shakes Some Reaction'

2   Parkes, 'Not Doing Things Is Soul Destroying'

3   Maconie, 'The Artery Of Noise'

4   Reynolds, *Blissed Out*

5   Savage, 'Feedback to the Future'

6   Fisher, 'My Bloody Valentine's *Loveless* And The Un-Invention Of Cock Rock'

7   Gourlay, 'We Became Seminal For Doing Nothing'

CHAPTER EIGHT

1   Johannesson, 'Life's A Picnic'

2   Dalton, 'The Sound Of Violence'

3   Powell, 'An Interview With Kevin Shields'

4   Grow, 'The Agony And Ecstasy Of *Loveless*'

5   Antonuccio, 'Twenty Years Ago: My Bloody Valentine's *Loveless*'

6   Petridis, 'Kevin Shields: We Wanted To Sound Like A Band Killing Their Songs'

7   Flint, 'Alan Moulder: Recording My Blood Valentine's *Loveless*'

8   Cavanagh, *The Creation Records Story*

9   Cavanagh, *The Creation Records Story*

10 Robb, 'Blown A Wish'

11 Di Perna, 'Bloody Guy'

12 Robb, 'Blown a Wish'

13 Parkes, 'Not Doing Things Is Soul Destroying'

14 Doyle, 'Classic Tracks: Only Shallow'

15 Tischler, 'Kevin Shields: From My Bloody Valentine To …?'

16 McGonigal, *My Bloody Valentine's Loveless*

17 Beaumont, 'The Making Of *Loveless*'

18 Gabriel, 'My Bloody Valentine'

19 Doyle, 'Classic Tracks: Only Shallow'

20 Di Perna, 'Bloody Guy'

21 Burgess, 'Loveless Twitter Listening Party Replay'

22 Reynolds, 'Valentine Daze'

23 McGonigal, 'Into The Abyss'

24 Beaumont, 'Creation Was Like An Asylum'

25 Bates and Beauvallet, 'La fleur du dragon'

CHAPTER NINE

1 Collins, 'World War Skreeeee!'

2 Hodgkinson, 'My Bloody Valentine'

3 Selzer, '*Loveless* Review'

4 Azerrad, 'The Sound Of The Future'

5 Collins, 'World War Skreeeee!'

6 Cavanagh, *The Creation Records Story*

7 'Fact! All The President's Men'

8 Cameron, 'Reading The Label'

9 Cavanagh, *The Creation Records Story*

10 O'Hagan, 'Daydream Believers'

11 Cavanagh, *The Creation Records Story*

12 Bonner, 'An Audience With … Kevin Shields'

13 Rogers, 'Diamond Gazers'

14 Cameron, 'Songs In The McGee Of Life'

15 Cameron, 'Songs In The McGee Of Life'

16 Dubrowa, 'Going Blank Again'

17 North, 'Kevin Shields: The Buddyhead Interview'

18 McCobb, 'No Love Lost'

INTERLUDE FOUR

1 Reynolds, 'POP VIEW: Dream-Pop Bands Define The Times In Britain'

2 Dubrowa, 'Going Blank Again'

3 Segal, 'Feed Me With Your Bliss'

4 Relyea, 'Sugar Rush'

5 Collins, 'World War Skreeeee!'

6 Collins, 'World War Skreeeee!'

7 Tischler, 'Kevin Shields: From My Bloody Valentine To …?'

8 Jones, 'Valentine's Day'

9 Roberts, 'My Bloody Valentine: Glide On Time'

10 Segal, 'Feed Me With Your Bliss'

11 Kuroda, 'Kevin Shields *Rolling Stone* Japan Interview Part 1'

CHAPTER TEN

1 Azerrad, 'The Sound Of The Future'

2 Peel, John Peel

3 Segal, 'Feed Me With Your Bliss'

4 Nation, 'My Bloody Valentine'

5 'Majors Court Indie Giants'

6 North, 'Kevin Shields: The Buddyhead Interview'

7 DeRogatis, 'A Love Letter To Guitar'

8 Reynolds, 'My Bloody Valentine: *Loveless*, The Lost Years, And The Resurrection'

9 Keenan, 'Invisible Jukebox: Kevin Shields / My Bloody Valentine'

10 Reynolds, 'When You Wake You're Still In A Nightmare'

11 Cameron, '(No) Sign Of The Valentines'

12 Reynolds, 'When You Wake You're Still In A Nightmare'

13 Dubrowa, 'Going Blank Again'

14 Raggett, 'My Bloody Valentine Interview At KUCI'

15 'My Bloody Valentine: Whore'

16 Thompson, 'Please Release Me!'

17 'About Bloody Time Too!'

CHAPTER ELEVEN

1 Bonner, 'Perfect Sound Forever'

2 'My Bloody Valentine: Whore'

3 *Beautiful Noise*

4 *Beautiful Noise*

5 Raggett, 'My Bloody Valentine Interview At KUCI'

6 'About Bloody Time Too!'

7 Raggett, 'My Bloody Valentine Interview At KUCI'

8 'My Bloody Valentine Interview AOL'

9 Robb, 'Blood On The Tracks'

10 North, 'Kevin Shields: The Buddyhead Interview'

11 'My Bloody Valentine Interview AOL'

12 Interview with Nick Hallam

13 'No Valentines This Year From Mr Shields'

14 Interview with Nick Hallam

15 Hewitt, *Alan McGee And The Story Of Creation Records*

16 Interview with Marc Marot

17 Cairns, 'Lost And Found'

18 McGonigal, *My Bloody Valentine's Loveless*

19 'My Bloody Valentine Interview AOL'

20 Murphy, 'Lost In Transmutation'

21 North, 'Kevin Shields: The Buddyhead Interview'

22 LaGambia, 'The Loveless Waiting Room'

23 Perry, 'My Bloody Valentine: Barbed Wire And Aliens In The Garden'

24 Leng, 'Kevin Shields Interview With Double J, 2021'

INTERLUDE FIVE

1 Lester, 'I Lost It'

2 Leng, 'Kevin Shields Interview With Double J, 2021'

3 Lester, 'I Lost It'

4 Lester, 'I Lost It'

5 McGee, 'The Twin Talents Of Charlotte Church And Kevin Shields'

6 Lester, 'I Lost It'

7 Reynolds, 'When You Wake You're Still In A Nightmare'

8 Hsu and Babcock, 'Perfect Sound Forever'

9 Mavromatis, *Hypnagogia*

10 Gregpore, 'Hypnagogia, The State Between Sleep And Wakefulness, Is Key To Creativity'

11 Huston, 'The Future Of … Rock: #8'

12 Savage, 'Feedback To The Future: My Bloody Valentine'

13 Bates and Beauvallet, 'La fleur du dragon'

14 Mavromatis, *Hypnagogia*

15 Bonner, 'Perfect Sound Forever'

16 Reynolds, 'When You Wake You're Still In A Nightmare'

17 'My Bloody Valentine Interview AOL'

18 Boinet, 'Kevin Shields, "I Have A Zero Compromise Policy."'

19 Leng, 'Kevin Shields Interview With Double J, 2021'

CHAPTER TWELVE

1 'Guitar Greats: Kevin Shields'

2 Cardew, 'In Another Way: My Bloody Valentine's Rhythmic Invention'

3 Parkes, 'Not Doing Things Is Soul Destroying'

4 McPherson and Steel, 'Unlimited Decisions: Record Label Battles'

5 North, 'Kevin Shields: The Buddyhead Interview'

6 Headly, 'KEXP Archives: An Interview With Kevin Shields'

7 Needs, *The Scream*

8 Marszalek, 'Vitamin Gee: Primal Scream's Bobby Gillespie Sees The Light'

9 Reynolds, 'Electric Warriors'

10 Hoskyns, 'The Angry Brigade'

11 North, 'Kevin Shields: The Buddyhead Interview'

12 Reynolds, 'Electric Warriors'

13 Reynolds, 'Electric Warriors'

14 Butler, 'The Art Of Noise'

CHAPTER THIRTEEN

1 Lester, 'I Lost It'

2 Strong, *Sofia Coppola: Forever Young*

3 Beta, 'How Composer Brian Reitzell Became Hollywood's Recluse Whisperer'

4 Murphy, 'Lost In Transmutation'

5 Beta, 'How Composer Brian Reitzell Became Hollywood's Recluse Whisperer'

6 Beta, 'How Composer Brian Reitzell Became Hollywood's Recluse Whisperer'

7 'Brian Reitzell At Red Bull Music Academy'

8 Cairns, 'Lost And Found'

9   Dansby, 'Kevin Shields On *Lost In Translation* Soundtrack'

10   Bonner, 'Perfect Sound Forever'

11   Robinson, 'Music Supervisor Report #2'

12   Reynolds, *Retromania*

13   Petridis, 'The Coral Sea'

14   Cameron, 'Of Sound Mind'

15   Cameron, 'Of Sound Mind'

16   Gillies, '*The Coral Sea*'

17   Walters, '*The Coral Sea*'

18   Huston, 'MBV Top—Kevin Shields And *Zidane: A 21st-Century Portrait*'

19   Hsu and Babcock, 'Perfect Sound Forever'

20   Gilbert, 'The Beat Up: Black Rays Defence'

INTERLUDE SIX

1   Johannesson, 'Life's A Picnic'

2   Morton, 'Live Review: My Bloody Valentine And Soup Dragons'

3   Thompson, 'Alive And Kicking At The Country Club'

4   *Rockin' In The UK*

5   Snub TV, *MBV Unedited Interview*

6   Anders, 'My Bloody Valentine: It's Quite Simple, Really'

7   Bates and Beauvallet, 'La Fleur Du Dragon'

8   Johannesson, 'Life's A Picnic'

9   Snub TV, *MBV Unedited Interview*

10   Boinet, 'Kevin Shields, "I Have A Zero Compromise Policy."'

CHAPTER FOURTEEN

1   *Upside Down: The Creation Records Story*

2   *Upside Down: The Creation Records Story*

3   Bromhead, 'Fender 60th Anniversary Classic Jazzmaster—Kevin Shields'

4   Bonner, 'Perfect Sound Forever'

5   Nichols, 'There's No Place Like Drone'

6   Pareles, 'Reunited, Loud And Finding The Love'

7   'Interview: Barry Hogan, Creator Of All Tomorrow's Parties'

8   Wray, 'The Oral History Of ATP'

9   Powell, 'An Interview With Kevin Shields'

10   Dombal, 'The Shoegaze Titan On The Strange Saga Behind My Bloody Valentine's Remasters'

11   Dombal, 'The Shoegaze Titan On The Strange Saga Behind My Bloody Valentine's Remasters'

12   Leng, 'Kevin Shields Interview With Double J, 2021'

13   Dombal, 'The Shoegaze Titan On The Strange Saga Behind My Bloody Valentine's Remasters'

14   Stubbs, 'My Bloodier Valentine'

15   Dombal, 'The Shoegaze Titan On The Strange Saga Behind My Bloody Valentine's Remasters'

CHAPTER FIFTEEN

1   Doran, 'Why My Bloody Valentine's *m b v* Has Come Too Late To Stop The End Of The World'

2   Anderson, 'Kevin Shields Reaffirm His Brilliant-Asshole Status'

3   Mejia, 'An Open Letter To Kevin Shields Of My Bloody Valentine'

4   Doran, 'Why My Bloody Valentine's *m b v* Has Come Too Late To Stop The End Of The World'

5   Butler, 'The Art Of Noise'

6   Stubbs, 'Feedback To The Future'

7   Dombal, 'Kevin Shields Speaks On The Long And Laborious Process Of Recording The Follow-up To *Loveless*'

8   Cameron, 'Of Sound Mind'

9   Bonner, 'Perfect Sound Forever'

10   Keenan, 'Invisible Jukebox; Kevin Shields / My Bloody Valentine'

11   'Now Let's Talk About Kevin …'

12   Parkes, 'Kevin Shields Discusses New MBV Album'

13   Cardew, 'In Another Way: My Bloody Valentine's Rhythmic Invention'

14   Pitchfork Staff, '33 Musicians On Their Favorite Albums Of The Last 25 Years'

15   Segal, 'Why You Should Still Give A Fuck About My Bloody Valentine'

16 Richardson, 'Kevin Shields Dissects His New *Loveless* Vinyl Remaster'

17 Dombal, 'Kevin Shields Speaks On The Long And Laborious Process Of Recording The Follow-up To *Loveless*'

18 Pearis, 'An Interview With Kevin Shields Of My Bloody Valentine'

19 Boilen, 'My Bloody Valentine's Kevin Shields Gets Deep Into *Loveless*'

20 Boilen, 'My Bloody Valentine's Kevin Shields Gets Deep Into *Loveless*'

21 North, 'Kevin Shields: The Buddyhead Interview'

22 Haagsma, 'Kevin Shields Excerpt From Passion For Vinyl'

23 Bonifacio, 'Full My Bloody Valentine Digital Catalogue Now Available For The First Time'

24 Dombal, 'The Shoegaze Titan On The Strange Saga Behind My Bloody Valentine's Remasters'

INTERLUDE SEVEN

1 Margulis, 'Music Is In Your Brain And Your Body And Your Life'

2 Boilen, 'My Bloody Valentine's Kevin Shields Gets Deep Into *Loveless*'

3 Richardson, 'Kevin Shields Dissects His New *Loveless* Vinyl Remaster'

4 Murphy, 'Lost In Transmutation'

5 O'Hagan, 'Daydream Believers'

6 DeRogatis, 'Valentine's Day Again'

7 Barnes, 'Come On Feel The Noise'

8 Dolphinblog, 'My Bloody Valentine Are Back!'

9 Taj, 'And Then Transcendence: My Bloody Valentine's Sensory Assault'

10 Sweeney, 'Not Your Bloody Valentine—My Bloody Valentine'

11 Barnes, 'Come On, Feel The Noise'

12 Canino, 'On Finding The Soul Of A Song'

13 Houseman, 'Hype: My Bloody Valentine'

CHAPTER SIXTEEN

1 DeRogatis, *Turn On Your Mind*

2 Stubbs, 'My Bloodier Valentine'

3 Lester, 'I Lost It'

4 Grow, 'The Agony And Ecstasy Of *Loveless*'

5 Sodomsky, 'Kevin Shields Talks New Album And Tour'

6 Gordon, 'Kevin Shields On My Bloody Valentine's Return'

7 Gordon, 'Kevin Shields On My Bloody Valentine's Return'

8 Canino, 'On Finding The Soul Of A Song'

9 Billboard Staff, 'My Bloody Valentine Back In The Studio?'

10 Roberts, 'My Bloody Valentine: Glide On Time'

11 Richardson, 'Kevin Shields Dissects His New *Loveless* Vinyl Remaster'

12 Bonner, 'Perfect Sound Forever'

APPENDIX TWO

1 Di Perna and Gore, 'My Bloody Valentine's Disposable Tunings'